Monarchy, Aristocracy and the State in Europe 1300–1800

Historical Connections

Series editors

Geoffrey Crossick, *University of Essex*
John Davis, *University of Connecticut*
Joanna Innes, *Somerville College, University of Oxford*
Tom Scott, *University of Liverpool*

Titles in the series

Monarchy, Aristocracy, and the State in Europe, 1300–1800

Hillay Zmora

London and New York

First published 2001
by Routledge
11 New Fetter Lane, London EC4P 4EE

Simultaneously published in the USA and Canada
by Routledge
29 West 35th Street, New York, NY 10001

Routledge is an imprint of the Taylor & Francis Group

© 2001 Hillay Zmora

Typeset in Times by
Florence Production Ltd, Stoodleigh, Devon
Printed and bound in Great Britain by
Clays Ltd, St Ives plc

British Library Cataloguing in Publication Data
A catalogue record for this book is available from the British Library

Library of Congress Cataloging in Publication Data
Zmora, Hillay, 1964–
    Monarchy, aristocracy, and the state in Europe 1300–1800/
Hillay Zmora.
        p.   cm.—(Historical connections)
    Includes bibliographical references and index.
        1. Monarchy—Europe—History.   2. Aristocracy (Social
class)—Europe—History.   3. Europe—Politics and government.
    I. Title.   II. Series.
    JC375.Z58 2000
    320.94′09′03—dc21   00–032311

ISBN 0–415–24107–3 (hbk)
ISBN 0–415–15044–2 (pbk)

To the memory of Mira Molchadsky

Contents

Series editors' preface

Historical Connections is a series of short books on important historical topics and debates, written primarily for those studying and teaching history. The books offer original and challenging works of synthesis that will make new themes accessible, or old themes accessible in new ways, build bridges between different chronological periods and different historical debates, and encourage comparative discussion in history.

If the study of history is to remain exciting and creative, then the tendency to fragmentation must be resisted. The inflexibility of older assumptions about the relationship between economic, social, cultural and political history has been exposed by recent historical writing, but the impression has sometimes been left that history is little more than a chapter of accidents. This series will insist on the importance of processes of historical change, and it will explore the connections within history: connections between different layers and forms of historical experience, as well as the connections that resist the fragmentary consequences of new forms of specialism in historical research.

Historical Connections will put the search for these connections back at the top of the agenda by exploring new ways of uniting the different strands of historical experience, and by affirming the importance of studying change and movement in history.

Geoffrey Crossick
John Davis
Joanna Innes
Tom Scott

Acknowledgements

It is frustrating to admit that these acknowledgements do little more than acknowledge the fact that I cannot adequately settle the debts I have incurred in writing this book. There is none the less a considerable pleasure in registering them. My greatest debt is to Dr Tom Scott who proposed that I write this book, then read the entire manuscript twice, offering invaluable criticisms accompanied always by equally invaluable advice. I am deeply indebted also to Professor Elena Lourie, who brought both her expertise and her erudition to bear on the manuscript, and made numerous illuminating suggestions. Dr Scott Dixon and Dr Chris Clark made some very helpful interventions at important moments in the gestation of the book.

Much of the preparatory work for the book was done while I was Research Fellow at St Catharine's College, Cambridge. I am grateful to the Master and Fellows for having given me the opportunity to pursue my research in such a congenial atmosphere. The book would have taken much longer to complete but for the largesse of Yad Hanadiv (the Rothschild Foundation). I am also grateful to the Fellowship Committee for having elected me to a Fellowship, and to the administrators, especially Ms Netanya Isaac, for their keen assistance.

Introduction

Nobility is subject to a bewildering variety of interpretations, notes Niccolò Niccoli, one of the personae in Poggio Bracciolini's celebrated treatise *On Nobility* (*c.* 1439–45). The Neapolitans, Venetians, Romans, Florentines and Genoese all have their peculiar conceptions of it, he says. The same is of course true of other European peoples. '[O]ur ideas about nobility are not uniform; they are different or even contradictory, so that there seems to be no sure basis for a definition of nobility.' The modern historians of nobility may, like Niccoli's interlocutor, resist his relativism and reject his intimation that nobility does not actually exist.[1] But they cannot but admit that the dissimilarities and heterogeneity with which they are confronted do indeed seem to defy systematization. Moreover, the problem is compounded by the fact that a major historiographical 'certitude' of past generations of historians has been repudiated. Until quite recently the reigning paradigm for approaching the various European nobilities has been one of a Crisis of the Aristocracy. This paradigm is now itself in what looks like a terminal crisis. Intensive research in the last three decades or so has shown it to be grossly simplistic and misleading. James Wood, whose study of the nobility of Bayeux, published in 1980, is an early showpiece of this historiographical shift, was quick to draw the implications:

> if the nobility was not declining, the personal and ideological struggles that plagued France during [the sixteenth and early seventeenth centuries] could no longer be interpreted as simple manifestations of a more fundamental struggle between a declining nobility and a rising bourgeoisie. The relation between the emerging state and the nobility would have to be reexamined.

The frequent frictions between them, he added, should be seen not as a sign of the nobility's alleged weakness but rather as a sign of its undiminished capacity 'to resist developments that were contrary to its interests'.[2]

Numerous studies undertaken since then have time and again borne out Wood's conclusions. Moreover, their findings formed part of a more general reassessment that had been going on for some time. It has become apparent, Anthony Molho has summed up, that those local, particularist institutions, which the early modern state was once supposed to have overwhelmed into submission:

> continued to thrive in the late medieval and early modern centuries. Indeed, these were not mere relics of a preceding political and constitutional order; they gave the early modern state its peculiar and idiosyncratic character ... [C]enter and periphery were often strengthened in tandem, in a process of mutual reinforcement that allowed the center new juridical and administrative powers but concurrently strengthened traditional freedoms that institutional and corporate bodies of the periphery had enjoyed in the past.[3]

With its traditional bases of power in the country and its array of immunities and privileges, the nobility naturally occupies a central place in the renovated picture. This is one main reason why, after years of relative neglect, it has so forcefully been put back on the scholarly agenda; why recent years have witnessed a spate of studies on various national, regional and local nobilities. Conversely, the cumulative results have forced historians to accept, sometimes despite themselves, that rather than embourgeoisement, Western European societies underwent a process of aristocratization.[4] It is no longer possible to dismiss the nobility as a phenomenon of secondary importance, for it has become clear that the nobility was not just another part of society, but a constitutive principle of its organization, and that therefore no adequate understanding of the latter can be formed without giving the nobility pride of place. However, what research on different nobilities has also brought to light is the prodigious richness of aristocratic experiences, which in turn renders the construction of a new overarching paradigm extremely difficult.[5]

The aims of the present volume are accordingly limited. Its focus is an experience which, though varied across times and places, was shared by all of the nobilities of Western Europe. Beyond this significant commonality, that experience was also literally formative. Indeed, it arguably had a greater impact on the lives of nobles than any other coeval development. It may thus be considered a crucial aspect of a more comprehensive understanding of the European nobility, and its exploration as a way of providing an outline of the evolution of that group. This was the process of state formation.

A central contention of what follows is that it was the transformation of the medieval kingdoms into states which shaped the nobility. The argument has two intertwined strands. The first has to do with the formal definition of noble status. Nobility, as it was commonly understood by the end of the period under discussion, was a juridical entity. Indeed, it has been observed that the early modern European nobility 'appears to have been a singular phenomenon in European history' by dint of its highly developed juridical character. It cannot be properly understood other than as an *ordre juridique*.[6] There is no other way fully to account for its special place in early modern society as there is no other way to define it without excluding some people who were deemed noble and/or including others who were not. Legal definitions were not watertight, of course. But over time they did tend to become increasingly tidy and demanding. And while the nobility did not emerge fully fledged at one specific point in time, but was subject to a continuous process of juridical elaboration, it is still possible to discern periods of crystallization. As Chapters 1 and 2 seek to demonstrate, the first crucial stage was the fourteenth century, and was an integral part of an equally crucial phase in the consolidation of states. Prior to that time, the nobles can be said to have constituted a nobility only in a very loose sense. Medieval nobles by and large lacked the explicit attributes, the more or less precise criteria of inclusion and exclusion, that distinguished them clearly and delimited the group. This means that in theory, if not in practice, anyone could become a noble.

This situation was undergoing a profound change in the later Middle Ages. Conceptual vagueness and the corresponding relative social openness began to give way to a more and more stringent definition of noble status, the *sine qua non* of the existence of nobles as a distinct social category. Thereafter, in theory if not in practice, not anyone (and according to some jurists, no one) could become a noble. The implied distinction between *de jure* and *de facto* status does not diminish the importance of the change, precisely because the drift was towards an effective identification between them. The intangible benefits which formal noble status conferred, such as social esteem, were increasingly qualifications requisite for obtaining concrete benefits. It gave access to both honour and 'honours', in the sense of entitlement to various kinds of personal and property rights, that was less and less available to non-nobles.[7] To gain that access, anyone not already noble had to have acquired noble status, which was far from impossible. But this too only serves to under-score the significance of the change under way since the closing centuries of the Middle Ages. This was not that the nobility was becoming an impermeable caste, albeit that the more exact criteria of nobility may have made movement into it more difficult. The point is that the change was a reflection of, and a factor in, the tran-sition from medieval to early modern society to whose structure and workings and self-image nobility was pivotal. Nobility was becoming a constitutive principle of the Old Regime, that social order based on privilege, differential prestige, and legalized inequality.[8] It is no coincidence that the English nobility, the least privileged in Western Europe, inhabited a society which is most resistant to classification as *ancien régime* type.

The explanation for this evolution of the estate of nobility is the second main strand of the argument. It is sought in the complex fabric of interrelations between monarch, state, and nobles. The underlying question is an old one. To borrow the words of Theodor Mayer:

> the great and critical problem of the [post-Frankish era] was how could the monarchical authority succeed in incorporating into the state of the king the great nobles with their dominions, to undermine their lordships, to make the autonomous lords into subjects.

Writing in 1959, Mayer assumed a contrariety between a strong monarchical state and a strong nobility; present students take comple-mentarity more seriously. As Bruce McFarlane, one of the historians most responsible for the subsequent change of perception, wrote of the relationship between king and nobles in England: 'In fact the area of possible conflict was extraordinarily small and any compe-tent king had no difficulty in avoiding it.'[9] Once the view of antithesis is rejected, however, two points call for clarification. One is the numerous and sometimes quite dramatic clashes between monarchs and nobles on which the older view rested. The second is how the widespread conflict on record can be reconciled with the ample evidence for close co-operation between monarchs and nobles which newer research has so emphatically stressed. These are principally the subjects of Chapters 3 and 4, which deal with the fifteenth and sixteenth century, respectively.

The key element in explaining the concurrence of conflict and collaboration is the nature of early modern state. In the first place, though the state had a pronounced patrimonial character, it must not be conflated (only) with the monarchy. Despite the early modern tendency towards identification of the two, they never fully fused.[10] King Louis XIV may have thought *l'état, c'est moi*, but one lesson he must have drawn from the *Fronde* was that he could not ride roughshod over the vested interests of the office-holders who manned the state. Thus, while the state was not yet impersonal, it did not appertain solely to the monarch; it did develop an existence inchoately distinct from the ruler, precisely because it was deeply penetrated by social interests and therefore not entirely distinct from some of the nominally ruled either. This character of the state was constitutive of the ambivalence in the relationship between monarchy and nobility.

The theme may further be developed with Machiavelli's help. In *The Prince* the state does nothing. The verbs with which *lo stato* is most frequently collocated are: to acquire, hold, maintain, take away, lose. It is an object, not a subject. Machiavelli uses 'the state' in an exploitative sense. To his mind it is an instrument with which to exercise command over men to one's own advantage. In *The Prince*, John Hexter has remarked, the state is essentially 'what is politically up for grabs'.[11] Although this meaning of 'the state' is not sufficiently wide for all the purposes of the present volume, it can be used to explain a good deal about the nature and development of the relationship between monarchy and nobility. To begin with, precisely because it was not an abstract, impartial public authority separate from the ruler, the ruled, at least some of them, could hardly allow the state to be completely separate from themselves. Conflict between monarchs and nobles was rife not simply because the state could be and sometimes was applied by the former to the subjugation of the latter, but because the state – being a tool of domination which could be captured, controlled, and alienated – had its uses also for the nobles. And the more it grew, the higher became the stakes, and the keener their interest in it. On the other hand, precisely these qualities of the state were also the source of numerous conflicts among the nobility itself over access to it, with the result that these two aspects often balanced each other: the ubiquitous struggle between nobles over a place in the state both encouraged alliances between some nobles and the ruler against other nobles, and enhanced his or her authority as an arbiter between them. The state apparatus 'was as much an arena for the regulation of conflicts inside the ruling class as an instrument of class domination'.[12]

The exploitation of the population to the mutual profit of ruler and ruling classes underlay much of the co-operation between them. As Chapter 4 will seek to demonstrate, this function of the state, mediated through the fiscal and financial institutions generated by the impetus of international wars, was the basis for the progressive integration of Continental nobilities into the state structure in the first half of the sixteenth century. The relationship between monarchy and a leading segment of the nobility turned from a loose alliance into an institutionalized interdependence embedded in the edifice of state. However, in the second half of the sixteenth century, the process of assimilation suffered a terrible setback in some countries. The momentous growth in the power of rulers in general, and in the wake of the Reformation in particular, lent harsh urgency to the question of authority, and provoked massive resistance. The state once again became an object of contention between monarchy and nobility, its divisive side overshadowing its integrative one, with exceptionally bloody consequences.

The reconstitution of the alliance, or, where it had survived, its reinforcement, was a defining feature in the emergence of absolutist regimes in the seventeenth century. Absolutism therefore needs to be reappraised: it was essentially a renewed accommodation between monarchy and nobility, not a radical restructuring of their relationship in favour of the former. As described in Chapter 5, it augmented and stabilized the power of both monarchy and a section of the nobility.

These conclusions do not on the whole apply to England. It is obvious that the divergence in the paths taken by the English and Continental states explains a good deal about the different kinds of relationship between monarchy and nobility. But the reverse is to some extent true as well.[13] Thus, the fact that in England no firm alliance formed between monarchy and nobility was at once a cause and a consequence of the English state being considerably more autonomous than those of mainland Europe. This, as Chapter 5 will try to illustrate, was decisive in giving England the edge over its giant rival across the Channel.

The English case indeed helps to throw into sharper relief the long-term implications of Western European absolutism. The rearrangement of the relations between monarchy and nobility which it involved amounted to something of a 'Faustian pact'. Shaped by an environment of unprecedently expanding scale of international warfare, it actually devitalized the state. Control over significant areas of government authority was in effect surrendered to those individuals and groups without whose 'private' political, military and financial resources the war effort would have been even more unsustainable. Research has revealed this phenomenon to have been so pervasive, and normative, as seriously to qualify and modify the prevailing thesis that early modern war acted as a catalyst of growth of state power. Rather than the instrument with which the monarchy shattered the might of the nobility, the state turns out to have been the instrument which the monarchy was forced to allow nobles (and other powerful people) to wield in their interest as well as in its own. On the other hand, the Continental nobles' very success proved to be a trap which left them vulnerable to a series of interlocking changes in the eighteenth century. The nature of this transition and the attendant decline of the nobility are sketched out in Chapter 6, which generalizes central points made throughout the book and takes the story, rather summarily, up to the nineteenth century.

1   The dawn of modern times

The modern state was born in Western Europe in the fourteenth century, the natural child of war and taxation. It is perhaps an historical irony that this type of state – in which law reigns and deifies human rights – has such brutish ancestry. But it is not a paradox. The wars upon which the English and French kings embarked around 1300, and which were soon to spill over to the Iberian peninsula, proved an altogether new, radically new, phenomenon: unlike earlier conflicts, they were effectively interminable. Neither monarch could meet the costs of war on a continuous basis out of his own resources: while the ordinary revenues of the English Crown were estimated in 1284 at £27,000, the expenditure on war in 1294–8 totalled some £750,000. And it stands to reason that neither monarch could afford the prohibitively expensive machinery necessary to coerce these resources out of the country at large. They all had to impress on their subjects the urgency of the situation, to persuade them that the common good was at stake, that they needed to contribute in taxes to an effort on a dauntingly exceptional scale. Frequently enough war itself did the talking, so to speak. The danger it posed to life and property made people readier than they would otherwise have been to part with their money so as to pay for their defence. In any case, a fiscal administration had to be developed to handle the complex operation of collecting and spending of tax monies, as well as to service the usually enormous debts left in the wake of the latter activity. Insistent pressure of war thus led to the creation or expansion of state apparatus, and to the multiplication of the personnel dealing with paying and supplying the army. Such swelling bureaucracy was itself a drain on economic resources, which in turn meant that more taxes had to be levied or new financial sources opened up, and so on and so forth. As Samuel Finer has put it in connection with the so-called Hundred Years War (1337–1453): 'The verdict

of history – at least European history – is that war calls out a super-
abundance of military, administrative, and fiscal overkills which
largely remain in place when peace returns. War has an adminis-
trative/fiscal ratchet effect.' On this account, wars made the states
that made wars on each other. Yet the impact of war was not everywhere the same; it had significantly disparate consequences in terms
of state forms.[1]

In England, the outbreak of war against France in 1294 was
followed by a revolt in Wales and then an invasion into Scotland.
The unquestionable emergency of the situation in the years 1294–7
enabled King Edward I to demand general taxation on plea of necessity. Taxes, previously sporadic, were now levied in three successive
years. To some influential people this seemed to be heralding an
expensive royal disposition, and before long a political crisis ensued.
The *Monstraunces* of 1297 complained that 'all the community of
the land feel themselves greatly aggrieved that they are not treated
according to the laws and customs of the land . . . , nor have they
their liberties which they used to have'.[2] Strong words, but the precise
legal platform for resistance to royal demands was yet to be worked
out. However frequent and enlarged in scope these demands grew,
they could be and were construed as a mere extension of incon-
testable royal prerogatives. They could not be rejected so long as,
because of war, evident necessity could be shown to exist. Precisely
this predicament made it imperative somehow to limit and regulate
the Crown's ability to trench upon the wealth of its subjects. This
could be achieved only through bargaining. Parliament was in effect
prepared to offer more money than royal prerogative warranted in
exchange for restraining the range of exactions that could be imposed
in the name of royal prerogative. In other words, money was traded
for constitutional power, whereby each party attained its immediate
goal.

The final stage of this process was reached in the 1360s, the
decade after the peace of Brétigny: the Crown, thanks to the habit-
forming effects of war and highly imaginative accounting by the
Exchequer, managed to bring Parliament to convert the wool subsidy
into a regular tax. Thus the crucial threshold was crossed separating
occasional wartime taxation from permanent peacetime taxation. The
price was that each grant required parliamentary consent, and that
direct taxation could from then on be sought for no other purpose
than the defence of the realm. Parliament became invested with the
authority to adjudicate whether the king's financial demands served
the common profit and should therefore be given the common assent.

A self-conscious political community came into being – the unintended and far-reaching consequence of the emergence of a system of public finance to pay war (it is noteworthy in this respect that it was in 1362 that Parliament pronounced English to be the official language in law courts). As early as 1370, then, England set off on that *Sonderweg* of co-operation which marked her political culture until the seventeenth century and beyond.[3]

In France, too, extraordinary taxes were converted into regular taxes around 1370. The turning point here was the capture in 1356 of King Jean II at the battle of Poitiers. Taxation was now irrefragably justified both by the doctrine of evident necessity and the ancient and honourable feudal tradition that obliged one to redeem one's lord from captivity. In late 1360 a royal ordinance established the *gabelle* (indirect tax on salt) and *aides* for six years to pay for the king's colossal ransom. As it happened, they were collected in all but two of the following fifty-seven years. Small wonder that the French *franc* takes its name from the inscription – *Johannes Dei Gracia Francorum Rex* – on a gold coin minted in 1360. The cessation of hostilities in the aftermath of the king's release had a second consequence extremely conducive to taxation: multitudes of soldiers, schooled in nothing but combat, were demobilized and took to roaming in lawless bands, living off the people. 'Robberies and pillages, arson attacks, larcenies, seizures of goods, violence, oppression, extortions [and] exactions' became the daily experience. This made paying taxes an attractive proposition as never before, if, as King Jean II declared, they would finance the suppression of 'the *compagnies* and the brigands'. In 1363 Estates representing Languedoïl consented to a *fouage*, or an apportioned hearth tax – the first direct tax to be raised in time of formal peace. In 1368 taxes were imposed also in Languedoc. They were designed to finance a military expedition led by Bertrand du Guesclin that would take the roving freelance soldiers out of the realm. These measures were as yet insufficient to form a convention, but they did set the decisive precedent of taxation with a view to maintaining an army in peacetime. After some vicissitudes in the following decades, these levies were restored in the fifteenth century to remain the basic royal taxes until the Revolution. As in England, war and taxation were turning the monarchy into a veritable national institution, thereby enormously expanding its potential. But unlike England, the years 1356–70 in France laid the foundation for an 'absolute' monarchy.[4]

In Castile of the fourteenth century a protracted war was no novelty. When, in the 1360s, the peninsula became a theatre of operations in the Anglo-French conflict, it had the formative experience of the *reconquista* behind it. And indeed, the pressures exerted from very early on by quasi-permanent warfare, coupled with the potent idea of crusading, made Castile fiscally precocious. They provided Castilian monarchs with a virtually unassailable justification for striking national taxes. This had already occurred under King Alfonso X (1252–84). But the really crucial date in this respect was 1342, when the *Cortes* granted King Alfonso XI the *alcabala*, a sales tax, for three years to defray the costs of the siege of Algeciras. During the reign of the first Trastámara king, Enrique II (1369–79), the *alcabala* appears to have been accorded every year. Under Enrique III (1390–1406) it was transformed into an ordinary source of income of the Crown, no longer requiring the prior approval of the *Cortes*. In 1394 the *alcabala* accounted for nearly 43 per cent of total royal revenue, and in 1429, 75 per cent. In the early sixteenth century it made up (together with the clerical *tercias reales*) some 80 or 90 per cent of the monarchy's income. Thus, as in France, the most important national tax in Castile was created in the mid-fourteenth century in response to the exigencies of war, and soon turned into a regular impost unfettered by an obligation to secure the consent of representative assemblies. This made all the difference between Castile with its absolutist monarchy and Aragon or Navarre, where the Crowns remained tied down by the *Cortes*. Neither Aragon nor Navarre was in a position to institute an army and bureaucracy capable of undergirding a modern state.[5]

Thus, a novel kind of war – endemic and incessant – imploded what remained of the decaying 'classic' feudal order in Europe. The personal, trans-territorial, segmentary feudal arrangements proved woefully inadequate to the new circumstances. Rulers therefore had to appeal for aid, in a consistent manner, to a much wider constituency than their greater vassals. The demands of each monarch now came to impinge on all those living in an area over which that monarch could make a tenable claim to supreme jurisdiction. The construction of a system of public finance to pay for war and the appearance of consolidated territory proceeded in parallel. Here lay the origins of the unitary, 'modern' state. The term 'modern' is not an absolute, and is understood variously by historians and sociologists. In one prevalent use, the 'modern state' denotes the democratic, liberal state whose history can be traced back to *c*. 1300.[6] But 'modern' may also be taken to mean primarily the effectiveness of the institutional organization of that state in comparison with other, contemporaneous states: a certain capacity to govern centrally and to mobilize human and material resources. It is true that in Western Europe the two aspects came to be wedded, and to have a certain causal relationship between them. But that is no good reason to confuse between them as necessary corollaries. Civil and political liberty, if allowed to take precedence over the needs of security and political control, might and sometimes did result in its own decline or even outright dissolution. 'It has long been a grave question,' President Lincoln pointed out during the Civil War, 'whether any government not too strong for the liberties of its people can be strong enough to maintain its existence in great emergencies.' In Western Europe this problem became massively relevant in the late fifteenth and sixteenth centuries, as an anarchic, multipolar system of states came into its own.

Italy and the Holy Roman Empire provide outstanding examples of failure to adapt to the new international environment. The successive waves of foreign invasions into Italy from 1494 onwards revealed that, for all their administrative sophistication, the Italian statelets were humiliatingly helpless in the face of so-called new monarchies. The French army 'conquered Italy with a piece of chalk', as Machiavelli put it: so weak was the resistance they encountered, that all the French needed to do was to mark houses where their soldiers were to be billeted.[7] With the Empire, too, all was not well. A long period without grave external military threat deprived the monarchy of such opportunities as its Western counterparts had to offer itself as a credible focus of common fears and aspirations. It is emblematic in this comparative regard that the famous Golden Bull of Emperor Charles IV was enacted in 1356. Although strengthening the monarchy towards the outside, the Bull, if only endorsing and regularizing an existing situation, confirmed in law the regalian rights of the seven electoral princes (*Kurfürsten*). It laid down, for example, that no subject of an elector could be summoned to any tribunal outside that elector's territory. The dualistic trend was not reversed in the fifteenth century, despite some experiments with general taxation. These miscarried one after another. The most ambitious attempt, the Common Penny of 1495, foundered like all the preceding ones on the opposition of the imperial Estates, especially the autonomous princes. These failures were compounded by the assumption by Habsburgs of the Spanish, Bohemian and Hungarian Crowns in the early sixteenth century. Their attention and resources spread thin, the Habsburgs were unable to achieve supremacy in the strategic core zone of southern Germany. These factors signalled that a centralized state, which in that period could only be constructed by and around a prepotent monarchy, would not come about in early modern Germany.[8] Politically fragmented like Italy, that inert mass of a Holy Roman Empire of the German nation was to succeed Italy in the seventeenth century as Europe's battleground, with horrific consequences to its inhabitants.

The German example raises with particular acuity the question of why the seigneurs in England, France and Spain did acquiesce in royal taxation that so prodigiously and conspicuously magnified the power of the Crowns. Was it not more in their interest to act like the German princes or the Polish magnates, and emasculate their monarchs? It is, after all, not for nothing that *panstwo*, the Polish word for 'state', derives from words referring to nobles (*pan, pany*) – so complete was their stranglehold on the monarchy. Were, in contrast, the Western magnates so myopic as not to realize that the power to tax would sooner or later give its possessor the power to coerce? The latter capability, at least in Max Weber's classic definition, is the constitutive feature of the state: 'a human community that (successfully) claims the *monopoly of the legitimate use of physical force* within a given territory'.[9] Perhaps Weber's formulation owed too much to his experience of Wilhelmine Germany, but it is nevertheless heuristically useful here as a point of departure precisely because it is so modernly categorical (and historically controvertible). From such a perspective, the lords, densely strewn over the Western European landscape, should have been the greatest single obstacle to state formation, to the reconstitution and consolidation of royal power after its breakdown in the 'feudal revolution' of *c.* 1000. Indeed, one of the twentieth-century's most influential German historians, Otto Brunner, argued that the medieval polity could not be classified as a state, precisely because what distinguished the lords of that period was their legally sanctioned right to resolve their differences by means of feuding. 'A world in which the feud is always a possibility,' he wrote, 'of necessity has a structure altogether completely different from the civil world of an absolute state which claims the monopoly of the legitimate use of force.'[10] The implication is that for non-state polities such as the medieval monarchies to become states, they had either to eliminate or at least subjugate those self-reliant, armigerous lords. But the question then is how they could accomplish either task when, not being states, they had not yet possessed a monopoly of the use of physical force, legitimate or not. The motto of the redoubtable one-eyed Breton lord Olivier de Clisson (1336–1407), *Pour c'est qu'il me plest*, is likely to have rung true in more than a couple of ears. But whereas he sided with King Charles VI of France, whom he boasted to have made 'roy et seigneur de son royaume',[11] many other lords were far less obliging.

Godefroi d'Harcourt, for instance: a puissant Norman lord, he picked a quarrel with King Philippe VI of France. In 1344 he was banished and his property confiscated. He went over to England, swore allegiance to King Edward III, and then facilitated the latter's invasion into Normandy. Such was d'Harcourt's clout, however, that when he later recanted, the French king was only too keen to embrace him.[12] This pattern of breaking oaths and shifting loyalties according to expedient was quite widespread among the lords of the late Middle Ages. But the trend-setters of disloyal conduct were actually nearly always and everywhere members of the ruling House itself.[13] And because the various European ruling dynasties were at once closely interrelated and constantly at each other's throat, powerful lords suffered no shortage of both compelling and contrived causes to involve themselves in succession and other disputes, support one pretender against the other, tergiversate if need be, and bolster their own position into the bargain. Philippe de Commynes related that, during the parley between King Louis XI of France and Duke Charles the Bold of Burgundy and allied princes, so many men changed sides that the place where these transactions were struck was called the Market. A textbook case is the conflict between King Fernando of Spain and his son-in-law, Archduke Philip the Fair. The Habsburg arrived in Spain in 1506 with the intention of claiming a share in government. He chose his time well: the grandees of Spain were by then utterly disaffected with the strong-willed Fernando. So when Philip disembarked at La Coruña they 'and so many other noble men, lords, knights and barons' waited there to give him a regal welcome. Left without political and military backing, Fernando agreed to abdicate the regency in favour of Philip and to leave Castile for good. It is reported that at Villafàfilla, where the treaty was signed, Fernando spotted his former councillor Garcilaso de la Vega (father of the poet), and exclaimed, 'You too, García?' A few months later, after Philip the Fair's sudden death, Garcilaso was restored to favour.[14]

To the modern eye such spectacles may appear rather quaint. Certainly they cannot be reconciled with modern legal concepts of the state. However, they should not necessarily be interpreted as indicating the non-existence of the state, nor otherwise its inveterate weakness. What they do point up is the very different characteristics and workings of the late medieval and early modern state,[15] which was shaped in large measure by the place of lords in it. In a scintillating chapter in *The Discourses*, Machiavelli theorized that the presence or absence of a class of lords was constitutive of the two main types of polity: a republic, presupposing a certain degree of social equality, can never flourish in the former condition; a monarchy thrives on it.[16] But between monarchies, too, there were significant structural differences, and in *The Prince* Machiavelli posited that the kind of lordly class on hand was a central factor in producing these differences:

> The whole Turkish Kingdom is governed by one ruler, the others all being his servants . . . But the King of France is placed amidst a great number of hereditary lords, recognised in that state by their own subjects, who are devoted to them. They have their own hereditary privileges, which the King disallows only at his peril. If these two kinds of state are considered, then, it will be found that it is difficult to overcome a state of the Turkish type but, if it has been conquered, very easy to hold it. On the other hand, in some respects it is easier to conquer a state like France, but it is very difficult to hold it.[17]

It was easy to conquer a state like France, Machiavelli went on to explain, because it was always possible to find and win over some malcontent barons who wanted to change the regime. Even on this rather negative view of the lords, the Western monarchies could not help being conditioned by that class of powerful people; powerful not only because they maintained their own armed retinues, but also because, in marked contrast to Russia, for example, they enjoyed a degree of autonomous legitimacy. As Richelieu (tendentiously) reminisced in his memoirs, 'the House of Montmorency, who from of old have been governors of Languedoc, have become so deeply imprinted on its people that they do not believe the name of the King to be but imaginary'. It is true that any ruler's power normally exceeded that of any of the greatest magnates, and that the magnates rarely wanted or were able to unite against the ruler. But no ruler, even if he or she wished so, could constantly resort to force and intimidation to induce compliance in his or her mightier 'subjects', for this would have been prohibitively expensive and, certainly in the long term, a self-defeating exercise. In this regard at least, all Western monarchies were limited in point of fact, if not in name. And it is mainly for these reasons that, to paraphrase Bruce

McFarlane, the real politics in the late Middle Ages consisted in the monarch's relations with the magnates. Any explanation, then, of how the modern state came about cannot avoid taking seriously into account the power and authority of lords, and the complex relationship between them and rulers. Any explanation that treats of these issues as merely sub-plots is as plausible as that given by the Baron of Münchhausen of how he managed to pull himself and his horse out of a swamp.[18]

In trying to explain the motives lords had to co-operate, whether passively or actively, in a project that augmented royal power, one is struck by the fact that the early phase of state formation took place at a time of pervasive crisis. The ravages of war and famines of the first half of the fourteenth century were disastrous enough; but they were minor irritants compared with the havoc wrought by the Black Death, the pestilence that reached Europe from central Asia in 1348. Sweeping through the continent, it wiped out, by a conservative estimate, a quarter of the population, in some areas up to four-fifths of it. A calamity of such magnitude could not have failed to produce cataclysmic effects. The most revolutionary of these was a reversal in the ratio of land to labour: land became abundant, labour scarce. Wages rose immediately and, slightly delayed, cereal prices plummeted – a development that benefited artisans and peasants. Also, the increased demand for labour bolstered their bargaining position and, in the agrarian sector, enabled peasants to improve tenancy terms. Correspondingly, the income of manorial lords from rents dwindled. Moreover, the circumstance that no comparable slump in the prices of manufactured goods occurred weakened further the lords' economic power. The lordly class fell on hard times.[19]

This is also the bottom line of the seminal Marxist, non-Malthusian interpretation of Guy Bois. While assigning no driving role to the plague, Bois argues that, for endogenous reasons, the revenues of the lords already started their descent at the beginning of the century. In the lords' ensuing impoverishment he sees more a cause than an effect of the general crisis that marked the fourteenth century. For the sole outlet available to them from the economic dire straits was participation in war, the growth industry of the time. Their manors no longer able to sustain them, the lords flocked to the royal armies. And, in a parallel move, on the shrinking seigneurial levy came to be superimposed the new centralized royal levy, which was then redistributed to the warriors in the form of salaries and pensions. The indigent lords, then, acted as a motor of war (and pillage), thus reproducing the necessity of royal taxation. In this way, Bois concludes (quoting Marc Bloch), 'it is not an exaggeration to say that it is through a crisis of seigneurial revenues that the Middle Ages come to an end and the modern times begin'.[20]

Bois's interpretation is highly suggestive in that it seeks to establish the mutually reinforcing links between economic problems, war and national taxation. Economic difficulties may well account for the alacrity with which some fourteenth-century lords, whose chivalric ethos anyway predisposed them to martial pursuits, lined up behind their belligerent kings. One moot point, however, is the assumed general correlation between destitution and enthusiasm for war. For there is no proof that all nobles suffered from economic adversity, nor that only impecunious lords joined the army. But even if it were the latter who formed the bulk of the armed forces, this does not in itself clarify why they agreed to pay taxes themselves and/or that their tenants would. Perhaps on the contrary: if anything, the 'crisis of feudalism' should have exacerbated competition between lords and monarchs over diminishing revenues. On the other hand, it is impossible to prove that at that early stage the lords were clear-sighted about the possibility that royal taxes imposed on commoners might regularly be siphoned off to them to such an extent as to make up for the dwindling seigneurial sources of revenue. This applies even to the greater lords who were more likely than their lesser fellows to make capital of taxation. In Castile, for instance, lords in revolt against fiscal novelties demanded also that the king increase their money benefices, which he of course could not do unless he kept up the novel royal impositions.[21] And indeed, throughout the first half of the fourteenth century, royal taxation was continually challenged in Europe. It was only in the latter part of the century that a change of attitude manifested itself among the lords: between 1350 and 1370, in both England and France, they ceased from protecting their dependants against royal taxation. And it is telling that this occurred at the very time when taxation was becoming a permanent feature.

The change was particularly swift and harsh in England, where it came as a direct reaction of the landowners to the crisis provoked by the plague. The Ordinance of Labourers and Servants was promulgated in June 1349; in 1351 it was followed by the Statute of Labourers. This was a piece of repressive legislation aimed at forcing all able-bodied labourers to work, and work 'in return for the salaries and wages which were customary . . . during the twentieth year of the present king's reign [1346–7] or five or six years previously'.

Moreover, the enforcement of the labour laws was entrusted precisely to those who stood to gain most from it. Indeed, the fines collected under statute were used to pay part of the subsidies granted to the king, thereby alleviating the tax burden on the propertied classes. Thus landlords, especially of the middling sort, made common cause with the Crown to keep their inferiors in their place, and squeeze their growing wealth. It is highly revealing that after 1350 the Commons stopped contesting the issues of prerogative levies and taxes on wool. They became agents, rather than critics, of royal government.[22]

In France, too, an instant attempt was made to legislate away the effects of the Black Death. But the connection between this and the lords' abandonment of their dependants to the tax-collector is not as explicit as in England. It may well be that the enhanced control peasants had gained over their own life made the effort of protecting them seem rather pointless. But France was anyway in the throes of a long-drawn-out political crisis, and the pestilence just complicated what was created by war, recurrent defeats, and power struggles consequent upon the capture of King Jean II. The result was a conflict between lords and commoners, a conflict which exploded into the *Jacquerie* of 1358. The revolt was put down, and it was after that that a decisive rapprochement took place between Crown and lords. This was facilitated by and reflected in the new tax structure. Whereas during the first half of the century the lords seemed to be losing ground to the pressure of royal taxation, after 1360 the burden of taxation was decisively being shifted onto other groups in the society. As historians have recognized, this was 'the keystone of the new pro-noble regime that took power in 1360'.[23]

In Castile, being anyway underpopulated, the impact of the Black Death was not overwhelming. Yet as in France it coincided with a period of political turmoil which it probably served to worsen. Three years after the *Cortes* of 1351, which tried to counteract the labour shortage and falling seigneurial rents, an aristocratic revolt erupted. It was led by King Pedro's bastard half-brother, Enrique of Trastámara. The civil war soon became part of the Hundred Years War, with the French (sending out those mercenaries who harried France) on Enrique's side and the English on Pedro's. After some dramatic turns of fortune, Enrique triumphed, the bloody struggle culminating, appropriately enough, in the murder of Pedro in 1369. Absolutely essential to the success of the Trastámara *coup d'état* was the backing of a number of lordly families whom Pedro managed to alienate and Enrique to win over. The change of regime meant that the lofty, authoritarian ideal of monarchy espoused by Pedro was supplanted by a more balanced relationship between king and lords. This received an immediate fiscal foundation. Countless rewards and annuities on royal income were distributed, and even shares in the proceeds from the *alcabala*, the mainstay of royal finances, began to be granted to lords as recompense for their support. It has been calculated that, in 1429, over 60 per cent of royal expenditure flowed to the aristocracy. Julio Valdeón Baruque has commented in this regard that, paradoxical as it may seem, this reinforcement of the standing of the seigneurs went hand in hand with a growth in royal power: 'the crises of the fourteenth century led to a reordering of the social and political structures of the Crown of Castile, whose most significant characteristics would be ... the advance of seigneurialisation and the approach towards the absolute monarchy'.[24]

Thus, despite differently configured sets of determinants, the crises of the fourteenth century had one similar net result in England, France and Castile: the formation of an alliance between the Crown and the lordly class – an alliance which strengthened both to the marked disadvantage of the lower orders. It is worthy of note in this context that the alliance gave unwonted prominence to lords of less exalted rank than the top magnates, and even to some of middling station. It is discernible in England, in the relationship between Crown and gentry, and the conferral on the latter of governmental responsibilities in the counties; in Castile, in the group families that were instrumental in the accession to the throne of the fratricidal usurper Enrique II; and in France, in the influence exercised under Charles V and especially Charles VI by the so-called *Marmousets* and their adherents among the military commanders.[25]

   This alliance was shaped by a shared reaction of the parties to the crises which threatened them. The immense strains generated by war and social and economic dislocation compelled the monarchy to extend its purview which it could not even begin to contemplate without the co-operation of the lords, still, despite everything, the most powerful men in society. If the turbulent reign of King Pedro of Castile had any lesson, it was the sheer futility and fatality of attempting to integrate the aristocracy into the state against their will.[26] But the prevalent unrest triggered by unremitting wars and unrelieved governmental demands gave lords occasions to demonstrate also their positive value to rulers. After all they were military experts, some of them possessors of strategic strongholds, men nurtured to exercise leadership, with feudal tradition of service, similar cultural certitudes and anxieties, and an interest in keeping down the common people. These were no mean credentials in that heyday of popular revolts in Western Europe: the *Jacquerie* in France in 1358, the uprisings in Flanders in 1379–82, the Peasants' Revolt in England in 1381, and many other smaller insurrections. In their search for order and stability the rulers fell back on the lords. And on the whole the lords acquitted themselves rather well: the count of Foix and the Captal de Buch 'mowed [the *Jacques*] down in heaps and slaughtered them like cattle', and their task was finished off by Enguerrand de Coucy (a future *Marmouset*); the suppressive activities of the earls of Buckingham, Kent, Salisbury, Warwick, Derby and Suffolk are attested in Wardrobe accounts of payments made to them to defray their military expenses in 1381; and the carnage of Roosebeke (1382) was the work of French knights (led by Clisson), who went on to reclaim the golden spurs taken by the Flemings eighty years earlier at Courtrai.[27]

The same disruptions that rendered them so indispensable to monarchs drove home to the lords the need to co-operate with the monarchs and acquiesce in their claims to greater powers. The cumulative effect of the various crises must have seemed intolerable to many lords: their own economic embarrassment coincided with a growing prosperity and self-confidence on the part of subordinates, resulting in a greater social mobility and loosening of seigneurial ties. The traditional order of society appeared to be breaking up. The Florentine chronicler Matteo Villani complained that:

> the common people, by reason of the abundance and superfluity that they found, would no longer work at their accustomed trades; they wanted the dearest and most delicate foods . . . while children and common women clad themselves in all the fair and costly garments of the illustrious who had died.

In England the Commons complained in 1376 that 'for fear of . . . flights, the commons now dare not challenge their servants, but give them whatever they wish or ask . . . – and chiefly through fear that they will be received elsewhere'. To stem the tide a concerted action was required, and that by definition called for central government action. This pressure combined with those generated by war that were transforming the feudal monarchies into national institutions. It was precisely the momentous growth in the scope and competence of monarchical authority that, if it provided outlets to those petty lords whose position had become vulnerable, was, more critically, opening up unprecedented opportunities to those greater lords whose ability to oppose the monarchy made their collaboration a requisite. It was the latter in particular who stood to profit from the expansion of the monarchical state. The allocation to Spanish lords of proceeds from the new *alcabala* tax has already been mentioned. French kings too took to sharing the yield from taxation with the great feudatories so as to secure their consent to levies in the territories under their control. By the same token, lords of somewhat lesser if still quite prominent rank, who were both willing and able to give the monarchy telling assistance, could expect to be invested with power and its rewards to a degree otherwise unthinkable. An example is provided, once again, by Olivier de Clisson. His wealth was an important factor in his nomination to constable of France, for it enabled him to pay of his own hundreds of troops, effectively lending money to the Crown; at one point he was owed by the treasury a sum that exceeded by 50 per cent the ordinary income of the Crown in 1374. But the constableship in turn was an important factor in allowing Clisson to increase his fortune to fabulous proportions, making himself one of the richest men in France.[28] It is true that such new power came with a price: it was more dependent on the monarch and inevitably entailed a certain loss of autonomy. But in the circumstances it was both revitalizing and more secure than the old form.[29]

This alliance, built in large part on the developing state institutions, fiscal and otherwise, was a reactionary, conservative solution to the problems of the age. But, like so many other attempts at restoration before and after, it produced far-reaching changes. It forged the nobility as a distinct socio-juridical category, laying the foundation of the *ancien régime* polities in Western Europe.

2 The changing face of nobility

In 1818 Ludwig van Beethoven was exposed as a fraud. Until then he had been presumed noble by Viennese society, the Dutch 'van' being mistaken for the German aristocratic particle 'von'. Beethoven, for his part, did not go out of his way to disown his gratuitous dignity. In 1818, however, he became party to a lawsuit that was heard by a court reserved for the nobility. Asked to prove his noble descent, Beethoven admitted that he could not, and was unceremoniously thrown out.[1] The incident is instructive as to what 'nobility' meant by the end of our period. That Beethoven, celebrated in his day, sank into utter despondency after he was denied noble status, indicates that 'nobility' represented a social ideal of formidable attraction. At the same time, 'nobility' was a social group, membership of which now was formally verifiable by means of simple, practicable tests such as the ability to produce a bona fide genealogy, testimony, or diploma. By the early nineteenth century noble status was controlled by explicit, unequivocal legal standards.

It had not always been so. Some four hundred years earlier noble status rested on different notions, and the question of what nobility meant was still open. Thus in 1408 a trial took place in the Dauphiné that revolved around the status of an innkeeper who laid claim to exemption from tax on the ground that he was a noble. A board of twenty-one people – two clerics, eleven nobles and eight commoners – were asked to give their opinion as to 'what is nobility'. The answers were of varied nuances and occasionally idiosyncratic. But in the main the responses converged on two points: a noble is he who pursues the military vocation and makes a living without having to resort to work. What is particularly remarkable is that only two on the panel believed that birth was a necessary (but not sufficient) condition for nobility. Nobility, in the eyes of these people, was essentially a matter of a distinctive way of life. By inference one might take up that style of life deemed noble and subsequently pass oneself off as a noble. Nobility, then, was informal and flexible – an amorphous quality. This raises a problem for the modern observer: given such fluidity, does it make any sense at all to speak of nobility in that period? Marc Bloch wrote:

> To deserve this name [scil. nobility], a class must evidently combine two characteristics. First, it must have a legal status of its own, which confirms and makes effectual the superiority to which it lays claim. In the second place, this status must be hereditary . . . To speak of nobility is to speak of pedigrees.

These Bloch did not find in the records. He concluded that 'pedigrees did not matter because there was no nobility' in Europe before the twelfth century.[2]

Bloch's thesis has not met with universal approval, and the debate over the medieval nobility is still going on. His critics have contended that the European nobility had a continuous and much earlier history than Bloch supposed, and that it had always been based on good birth.[3] But things are not that simple. For one thing, medieval people did not feel until quite late a need to define nobility. The Latin word '*nobilitas*' did not denote a social group but a collection of qualities, and *nobilis* was not a noun but an adjective. For another, the concept contained various elements whose relationship to each other was complex and unstable. It has been shown, for instance, that great French dynasties of the eleventh and twelfth centuries fabricated their genealogies so as to claim descent from a very recent but audacious and valorous ancestor, whereas their true origins went back to Carolingian or even Merovingian times. What this curious case suggests is the growing influence in the eleventh century of the idea of virtue as the basis for high rank. It may have helped to modify the criteria of nobility in allowing greater scope for talent.[4]

The rivalry between virtue and birth was as old as the notion of aristocracy itself, going back to ancient Greece and Rome. It is not surprising therefore that the controversy was taken up again in the Renaissance. Already Dante let fly in *The Convivio* at the 'opinion of the vulgar' that associated nobility and heredity (trattato IV, xix–xxi). The Humanists made the theme of personal merit their own, and they had all the compelling authority of the venerable Aristotle to call on. And the philosopher's formulation that 'good birth . . . [was] only ancient wealth and excellence' indeed found its way into numerous treatises since the translation into Latin of *The*

Politics around the mid-thirteenth century.[5] One might have been tempted to dismiss the 'personal virtue' doctrine as merely the conceited casuistry of pen-pushing 'new men' engaged in a project of self-aggrandisement, were it not for one significant fact: quite a few noblemen not only took interest in the polemic, but also took the line that individual achievement was at least as important as birth. It was John Tiptoft, Earl of Worcester, who around the mid-fifteenth century translated into English Buonaccorso de Montemagno's *De nobilitate*, a work which advocated 'nobility of virtue'. The German noble Ulrich von Hutten, in his dialogue 'The Robbers' (1521), made one of the characters say: 'I am of the opinion that virtue is not hereditary and that he who has to reproach himself with ignominious deeds should in no way be counted among the nobility, even if he were a prince.'[6]

A literary text may not carry sufficient probative weight; but in this case the ideal had close correlation to the real. Virtue played an important ideological role which, as Maurice Keen emphasized, 'gave to the notion of nobility a positive dynamism . . . and ensured the recognition of the desirability of some degree of social mobility'. Another manifestation of the importance attached to the noble way of life was the idea of *dérogeance* which appeared in the second half of the fourteenth century. A noble found engaging consistently in activities perceived as at variance with noble status forfeited his status and privileges (these could later be restored contingent upon abandonment of the derogating activities). High birth had thus provided no insurance against sliding into the commonalty.[7] By the same token, low birth did not disqualify a man from becoming a noble. It could not in fact be otherwise, for noble families were dying out at a rate of 50 per cent every hundred years. Replenishment was therefore too vital to the survival of the noble species for heredity to be allowed to operate as the overriding criterion of affiliation. And indeed, in law codes and law courts as well as in literature, both ancestry and 'living nobly' were often enough adduced simultaneously as equally sound proofs of nobility.[8] 'Birth' or 'blood' was rather a cultural idiom exploiting images of nature to justify the social order. It aimed at imparting a sense of necessity and constancy to social arrangements that in effect all but lacked these qualities.[9]

The preceding discussion suggests the indeterminacy and fluidity – both conceptually and sociologically – of nobility in the late Middle Ages. The aplomb displayed by many historians in proposing neat definitions with which to pin down the late medieval nobility seems, perhaps more than anything else, a measure of the remarkable success of nobiliary ideology. But this ideology, which was beginning to form just then, should not uncritically be projected onto the fourteenth century. Noble identity was at that time in a state of flux and often in contention. This situation was, for whatever reason, apparently not perceived as an inconvenience throughout most of the Middle Ages. It is therefore significant that towards the end of this period nobility became an issue and that a change got under way that would eventually give it sharper, formal contours. Indeed, what Bloch specified as a precondition of a real nobility, namely a transmissible legal status, whose appearance he reckoned from the twelfth century, seems to have taken clear shape only as late as 1400.

In the frontier society of Castile, social boundaries were still open in the thirteenth century, and there is no evidence that this gave rise to anxiety. But towards the end of the next century a conspicuous change occurred. In 1371 a special Judge of the Nobles (*alcalde de los hijosdalgos*) was installed to hear cases of noble status. He was a jurist trained in Roman rather than feudal law, and his was a permanent chamber and part of the central court. Who qualified as noble and who did not must have become a pressing question. The first known legal dispute over noble status took place in 1395. The next two centuries saw an exponential multiplication in the number of cases brought before the Court of Nobles. The vast majority of them resulted from claims to exemption from direct taxes. This privilege, then, crystallized early on as the distinguishing trait of nobility in Castile, and remained so until the mid-sixteenth century.[10]

As in Castile, noble status in France became an issue in the fourteenth century. This was in large part due to the advent of royal taxation which turned the social distribution of the fiscal burden into a political battleground. The crisis-ridden reign of the intermittently insane Charles VI was decisive in this respect. Factional strife at Court was rife, and the competitors vied for the support of the nobles. So when the king's uncle Duke Philippe of Burgundy took over the governance of France, he used tax concessions to secure their goodwill, thereby validating and concretizing their status. The royal ordinances promulgated under his aegis in 1388 and 1393 represented a fateful reversal of policy. They exempted from the *taille* 'nobles of noble lineage who do not engage in trade and who pursue arms, and those of this condition who had once pursued arms but can no longer do so on account of injuries, maladies or old age'. Another important decree was ordained in 1396. It concerned hunting, probably the single activity that in subsequent centuries would come to be relished by all nobles as a mark of their special status. The decree, for the first time ever, barred commoners from the chase, and restricted the right to it to 'persons noble or having free warrens or privileges'. The reasons cited were the need to curb the poaching stimulated by the political disorder, and to prevent dereliction of agricultural labour and commerce.[11]

This commonplace argument was deployed by the English Parliament in 1389, when it passed the first qualification act regarding the right to hunt game. This forbade all persons with land worth less than forty shillings a year to take 'other gentlemen's game'. The thinking behind it was that servants and labourers go out hunting too often and that 'sometimes under such colour they make their assemblies, conferences, and conspiracies for to rise and disobey their allegiance'.[12] The Black Death and its aftermath in the Peasants' Revolt, it is clear, provoked in the propertied classes an intense concern with establishing safe social distance from their inferiors. This brought about a refinement of social nomenclature and a greater definition of status, as attested by the 1413 Statute of Additions. But this process did not proceed so far as to allow the gentry to set itself apart from the lower orders to the same degree as their Continental counterparts. Not for nothing did Shakespeare portray in *Henry V* the French chief herald as mortified at the sight of dead nobles lying pell-mell with dead commoners (Act IV, sc. VII). The reason for this cultural difference was that in England landed wealth had been and remained the most important yardstick of gentility, and this made for relatively uncomplicated entry of newcomers into the gentry.

Ironically, the one social boundary that was drawn with any rigidity divided the gentry from those above them. So much so that Bruce McFarlane stated that the gentry, rather than rising in the later Middle Ages, fell from the nobility to which they had once belonged:

> In the reign of Edward I [1239–1307], a dozen earls, the dwin-
> dling survivors of a seemingly obsolescent baronage, shared their
> nobility with an undifferentiated mass of some three thousand
> landowners, each of whose holding were said to be worth £20
> a year or over. By the beginning of the sixteenth century a small
> and graded upper class of 'lords' numbering between fifty and
> sixty had emerged in possession of rank and privileges which
> marked them off from lesser men.

McFarlane may have overstated the pristine uniformity of the English landed class under Edward I. Yet there is no gainsaying that during the fourteenth century, and at an accelerated pace towards its end, a far-reaching change occurred: the emergence of the 'titled nobility' as an officially discrete group comprising those men summoned to Parliament by personal writs. As time wore on, the parliamentary lists of summonses came to serve as an almanac of nobility, as it were, creating a situation whereby a man was unlikely to be summoned to Parliament – and hence to be considered a peer – unless his forefathers used to be summoned.[13]

A hardening of class barriers in the late fourteenth and early fifteenth centuries was the experience of the German lands also. A particularly telling body of evidence for the trend there comes from Franconia. In the ecclesiastical principality of Würzburg, the year 1400 saw the climax of turbulent decades during which the local towns united in a league in a bid to gain independence from the prince-bishop. The conflict was decided at the Battle of Bergtheim. The prince's army, which included most of the local lords, won the day and dashed the cities' aspirations. When a few months later a new princely register of fiefs (*Lehenbuch*) was redacted, it introduced a significant novelty. Henceforth vassals were registered not primarily following the chronological order of their enfeoffment, as had been the custom hitherto, but according to their social estate. Noble feoffees were lumped together in one section. Each rank – princes, counts, barons, untitled nobles – was then recorded in a subdivision. Burghers and peasants, grouped together in another section, were entered in the *Lehenbuch* following their geographical origin. Thus, at one fell swoop, the two groups were separated and subjected to different taxonomic principles: the one feudal and personal, the other territorial and regnant. Similar bureaucratic procedures were set up at roughly the same time in the adjacent principalities of Bamberg and Brandenburg-Kulmbach. Only against this background is it not surprising to find out that the German word *Adel* had not come to designate the Franconian nobility as a social formation before the fifteenth century. Complementarily, the social cleavage between nobles and commoners widened over the century. The closer the links one had to burgher families, the less likely one was to be accepted as noble by other nobles, or conversely the more likely one was to be demoted from the nobility. This was also the period when cathedral chapters all over Germany began to insist that prospective entrants be of immaculate noble parentage. In Speyer, for instance, applicants were required, since 1442, to produce a written proof of ancestry. Erasmus, having been familiarized with the most exclusive cathedral chapter of Strasbourg, remarked that 'it would not have admitted even Christ himself'.[14]

Hiving off the nobility alongside degrading the commonalty was thus a phenomenon not confined to so-called 'new monarchies'. It was, however, confined to monarchies. In republics, the place of the nobility was radically different. The thrust of the laws with which the self-governing Italian towns hedged round noble status was diametrically opposed to that exhibited in monarchies. In Florence, for instance, the Ordinances of Justice of 1293 turned nobility into a liability: the law excluded those it identified as magnates from the most important civic offices; it forbade them to bear arms in the city; it also rendered conviction easier of magnates accused of crimes against *popolani*. Thus, in a complete inversion of the tendency in monarchical states, the 'popular' governments in Italy treated nobility as a threat to the body politic. Society's defenders were here the people, the citizens.[15] As Machiavelli averred, a republican regime and real nobility were irreconcilable. The latter was a monarchical institution:

> [W]here considerable equality prevails, no one who proposes to set up a kingdom or principality, will ever be able to do it unless from that equality he selects many of the more ambitious and restless minds and makes them [lords] in fact and not in name, by giving them castles and possessions and making of them a privileged class with respect both to property and subjects; so that around him will be those with whose support he may maintain himself in power, and whose ambitions, thanks to him, may be realised.[16]

Machiavelli's timeless observation seems a fitting encapsulation of the social process that gripped monarchical Europe around 1400: a stricter, more explicit hierarchical division, upgrading the nobility, accompanied by the drawing of an ever more definite cut-off line between nobles and non-nobles. That this development may actually have been a mere formalization of principles already implicit in the life of those communities does not diminish its importance in the slightest. On the contrary, it is precisely such formalization that is characteristic, if not constitutive, of an *ancien régime* society, granted one takes the term to mean a society based on institutionalized inequalities which are articulated through an ideology of exaggeration: in contradistinction to modern societies, theory emphasizes differences, hyperbolizes the imperviousness of the boundaries between strata, making them appear incomparably less porous than they are in practice. Yet at the same time, the very standardization of distinctions, the ideological accentuation of inequalities, creates a frame of reference for examination and scrutiny. This in turn is likely to make social immigration and assimilation into the upper reaches of society a more arduous journey than before. And in fact, a number of studies have shown that advancement into the nobility became more problematic during the early modern period than it had been during the Middle Ages.[17] To define the nobility was in a sense to close it.

This greater and favouring definition of noble status, its increasing juridical elaboration, seems to have been the product of the alliance between rulers and lords that was forged in large part in reaction to the crises of the fourteenth century.[18] The process was, it would appear, impelled by an attempt – typical of pre-modern, organic societies – to create or restore order by fixing people into prescribed positions through minute specification of rights and obligations and restrictions. At the heart of the matter lay the privileges that came to be associated with nobility: exemption from certain taxes; the right to be tried by special courts; entitlement to certain offices; the right of French nobles, according to Claude de Seyssel, 'to bear arms everywhere even in the king's chamber'; the right of the Spanish grandees to keep their hats on in the presence of the king and to be addressed by him as 'cousins', as was the right of members of the Order of the Golden Fleece – and myriad other rights, property and otherwise.[19] There are three main points to be made about noble privileges. First, they were inexorably predicated on the state and its law and/or on the person of the ruler, and were guaranteed by such authority. Second, they were as much the consequence as the cause of nobility, its stigmata, as it were. Exemption from taxation, for instance, was not only a privilege accorded to nobles, but often also served as proof of nobility. But, third, at the same time as privileges signalled a state of social grace, they also underlay the nobles' pretension to hegemony in the polity. Hence the juridical stabilization of noble status could not but raise the stakes involved in what it meant to be a noble. A dissonance between one's claim to nobility and the material and normative justification for this claim was now less likely to be tolerated; and, with controlling mechanism afoot, both more susceptible to detection and easier to penalize. As the petty nobleman Gouberville noted in his diary in 1555–6, 'last year those who were unable to furnish proof of their nobility were condemned to pay six years of their income'. He himself, no longer able to take it for granted that his nobility would be taken for granted, rummaged desperately through his papers until he emerged with the title deeds which enabled him to continue to enjoy tax exemption. Such episodes could not but reinforce the nobility, socially and mentally. It has indeed been suggested that it was growing harder over the early modern period not only to join the nobility but also to stay in it.[20]

That the nobility was an *ordre juridique* is nowadays something of a historiographical common property, all the more so given its obvious methodological advantages. James Wood, for example, has asserted that 'given the diversity of noble types, it should be clear that their legal standing as nobles was the only characteristic that simultaneously was shared by all nobles without exception and clearly divided nobles from commoners'.[21] It should perhaps also be clear that, in a certain sense, this is to beg the question. For was the juridical definition of the nobility not tantamount to closing it, and closing it in turn a necessary condition for the group to qualify as nobility? As a sociological type the nobility presupposes its demarcation: whereas the sociological peculiarity of the middle class subsists in being open at both its bottom and its top end, 'that of the nobility subsists in being sealed at both'.[22] This state of affairs did not effectively obtain in Europe prior to the fifteenth century. Either there was no nobility as a social category during most of the Middle Ages, or else the nobility of the early modern period was of a very different kind.[23] In any case, by 1400 noble identity was no longer embedded predominantly in autonomous power. It was coming to be heavily dependent on relations with the state.

A remarkable corollary, and presumably also a contributing factor, to this sea change was the overwhelming wave of extinction of grand old families in the late Middle Ages, and, on the other hand, the nature of the rise to prominence of the ones which supplanted them.[24] Of 136 English families whose heads had by 1300 been summoned to parliament, a mere sixteen were still in existence by 1500. Of 120 baronial or comital families in Westphalia in the mid-twelfth century, only nine survived to the mid-sixteenth century. Of thirty-three such families in eastern Switzerland at the beginning of the thirteenth century, thirty-one had died out by 1500. Of thirty-four leading ancient Castilian lineages in the twelfth and thirteenth centuries, eighteen had become extinct in the male line by 1369.[25] These families were medieval Europe's 'social dinosaurs': they antedated the state, and the greatest among them derived their legitimacy and power from their ancientness and, usually, blood ties to royalty. The families that in the next period came to replace them at the pinnacle of society were mostly of a different cast – a cast that both reflected and helped to fashion the new political structures. To illustrate this it may be helpful to pick up some illustrious individual nobles and noble families of the early modern age and then work backwards in an attempt to pin down the pattern and determinants of their ascent.

A striking example is provided by the Mendoza family, one of the three richest among the Spanish titled nobility in 1550–1600. In the mid-fourteenth century, the Mendoza were one of those up-and-coming families which, after much vacillation, threw in their lot with the pretender Enrique of Trastámara. They therefore suffered the bad luck of taking part in his initial defeat at the Battle of Nájera in 1367. That military fiasco proved a formative event in their rise to eminence. From captivity they emerged Trastámara stalwarts, equipped with a set of political and marital bonds to other Enriquistas who shared their experience. When Enrique II came to the throne in 1369, this group – which historians have taken to call the 'new nobility' – came to the fore as the major beneficiaries. The new king (and his immediate successors) lavished on them the *mercedes*, or rewards, and offices that formed the foundation of their families' tremendous wealth and influence. And with requisite royal approval they began to found *mayorazgos*, or perpetual entails of their estates, which helped them stay at the very top in the next centuries as well. A famous exemplar of this group is Fernando Álvarez de Toledo, third Duke of Alba (d. 1582), the ruthless commander of the Spanish army dispatched to suppress the Dutch Revolt. The outstanding Spanish grandee under King Philip II, he too traced the prominence and riches of his family back to a not-so-distant ancestor, Fernán, who was bold and discerning enough to wager on the political and military skills of Enrique II.[26]

The third Duke of Alba is an interesting figure also because he manifested, with grim resolve, an ethos of royal service which contrasted sharply with the unabashed opportunism of Fernán. He did not flinch even from condemning to death two leading Netherlandish nobles, the Counts Hoorne and Egmont, the latter a one-time boon companion; and the story may well be true that, watching the execution from the balcony of the Hotel de Jassy in Brussels, Alba for once failed to contain his emotions and burst into tears. The beheading of Egmont and Hoorne was all the more sensational because they were members of the Order of the Golden Fleece. As such, they enjoyed the privilege of judgement by peers. It was curtly suspended by Alba in the name of reason of state. Here was apparently a dramatic clash between the new principle of sovereign authority and the older aristocratic principle so fully represented in the array of privileges of the Order of the Golden Fleece. It is ironic therefore that that most glittering of chivalrous brotherhoods was initially as much an instrument of state building as a bastion of nobles elevated to distinction in circumstances reminiscent of those which Alba's ancestor turned to such good account.[27]

The social make-up of the Order in its early phase under the Valois dukes of Burgundy speaks volumes. Contrary to what one might expect, it was not the nobility of Burgundy proper which supplied the Order with the largest number of fellows between 1430 and 1477, but rather the Picards. The reason for this preferential treatment is not far to seek: Picardy was the contested border region between the kings of France and the dukes of Burgundy. The allegiance of the Picard nobles was therefore solicited by each side so as to create a bulwark against the other. Some local families made a brilliant career out of that competition. A case in point is the Croys. They are a particularly interesting example because in the early sixteenth century one of their number reached an altitude of political influence to beat the band. This was Guillaume, Marquis of Aerschot and lord of Chièvres (1458–1521), the tutor and Grand Chamberlain of Charles V. So dominant was his position that contemporaries regarded him as a second king (*alter rex*), and 'it seemed as if [he] were the king, and the king his son'. Charles V himself later acknowledged that 'Mr de Chièvres held sway over me'. The Croys were a success story, becoming dukes in 1560. Yet two centuries earlier they were still a modest Picard family. It was not until 1398 that they first made an impression, when Jean de Croy (Guillaume's great-grandfather) was appointed chamberlain of Duke Philippe of Burgundy. It was he who founded the family tradition of ducal state service which, within a few decades, had lifted the family to unanticipated grandeur. The Croys, though, were not unique. Looking again at the sixteenth century, one cannot fail to notice that the Netherlandish high nobility consisted of families risen in the employ of the Burgundian dukes.[28]

Not quite a second king, but surely a kingmaker, was Richard Neville, Earl of Warwick. The history of his political ascendancy and downfall is too well known to be recapitulated here. But the early record of his family is less familiar. This is hardly surprising: it is the tale of an humble family, doggedly making its way upwards by means chiefly of royal service. The early Nevilles were nearly all active as sheriffs, and conformed almost too well to the model of ambitious upstarts which medieval chroniclers loved to vilify as 'men risen from the dust'. The later Nevilles, while never breaking with the royal forest administration, moved into higher offices and closer to the king. It was through these offices and the attendant royal patronage that the Nevilles put together the landed power base in the North on which the Kingmaker's position would eventually repose. So even if Warwick himself was a magnate in a league of his own, there was none the less nothing particularly out of the ordinary in the ascent of the Neville family. Royal service, as Lawrence Stone has pointed out, was often the most important factor in the progression of most aristocratic families. By 1559 the majority of peerage were recent promotions. The same is true of some of the most influential men under Edward VI, Elizabeth I, and James I. The origins of William Cecil, Lord Burghley (1520–98), despite the 'immense pains . . . taken to construct a long pedigree of the family', cannot be traced back further than his grandfather, sherrif of North-amptonshire. Sherrif was also the grandfather of George Villiers, the notorious courtier and first Duke of Buckingham (1592–1628), whose family was described by his first biographer in 1672 as 'rather without obscurity than with any great lustre'.[29]

The sample of examples for the enormously invigorating impact on pre-modern families of state service in its diverse forms can be extended to include some very well-known names: the Liechtensteins, who through utility to the Habsburgs amassed prodigious wealth: in the mid-seventeenth century they were masters of 19,000 tenants (20 per cent of the total) in Moravia and 18.2 per cent of the land; and in 1719 their lordships of Schellenberg and Vaduz were converted into the principality of Liechtenstein. Or the Farnese, originally military adventurers from Orvieto, who through connection with the papacy metamorphosed into dukes of Parma and princes of international stature. There were some more families with similar histories whose splendours and riches have left a still visible imprint on their homelands.[30] But sufficient genealogical dossiers have been compiled to permit one or two general conclusions.

The greatest nobles throughout most of the Middle Ages were commonly their kings' proximate relations. In England, the highest title of duke was introduced in 1337 for the benefit of the Black Prince, and the first non-royal duke was created as late as 1397. In Spain, no hereditary title of nobility was granted outside the royal patrimony before 1438. The mystique of blood royal had not by then faded away, of course, as attested by the astounding fortunes of that unassuming Welsh family, the Tudors.[31] The few surviving ancient dynasties with ties to princely or royal Houses still commanded unparalleled reverence in the early modern period. But they were no longer alone at the apex of their class, and not the majority either. The nobility, in short, had been transformed: its upper echelons now were populated with families whose standing was inextricably bound up with the state and its service. Little was left of the erstwhile feudal autonomy. This new situation was reflected in the income structure of nobles: it appears to be almost the rule that the higher the position of a noble, the larger the proportion of his revenues that was derived from the state. The size and sources of Don Álvaro de Luna's income indeed vindicate his description by an eighteenth-century biographer as 'the top favourite I have anywhere met with in History': 3,239,760 *maravedís* accrued to him from the Mastership of Santiago alone, and a further 1,130,112 from various other offices and royal grants. All in all, his income in 1453 stood at 9,532,381 *maravedís*, or nearly 12 per cent of the Crown's ordinary receipts in that year. Guy de Brimeu, who used to read classical bed-time stories to the adolescent Charles the Bold, had an annual income of approximately 32,000 *livres* in 1473–6; around 5,000 were from his patrimony, most of the rest from his position at the Burgundian Court and in the territorial administration. Antoine de Chabannes (born *c.* 1408) netted 25,000 *livres* every year as a *grand maître* under Louis XI of France, while his independent sources brought him 10,000. William Brereton, a groom of the privy chamber, managed by 1534–5 to arrange for himself a gross income fit for an earl, £1,236, of which over £1,000 were from Crown fees, farms and annuities. In 1546 Henri II d'Albret drew 37.1 per cent of his income from his domains (and a further 4 per cent from gambling wins), but 48.4 per cent from the French Crown for service as governor. The French Crown also looms very large indeed in the ledgers of the Constable Henri I de Montmorency: while his ordinary and extra-ordinary revenues (including sale of assets) in 1601 were just over 41,000 *écus*, royal pensions and *octrois* accounted for some 70,500 *écus*. For Antonio Alonso de Pimentel, sixth count of Benavente and commander of the Imperial Guard, *alcabalas* represented nearly 48 per cent of the return from his estates in 1536, as they did (together with *tercias*) for the duke of Béjar in 1630. Richelieu's income reached a staggering 1,099,000 *livres* in 1640, of which some 360,000 *livres* flowed from royal offices (and a further 300,000 from church benefices). It is appropriate, perhaps, to end this series of examples with a non-noble who, in this area at least, outshone even Richelieu: his successor Mazarin. At the end of his life he was in possession of cash reserves greater than those of the Bank of Amsterdam. The origins of this wealth are betrayed by his insistence that a public inventory of it was not in the interest of the state.[32]

Translated into words, these figures indicate how exceedingly large the state loomed in the lives of early modern nobles. Its expansion ushered in a new era for nobles. It came to represent a preponderant source of hopes and frustrations. The chronicler Philippe de Commynes related how Jean Daillon, Lord of Lude, told him in 1477:

> Now, are you leaving at the very moment when you should be making your fortune, or never, considering the great things which are falling into the hands of the king [Louis XI], and with which he can bring advantage and riches to all those whom he likes? And as for myself, I expect to become governor of Flanders and to turn myself into gold!

Such a statement of intent would have made no sense whatever two hundred years earlier. Similarly, one can hardly imagine a thirteenth-century Castilian *rico hombre*, or an English baron for that matter, meditating on political life in the way Alba was to do in the late sixteenth century: 'kings use men like an orange', he said, 'squeezing out the juice and throwing it away'.[33] The state, in other words, shifted the ground on which nobles' power stood and redefined their relationship with the ruler. Success or failure in that aggressive aristocratic world came to depend very heavily indeed on one's function in and usefulness to the state. But the facts and figures cited above can sustain another, complementary reading. They suggest also that the growth of the state opened up for nobles entirely new vistas; it presented them with political and economic opportunities on a vaster scale than anything their stateless forebears had been accustomed to. Those of them who were capable of catering to the revolutionary demands which the state made on society, who managed to make their services indispensable, gained access to resources of power unavailable before the state invented them. In the state they discovered a domestic El Dorado. Such nobles were incomparably more influential and affluent than their predecessors. Looked at from this standpoint, the alliance between state and nobility that began to form in the fourteenth century magnified the power of both without making them mutually exclusive.

Few historians nowadays persist in the belief that the nobility was the Anti-state. British historians in particular, in the wake of the

McFarlane revision, have developed cogent representations of abiding co-operation between monarchy and nobility as the essential feature not only of their relationship but generally of the late medieval and early modern polity.[34] Rulers and nobles are seen in this light not as inveterate rivals playing a zero-sum game, but as a community of interest. Yet this new line has one especially disturbing implication: conflict has little or no place in it other than as the odd disruption in a normally harmonious cohabitation. While the older view tended to make great play with clashes and misrepresent them as symptoms of a general opposition of nobles to the state, the new one comes perilously close to seeing every conflict as just an individual, isolated event. The problem here is not mainly of an imbalance which has to be redressed. Rather, it is that the new perspective obfuscates the fact that the state could become an object of fierce contention between monarchs and nobles not only (or even primarily) because it posed a threat to the latter's authority, but in large part because it also held out crucial advantages which amplified their authority. Indeed, much of the early modern political process consisted of managing and regulating the resulting tensions and contradictions. Alongside dialogue and co-operation there was an ongoing struggle over the terms and conditions of this dialogue and co-operation – over the precise place of nobles in the body politic.[35] The decades immediately following the end of the Hundred Years War witnessed a new stage in the attempts at coming to grips with this problem.

3 A question of definition
State power and aristocratic authority

Out of the crucible of decades of continuous war the Western monarchies emerged, by the second half of the fifteenth century, armed with some of the more important paraphernalia of state. The precedents set in the previous century of taxation and regular armies were solidifying into reality. This was a revolution in government, and it was nowhere more readily apparent than in France. On 2 November 1439 King Charles VII promulgated at Orléans an ordinance with a view to overhauling the French military organization. The first clause announced that 'very many captains have exceeded their authority and gathered a large number of men-at-arms . . . , from which great evils and troubles have arisen'. The king therefore selected some captains and assigned them to the conduct of war. It was forbidden for 'anyone else to be called, or carry the title of, captain'. Clause 3 specified that no one, 'of whatever estate he may be, on pain of lèse-majesté', was allowed to raise and command a *compagnie* without the king's permission. Conversely, no one was to serve in a *compagnie* under any unauthorized captain. The king, in short, claimed a monopoly over the legitimate use of physical force. But that was not all. Clauses 30 and 31 enjoined lords holding strong places and garrisons to disband their forces or else keep them at their own expense, that is without levying impositions on the local population. Whereas in the past, 'under pretext of defending their positions', numerous lords, barons, and other military leaders used to extract their upkeep from the local people and travelling merchants, the king now declared all these exactions unlawful and punishable by forfeit of life or property. Finally (Clauses 39–42), the edict ordered the lords to desist from collecting taxes, from resisting the collection by royal agents of the *taille*, or from retaining a cut for themselves.[1] The claim to a royal monopoly over the means of coercion thus came together with a claim to a royal monopoly over

taxation. The two claims, fundamental to state power, were insepar-
able. And it is highly revealing that the military reforms required to
expel the English from France presupposed the assertion of royal
authority over the lords.

The implications of the 1439 ordinance were not lost on the great
lords, nor did they lose much time in working against it. In 1440
the Duke of Bourbon led a rebellion – known as the Praguerie –
against Charles VII.[2] The revolt was unsuccessful. Five years later
a standing army was instituted. The circumstances were similar to
those which in the 1360s allowed the introduction of 'permanent',
peacetime taxation. In 1444 a truce with the English was concluded,
and the demobilized soldiers again posed a serious threat to society.
The army created by the military *ordonnance* of 1445 was recruited
from among the unemployed men-at-arms. The cost of maintaining
that host, initially some 1,500 cavalry *lances* (a unit of six combat-
ants), was huge.[3] The burden of tax was accordingly heavy, but
presumably not as crushing as thousands of jobless soldiers at large.
There was thus something of a racket to the establishment of the
standing army, offering protection from itself. But once this force
was set up, a further and radically different stage was reached – the
coercion–extraction cycle came into being: funded by taxes, the army
could now be used actively to coerce the payment of the taxes which
funded it, and so on. The chronicler Thomas Basin (1412–90), Bishop
of Lisieux, was acutely aware of the novel danger. He argued that
once the English had been beaten off, a standing army was no longer
necessary. Any prudent person could see what a ruinous burden on
the realm the army was. The real reason why it was not disbanded
was that tyrants relish having

> in their pay a great army whose function it is to keep the common-
> wealth and the entire realm in terror ... These tyrants, when
> they impose on their subjects new taxes to finance the army, are
> not content with what is necessary, but crush their subjects with
> enormous and veritably unsupportable taxes under the pretext of
> the public profit and the general interest ... Thus the kingdom
> of France, once noble and free, has, under colour of the neces-
> sity to maintain a paid army, been cast into that abysmal servitude
> of tributes and exactions, to the point that all its inhabitants are
> publicly declared taxable at the will of the king ... no one
> braving to speak against this nor even to say a prayer ... To
> raise doubts would indeed involve a greater peril than to deny
> the truth of the Faith ... The army, in effect, is the preserver

of servitude, and so long as it exists the realm will doubtless be unable to shake off its yoke, and will continue to languish pitiably under it.[4]

And indeed, some fluctuations notwithstanding, the army was steadily growing in size; the number of cavalry *lances* rose to about 1,800 in a matter of few years. In 1451 King Charles VII commanded more than 20,000 fighting men.[5]

'The power to tax involves the power to destroy,' Chief Justice John Marshall once said. In King Louis XI (1461–83) the nobles had an approximate embodiment of the principle.[6] So in 1465 came an aristocratic reaction with a vengeance. The princes of the blood and great feudatories united in the League of the Public Weal. In March they moved to attack the king. Their nominal objective was a reform of government in the interest of the common profit. They had the means to press their views. According to one chronicler, the coalition army numbered 51,000 warriors, more than a match for the king's *gendarmerie*. On 16 July they fought the bloody but inconclusive Battle of Montlhéry. Louis XI, having retreated to a besieged Paris, was forced to seek a negotiated settlement. So hopeless was his position that he acceded to all of the lords' demands. These demands betray what the revolt really was about. Some wanted sweeping territorial concessions: royal disclaiming of the regalia in Brittany in favour of the duke; returning of the recently redeemed Somme towns to the Count of Charolais, the future Duke Charles the Bold of Burgundy; and, perhaps most damaging of all, ceding of Normandy to the king's brother Charles (a dupe of the other lords), thereby depriving the Crown of one-third of its revenues. Jean of Anjou, Duke of Calabria, insisted on receiving financial assistance and 12,000 men-at-arms until such time as he had managed to conquer the kingdom of Naples. Indeed, the royal army was a major prize. The king was not to have the 1,700 cavalry *lances* under his direct command, only 800 of them. The other 900 *lances* were to be distributed as follows: 400 to the new Duke of Normandy; 200 to the Duke of Brittany; 100 to the Duke of Bourbon; 100 to the Count of Dunois; the rest were to be shared between the Count of Dammartin and the Bastard of Bourbon. Another reform measure was the setting up of a board of thirty-six councillors, of which eighteen were to be appointed by the lords, the other half by the king. The board was to have authority to reform the administration of justice, reduce taxes, and remedy all sorts of perceived malpractice. In short, the lords were out to cut monarchical power down to a convenient size. Their idea of the proper polity, it seems, was one of royal government at the nobles' command. As the Milanese ambassador to Louis's Court remarked, if the lords were to have their way, 'they would pluck so many of the king's feathers that he would no longer be able to fly'.

Louis XI's handling of the crisis did full justice to his reputation as an artful king of the first water. All the more so as no one suspected him of being scrupulous in keeping promises. And he was in no position to renege on his word. In a cool-headed *volte-face* Louis chose to convert into an ally the most powerful member of the League: Charolais. He offered him more territorial rights than Charolais dared ask for; he went out of his way to show him favour, confirming him as the first among the princes; he nominated Charolais's friend, Count Louis of Saint-Pol, to a Constable of France; and he offered Charolais the hand of his daughter. And sure enough, an almost miraculous amity soon began to flourish between the two men. The Dukes of Brittany and Bourbon received a similar treatment. With the goodwill of these lords secured, the other Ligueurs could then be dealt with in a rather less debonair manner. Jean of Anjou was hectored into breaking camp without having brought the king to finalize his promises. None of his allies took up the cudgels for him. The Count of Armagnac was offered far less than he was willing to settle for. None of his allies interceded on his behalf. Back in the lords' camp he fumed at them, uttering the words which Philippe de Commynes would borrow and immortalize in his memoirs: 'the Public Weal had been turned into private interest'.[7] The rebels' solidarity collapsed. The League shattered into so many particularisms. Louis's discriminatory capitulations defused a crisis that might have irreparably debilitated the French monarchy. In January 1466 Normandy was recovered, with the Duke of Bourbon at the head of the royal forces.

In the same year, 1465, on 5 June, a not dissimilar confrontation between king and nobles reached its climax in Castile in the so-called 'Farce of Ávila'. A group of dissident nobles placed on a platform a wooden statue representing King Enrique IV, complete with sham royal insignia. The statue was forced to listen to a long list of accusations. Then Alfonso Carrillo, Archbishop of Toledo, took the crown off the effigy; Juan Pacheco, Marquis of Villena, took away the sceptre; Alvaro de Stúñiga, Count of Plasencia, grabbed the sword; the Counts of Benavente and Paredes kicked the statue down. The king was deposed. As a new king they declared the *Infante* Alfonso.[8]

Conspicuous among the cast at Ávila was Juan Pacheco. As the favourite of Enrique he was actually the focus of the aristocratic discontent that eventually led to the mock deposition. His ascendancy with the king threatened and alienated other powerful nobles. These formed a league in 1460. In 1463 Pacheco fell from grace, not least due his own excessive machinations, losing his influence to the Mendozas. It was now his turn to form a faction of malcontent nobles. In Enrique IV they found an almost perfect king to defy: listless, hesitant, and worst of all, something of a pacifist. So after some open hostilities, he concluded an inordinately conciliatory agreement with the rebels in late 1464. The *Infante* Alfonso was confirmed as heir designate and given Pacheco for a tutor. A board of five was appointed with a view to reforming the government (Pacheco being one of them). On 16 January 1465 the commission put out the Sentence of Medina del Campo. This called for a committee to be set up whose consent the king would need in order to have a noble imprisoned. It sought to limit taxation to times of manifest urgency, while insisting that royal stipends be paid from money levied in the very domains of the grantees. To cap it all, the king was required to scale down his army from 3,000 to 600 *lanzas*. This was too preposterous even for Enrique. He rejected the Sentence; the rebels staged the ritual dethronement at Ávila; and civil war broke out.[9]

The demands of the rebellious lords in Castile were thus remarkably similar to those of the initiators of the Public Weal movement in France. This was so because government in Castile and France had some fundamental traits in common. By the second half of the fifteenth century both monarchies were already possessed of some of the hallmarks of 'absolutist' monarchies: in particular, the right of kings to tax on their own, which enabled them to maintain a standing army. For nobles, especially great ones, this posed an unprecedented threat. It jeopardized one of their chief sources of power: the preponderant influence in the localities which gave them the key role of mediators between king and populace. In a modern society the test of power is very much 'who decides?'. The putting into effect of a government decision is normally a technical matter and only encounters particular difficulties when the decision is extraordinarily controversial. In early modern Europe the ability to participate in the process of decision-making was of course also a critical test of power. But a no less, and sometimes more, important criterion of power was the ability to kill a decision – or help it along, as the case might be – when it came down to the ground.

The lords had what it took to do both. To borrow a Chinese proverb, 'the mighty dragon is no match for the local snake which knows the ins and outs of the place'. It is more or less this idea that the Mendoza Count of Tendilla conveyed to King Fernando when he reminded him of the maxim that 'advice should come from where the action is'.

The lords were of course more than just well-informed locals. They also had landed estates, vassals, clients, and other dependants. Hence, as far as monarchs were concerned, the power bases of the lords were essential to their own ability to govern the country, and at the same time a potential danger to it. Thus, while Louis XI sought to curtail the influence of the La Trémoille family in the west of France, François I later entrusted them with the defence of that very area. In nominating one de La Trémoille to his lieutenant he explained that he did so because of the latter's loyalty and capability, but also because of 'the power, credit and authority which he possesses in that province, where he holds many places, towns and castles of importance, by means of which he will better be able to serve us'. Whether a security hazard or a security asset, the lords' local power was a matter of crucial importance to the centre, for without peripheries the centre was not at all central. Now a standing army under full royal control was bound to change the relationship between centre and provinces. Commands could be enforced more directly, reducing the need to rely on the lords' intermediary assistance. Conversely, it could serve to punish recalcitrant lords. It was unlikely to make them redundant, but almost sure to undermine their prominence. It is against this background that both the Castilian civil war and the League of the Public Weal should be viewed. What the great lords in both countries were coming to fear was a monarchy not dependent on their co-operation, a monarchy that could act effectively without and against them.[10]

On the other hand, an effective monarchy was vital to nobles, save, perhaps, the very grandest among them. Like almost anyone else, nobles needed a minimum of law and order, but in their case the stakes were higher. Their wealth was in large part landed wealth, and therefore exposed and vulnerable in the myriad conflicts nobles had with each other over landed wealth. A certain degree of stability was essential for its preservation. This could be provided only by a monarch who was strong enough to govern impartially. A weak monarch might prove a disaster in that he or she was not only less able firmly to intervene and arbitrate in conflicts among nobles, but also likely to be under the partisan spell of a favourite or faction.

There was hardly any situation more unacceptable to most nobles than that, and hence more likely to perturb the political arena. The civil war in Castile was in large part the result of the overweening predominance of Pacheco. And King Enrique IV lost his last supporters when he embraced Pacheco again. The Wars of the Roses in England were caused fundamentally by a long reign of the nonentity Henry VI. There was no one but nobles to direct the nobles, and law and order collapsed.[11] If the nobles did not want too powerful a monarchy that could reduce them to subservience, they were well advised to wish for a powerful enough monarchy to protect them and enable them to thrive – a 'vaccine monarchy'.

In the case of France and Castile there was a further factor which made a strong monarchy worthy of noble support. A monarchy with a well-established right to tax its subjects' wealth was an immensely attractive proposition to many lords – provided, of course, they had a say in the redistribution of the takings. Not surprisingly, at this early stage, nobles were quite ambivalent about the new state of affairs. The leaguers of the Public Weal talked of reducing taxes while seeking to secure command over an army that could not be sustained otherwise. The rebel magnates in Castile also talked of reducing taxes, yet demanded that the relevant portions of royal taxes levied in their domains be paid directly to them as pensions. The eagle was certainly a menace, but it was now laying golden eggs. Taming it was the best course of action. That is why representation in the royal council was a top priority of the lords. It was the place where political decisions having major consequences were taken, including such that could impinge on lordly local influence, and where the spoils were apportioned. Thus in 1442, Castilian magnates, then a majority in the council, pushed through an act which barred the king from granting a donation worth over 6,000 *maravedís* without conciliar approval. In France in the same year, the lords of the Praguerie asked to lead Charles VII's royal council.[12]

The nobles' concern with the council indicates the degree to which they had, by the second half of the fifteenth century, acquired vested interests in the state. This was one main reason why there were usually some nobles who supported the monarch against those who opposed him, and why those who opposed him were unlikely to strive to dismantle the monarchical state. Once the state was worth fighting over, there was less point in fighting against it. As the humanist Fernán Pérez de Guzmán (*c.* 1377–1460) said of his fellow Castilian nobles, 'they will consent to the imprisonment and death of a friend or a relative in order to have a share in the booty'. The power struggle between nobles and monarchs was attenuated by the attendant power struggle between nobles whose objective it was to secure access to the state. This was a costly political system. Enrique IV, in the first half of his reign, made on average eight grants to individuals a year. In the second, crisis-ridden half the annual average nearly doubled. In 1465, the beginning of the civil war, he created seven new titles for supporters, as against an annual average of just over one title throughout the reign. The result was an alarmingly depleted treasury – royal income in 1465 was 45 per cent lower than in 1429.[13]

Yet the fact that the state lent itself to making some nobles influential and rich to a degree otherwise unattainable, often at the expense of its own authority and revenues, was not a fatal weakness. On the contrary, it may be considered as one of its greatest strengths at this early stage of development. Not only did it win adherents, it also possibly helped to preclude a more intractable situation whereby the noble class as a whole controls (and paralyses) the state, as happened in Poland in the late seventeenth and eighteenth centuries; or a situation whereby the nobles have relatively little direct stake in the apparatus of state and therefore little to lose from stymieing royal fiscal policies, as happened in England in the seventeenth century. Louis XI's handling of the League of the Public Weal is an object lesson. Another remarkable example of the mechanism at work is provided by the Count Lamoral of Egmont's mission to Spain in 1565. Its aim was to bring pressure to bear on Philip II to accept a plan that would have placed The Netherlands Council of State under the nobles' domination. Philip absorbed the pressure with magnanimity. He reportedly went out of his dour way to charm Egmont, according him financial favours and promising royal assistance in marrying off grandly the count's eight nubile daughters. Egmont returned home mightily satisfied and convinced of the success of his embassy, only to be reprimanded by William of Orange that he allowed himself to be inveigled into putting his private well-being above the public good. Orange's reproach was not entirely free from double standard. He was using a political vocabulary which he only very recently – and quite reluctantly – had acquired. He too used to be agreeably implicated in the coalescence between the public and private spheres that had been in progress at the upper levels of the sociopolitical order and that, for the time being, was bringing great benefits both to the incipient absolutist monarchies and to their greater nobles.[14]

England emerged from the first phase of state building with much less, if at all, of a New Monarchy than France and Spain. The constitutional principle that national taxation could not be levied other than for actual or potential war was still in force.[15] The king had no standing army. The English magnates, unlike the French and Castilian, might well have had little to worry about the monarchy, were it not for the fact that Henry VII, the first Tudor king (1485–1509), worried keenly about them. Henry may in part simply have applied to English politics lessons he learned from Louis XI of France, where he lived until his accession to the throne. Moreover, being a usurper, he initially had a precarious hold on power and fears to match. At any rate, his political strategies betrayed an ingrained distrust of the nobles. Building on Edward IV's anti-retaining legislation, Henry set about stripping the magnates of their military capacity. A second strategy to reinforce his authority was in effect a replication of Richard II's innovative policy of the 1390s (incidentally providing another argument against 'New Monarchy'): both kings tried to rule the country through their own agents rather than the magnates. There was one important difference: while Richard II failed and lost his crown, Henry VII succeeded. The contrast was not primarily one of personality. It reflected the changes that had taken place in the intervening century, and it illuminates the differences between England and the Continental monarchies.

The legacy of previous centuries, the English monarchy rested on a much wider, and centralized, sociopolitical foundation than its Continental counterparts. The co-operation which English kings expected from the magnates was less conditional than that which their Castilian and especially French opposite numbers received. They were therefore not as dependent on the nobles. This is not to say that the great lords of England were not important in translating royal directives into reality in the shires. But they had limited leeway, not least because to fulfil this crucial function effectively they in turn had to be able to carry with them at least the more significant elements among the lesser landowners, the gentry. These were people with a strong tradition of local participatory politics and experience of local offices. They were by no means under the magnates' thumb, even though they did look up to them for leadership. However, it appears that the Wars of the Roses transformed this structure of relations. The involvement of the magnates in the wars and crises after 1450 estranged the gentry who subsequently took to running local society with less and less reference to their betters. This coincided with a momentous expansion of the royal demesne which began under

Edward IV and which increased the number of lesser landowners under the king's lordship. Henry VII took advantage of this widening stratum of self-reliant gentry to work with them directly, without having to bring the magnates too often into play. Conversely, as Steven Gunn has written, a new kind of regional magnate rose 'whose power rested not so much on his own landholdings as on his responsibility for the Crown's lands in the area where he held sway'. As the great lords' role as self-governing intermediaries between king and localities diminished, the balance of political power necessarily tipped towards the centre. Algernon Sidney wrote of this change that it 'exceedingly weakened the nobility . . . and was a great step towards the dissolution of our anteint government'. Tudor England was to be governed predominantly from the Court.[16] Paradoxically, then, the Wars of the Roses ultimately worked to strengthen the Crown at the expense of the great nobles. The English monarchy, thanks to a peculiar social structure and a peculiar political tradition, emerged as internally much more powerful than either France or Castile.

Lawrence Stone has remarked that, in 'England, unlike France or Brandenburg, a firm alliance of mutual self-interest between a highly privileged nobility and an authoritarian Crown was not given time to mature'.[17] The reign of Henry VII, it seems, marked a watershed in this regard. In France and Castile, on the other hand, the trials of strength that rocked both countries did not end in a similar break. Significant changes did occur in the relationship between monarchy and nobility, but the net result was essentially a reciprocal adjustment, a working arrangement.

A telling example is provided by the 1480 fiscal *mercedes* reform of Fernando and Isabel. It used to be regarded as a successful vindication of royal authority, reclaiming sources of income alienated from the Crown during the troubled period of the Trastámara kings. It is true that, in absolute terms, the nobility's revenues from royal grants and concessions declined (from 32,789,822 *maravedís* to 17,118,613). But so did the revenues of anyone else with access to the royal trough. In relative terms, however, the fifteen great magnate families increased their proportion of total *mercedes* holding from 34.9 per cent before the reform to 43.9 thereafter. The proportion of *mercedes* in the hands of the nobility as whole, i.e. both magnates and lesser nobles, rose from 55.5 to 62.61 per cent. The share of officials and professional 'middle class' fell from 4.5 per cent to 4 per cent. Moreover, those sources of income that did remain in noble hands now acquired legal force. If anything, the nobles' grip on royal taxation was now more secure than before. Another measure taken by monarchs that had customarily been interpreted as detrimental to the nobility was the institutionalization of the Holy Brotherhood (*Santa Hermandad*), the royal police force that would develop into an army. It is true that the nobility objected – to no avail – to the Brotherhood, which they said was 'an abomination to the great'. But it is only in legend that the Brotherhood forces were used to discipline the nobility *qua* nobility. Moreover, some 30 to 45 per cent of the army assembled by Fernando and Isabel for the conquest of Granada was provided by the magnates. Finally, it is also true that the Catholic monarchs barred the greater lords from the royal council, a policy inspired by the experience of crippling infighting in the reigns of their predecessors. Yet nobles were by no means removed from the hub of power. There were many nobles at Court who served the monarchs in various administrative capacities. Among these there was an inner ring of nobles whom the monarchs trusted and quite often called upon to perform important political and military duties. In 1498, having left for Aragon, the monarchs invested Fadrique Álvarez de Toledo, Duke of Alba, and Bernardino Fernández de Velasco, Constable of Castile, with viceregal powers. In 1499, as they embarked for Andalusia, they deputed the Counts of Feria and Cabra to govern together with the Royal Council. They also appointed more nobles to royal offices than their predecessors Juan II and Enrique IV. Thus, under Fernando and Isabel, a kind of tacit understanding between monarchy and nobility came into being. The nobles accepted in principle that they should pursue their private and public goals within the political bounds demarcated by the monarchs. The latter guaranteed the nobles' fundamental interests, sanctioned formally their special position in the state, and helped to stabilize their predominance.[18]

A *détente* between monarchy and nobility took place also in France. The monarchy's narrow escape in the War of the Public Weal demonstrated that the only way for it to bring the greater lords under its authority was to win them over. Largesse was one tested means. In 1470, Louis XI's expenses on pensions to princes of the blood, knights of the Order of Saint-Michel, courtiers and other dignitaries, came to 642,000 *livres*, which amounted to about one-third of his net revenue that year (compared with 934,000 *livres*, or 47 per cent, on the military). In 1497 Charles VIII spent 498,000 *livres* on pensions, which represented nearly one-quarter of the royal income from *tailles* as of 1498.[19] Another, related means of eliciting commitment to royal government were seats in the royal council. When

Louis XI inherited the Crown in 1461 he found a council dominated by fifteen highly influential persons, men such as Jean, bastard of Orléans (Count of Dunois), Charles of Anjou (Count of Maine), Duke Jean of Bourbon, Count Gaston of Foix, and others. Louis carried out a purge. Only Bourbon, perhaps because he was the king's brother-in-law, was allowed to continue in office. But after the War of the Public Weal Louis began to relax this policy of exclusion. Charles VIII (1483–98) and Louis XII (1498–1515) reversed it. They co-opted the grands into the council and used it to induce the greater men of the realm to co-operate with the monarchy. Among the fifty-two most active councillors under Charles VIII, at least thirty-six (69 per cent) were nobles. Ten of these thirty-six were princes of the blood and/or grand feudatories; most of the rest were very prominent seigneurs. Among the twenty-one most active councillors under Louis XII, twelve (57 per cent) were nobles. The clout of these councillors becomes startlingly evident when one considers the other posts they occupied. In the 109 archbishoprics and bishoprics in France in 1483–1515, forty-four episcopacies were held by members of the royal council, and a further eighty-eight by members of their families (altogether 70 per cent of the available terms of office). What is more, members of this 'central oligarchy', as Mikhaël Harsgor has dubbed it, headed between them nearly half of the ninety-seven *bailliages*, *sénéchaussées*, and *gouvernements*. The latter make a particularly revealing case. At the end of the period under discussion (1515), there were eleven major provincial governorships. They were the top positions in the territorial administration of France. The major governors were most commonly also captains of *compagnies d'ordonnance*. It is therefore interesting to note that governorships, from the late fifteenth century onwards, were entrusted without exception to men whose social and political profile was similar to that of the lords who made up the League of the Public Weal.[20]

Before drawing some conclusions, it may be worthwhile to consider the case of the Holy Roman Empire. The point may bear re-emphasizing that the political history of the late medieval Empire was not one of a disintegrating central authority. For before 1470 there was virtually no centre that could fall apart under pressure of centrifugal forces. In truth, after 1470, the Empire was becoming a more, rather than less, cohesive conglomeration. But this did not take the form of a unitary state. What evolved was a dual structure. Political authority was being reinforced at both the level of imperial dynasty and of the Empire's constituent parts, most significantly the princes.

While the princes derived their position from the imperial constitution, they had by the fifteenth century emerged as rulers with regalian – if theoretically delegated – rights in their territories.[21] And like any other ruler, they faced the challenge of extending their jurisdiction over the nobles in their respective principalities. The process generated a good deal of friction.

The conflict had different upshots in different geopolitical areas. In Bavaria, for instance, a revolt triggered in 1489 by Duke Albrecht's taxation demands ended in 1493 with the prince confirming the nobles in their traditional immunities. In 1557 the nobles agreed to contribute the very large sum of 812,000 *Gulden* towards retiring the duke's debts in exchange for the so-called 'Nobleman's Liberty' (*Edelmannsfreiheit*) which licensed the extension of their seigneurial rights at the expense of the ducal ones. It accorded them a privileged position within the Bavarian state, a sort of 'dependent autonomy' not unlike that enjoyed by French and Spanish nobles.[22]

A radically different outcome, indeed a quite uniquely 'German' one, occurred in the core zone of the Empire in the rich German south. This zone consisted roughly of Franconia, Swabia and the Middle Rhine – areas with a tradition of *Königsnähe*, or political proximity to the King of the Romans. This made them amenable to the monarch's influence in a way that Bavaria never was. It is revealing of the disparity that the Wittelsbach Dukes of Bavaria based their claim to legitimacy on the self-referential antiquity of their House, requiring no higher instance to bear them out. In contrast, the Hohenzollern Margraves of Brandenburg-Ansbach-Kulmbach in Franconia based their claim on their distinguished record of service to emperors and on the imperial franchises and privileges which they received in return.[23] This was a symptom of the limiting effect on princely authority of the relatively strong imperial presence. This problem of disabled 'sovereignty' was compounded by the fact that political authority in this zone was widely fragmented and contested. In Franconia, for example, there was a constant and rather inconclusive territorial struggle between the three major local princes (not to mention the counts and the imperial cities). All this carried far-reaching implications for the relationship between princes and nobles. For the gallimaufry of intersecting, competing princely territories allowed the nobles ample interstitial room for manoeuvre. As one noble councillor of the margraves of Brandenburg wrote of his fellow nobles: 'The knightage [*Ritterschaft*] ... are provided with many princes; when one is not pleased with a prince's ... judgement he goes over to another prince'. Any attempt by one of the princes to subject the nobles in his purported catchment area and thereby strengthen his hold on it was likely to backfire by driving them into his rival princes' camps and thereby weaken his hold on it.[24]

This tradition of noble independence came under unprecedently massive attack in 1495. The reforms introduced at the Imperial Diet of Worms lent a tremendous boost to princely power, partly at the expense of the emperor, mainly at the expense of the non-princely nobility. The statutes revoked the nobles' customary right to feud and laid it down that in disputes between princes and nobles, the latter would have to come before the princely aulic court of law (*Hofgericht*). To rub salt in the wound, the reforms were to be financed by the new Common Penny tax, from which nobles were not to be exempt and which was to be collected by the princes themselves. Both the lesser nobles and the counts and barons objected to the entire scheme vehemently. They resolved, as one of them later recalled, 'that they would not let themselves be put on a level with the French [nobility], who once were also free'. To this end they set about building regional leagues in Swabia, Franconia, and the Middle Rhine. They jointly vowed not to pay the Common Penny and made concerted military preparations should an attempt be made to coerce them.[25] The princes perceived these measures as a direct threat. There followed decades of struggle which only served to turn the leagues from the *ad hoc* associations that the nobles intended them to be into durable territorial organizations. The nobles in effect placed themselves beside and outside the forming princely states.

What enabled the nobles to elude the tightening grip of the princes was imperial patronage. The emperors had always had an interest in helping the nobles maintain some independence from the princes. This secured them a clientele of lords who depended on their support and who could be used as conduits of imperial will and as checks on princely expansionism. Thus, in 1510, Emperor Maximilian I pronounced against the landgrave of Hesse that his, the landgrave's, wine toll rights, which he exploited to stake out territorial claims, could not be exercised in the domains of the neighbouring Wetterau counts. Imperial protection, though, had its price. In 1532 the Swabian and Franconian knights agreed to contribute in taxes to the war effort against the Ottomans, albeit making a point of naming the payment *subsidium charitativum* so as to underscore its optional character. In 1542 they consented to the Common Penny, revivified to help finance King Ferdinand I's war in Hungary. In return Ferdinand declared the knights as 'subordinate to a Roman Emperor and King without any intermediary'. The counts and barons were admitted as an Estate to the *Reichstag* and were given a vote. Neither they nor the lesser nobles were to be constitutionally subject to the principalities. They continued to serve the princes as vassals and officials. Indeed, they still retained vested interests in the princely states. But they did not recognize the princes as their sovereign overlords. Impelled by imperial fiscal demands and under imperial aegis, the regional associations which they formed were institutionalized as corporate bodies endowed with a central administration and power of taxation. It is said that as Frederick the Great passed through the puny territory of one of those petty imperial knights, the latter came out and welcomed the king to his 'state'; Frederick responded in kind: 'Ah, deux souverains qui se rencontrent.'[26]

The second half of the fifteenth century was a critical juncture in the evolution of the relationship between monarchy and nobility, and by extension, in the history of state formation. In Central as well as in Western Europe rulers emerged from the primitive phase of state building with enhanced claims to sovereign powers and with more adequate means than hitherto of making them good. The result was a series of quite similar confrontations between them and nobles over the relative scope of their authority, the nature of their rights and obligations. The War of the Public Weal is not only a testimony to how serious these conflicts were; it is also a reminder that they were not a foregone conclusion. The case of the core zone of the Empire in Germany may serve as an example of one possible geopolitical outcome the War of the Public Weal might have had. But precisely the basic similarities between the various cases throw into relief their differences.

Like the nobles in France and Castile, or for that matter Bavaria, the nobles inhabiting the imperial heartland in Germany regarded politico-juridical privileges as central elements of their status, and guarded them equally ardently. Yet the resolution of these issues led in their case to an abandonment of the princely states as their main frames of reference. What is so striking is not only that the incentive to reach accommodation with the princes was not strong enough, but that they found the alternative more attractive. The consequence was the survival of imperial influence in these areas – in effect reproducing a root cause of this situation. While this was an apology for imperial sovereignty, it was enough to incapacitate the local princes. They were no more able fully to consolidate their power in their domains than the emperor was able in the *Reich*. The emperor could not offer the princes, nor could the princes offer the nobles, what the French and Castilian monarchs could turn into such a good account in their relationship with their nobles: a big stick that at the same time was miraculously an equally big carrot. In sum, neither the Habsburg *Großdynastie* nor any other princely House could impose itself on the zone which might have served as a springboard for the forging of a centralized state in Germany.[27] This indirectly accounts for the great lengths to which French and Castilian monarchs could and were prepared to go in order to incorporate nobles great and small into their states.

The control, however tenuous, which the Castilian and French kings had acquired over the nation's wealth and military forces was at first a mixed blessing. A crucial advantage, it immediately invited trouble, for it both threatened the mighty and whetted their appetite. This ambivalence suggested its own solution: if royal resources were scarcely sufficient to quell opposition, they were quite enough to buy it out. For the nobles to have a share in these resources meant not only that these were less likely to be used against themselves; it also held out the prospect of more wealth and influence than afforded by the peaceful enjoyment of 'feudal autonomy'. This was one reason why the struggle was now not over the authority of the monarchical state as such but over who exercised it and to whose benefit. Hence also, as the contests over the royal council indicate, the assimilation of the nobles into the French and Castilian monarchical state could only be achieved through making spacious room for them within it. Thus, some of the most effective instruments that these monarchs could employ to assert their authority over the nobles were the very ones that the nobles could in turn use to enhance their own authority. This was the basis for the political equilibrium that had been established in France already by the latter part of Louis XI's reign and in Castile under Fernando and Isabel. Monarchy and nobles were learning to accommodate each other, however tentatively. The tensions between them had subsided somewhat. The nobles came to accept the state and the novel powers it conferred on their monarchs, but in return they received a substantial share in the exercise of its power and in its revenues. The last decades of the fifteenth century and the first of the sixteenth brought to a close the formative period in the making of an alliance between nobility and state that would underlie the *ancien régime* in France and Castile.

Such politics of bargaining was by and large alien to England. The English monarch needed to buy out his greater subjects only in exceptional circumstances, such as prevailed under Henry IV or in Edward IV's early years. In normal times there was no 'budget of noble assistance'. It has been calculated that the annual cost of pensions paid by the English Crown during the second half of the sixteenth century was less than one tenth than that borne by the French Crown in the mid-1570s. There were quite a few factors preventing such liberality. England's early unification, the pattern of participatory politics in the counties, and, after 1450, the 'divorce' of peers and gentry, combined to provide kings with a comparatively wide sociopolitical basis which, as discussed above, Henry VII exploited in order to subdue the magnates. This was well reflected in the composition of the Tudor Privy Council. In 1536–7, only six of the nineteen councillors were nobles in the second generation. In the early years of Edward VI's reign (1547–53), it was of nearly perfect *arriviste* complexion: of the twenty-eight councillors, only Arundel was the son of a peer. Eleven were of the upper gentry, a further nine of the lesser gentry; the rest were of a lower station still. These people clearly were the monarch's creatures. It was their submission and loyalty that earned them a place in Council, not the need to draw them into the monarch's orbit of influence.[28]

The English king, then, though he governed in conjunction with Parliament without whose consent he could not make laws, was not as weak as he might have seemed from the perspective of the Continent. Louis XI of France would surely have admired the despotic techniques of Henry VII – who placed forty-six of the sixty-two peerage families under financial bonds – but was in no position to do the same. A Venetian envoy could not help notice in 1497 the limited judicial authority of the English nobles and that they had no castles. He was not quite sure whether they deserved to be counted as nobles. There is a striking contrast between the limited capability of English monarchs to wage international war and the strength of their domestic authority, particularly in relation to the nobility. This contradiction was perhaps at its most glaring under Henry VIII. His military interventions in Europe showed England to be a second-rate contender; yet it was under him, historians have speculated, that the English monarchy, having just treated itself to vast Church lands, had its greatest chance of taking the path to absolutism. The chance was literally squandered in Henry VIII's disastrous excursions across the Channel. The costs of European wars were so high that the Church properties had to be put up for sale. It has been estimated that perhaps 70 per cent of Henry VIII's extraordinary income came from this as well as from debasement of coinage. Gone was the opportunity to gain financial independence from Parliament, and in turn this was to dampen any future monarchical enthusiasm to join in the European fray. Only after 1640 would the English state have sufficient income from taxation to allow the pursuance of an aggressive rather than merely defensive foreign policy.[29]

The failure of the English monarchy to emulate the French and Spanish ones did not, however, entail an aristocratic comeback. For one thing, in the longer term, the disengagement from European warfare blunted the English nobility's martial instincts, one traditional asset wise rulers had to reckon with. By 1576 three out of four peers lacked military experience. For another, and more importantly, the fact that England did not try to fight wars with inadequate means of financing them meant that it did not have to resort to the same expedients as used by the French and Spanish monarchies at the expense of their own future well-being.[30] As a result, the English state remained comparatively immune to moneyed, vested interests, among them the nobility, which in other countries penetrated and then monopolized the governmental and financial systems.[31] That the English state had not come to represent an economic and political enterprise for powerful groups was, as already intimated, destined to cause grave difficulties to the monarchy; but for the English state itself, for society, and even for the aristocracy, the consequences turned out in later centuries to be very felicitous indeed. To European and world history they were downright fateful.

4   From consensus to conflict

Monarchy and nobility between war and religion

With the French invasion of Italy in 1494 began the long and revolutionary sixteenth century. The incursion betokened also the emergence of a European system of national states whose formation has been seen as 'the dominant political fact of the last thousand years'.[1] This system was right from the outset as devastatingly expensive as it was brutally competitive. The struggle for mastery that nourished it dwarfed in scale and costs the Hundred Years' War. Indeed, the fisco-military effort could be too strenuous. While war in the fourteenth and fifteenth century generally invigorated the states involved, in the sixteenth century it threatened fatally to sap ambitious belligerents. Moreover, religious schism in the wake of the Reformation stretched in some countries an already tried consensus to breaking point and compounded the strain on governments. These exigencies profoundly shaped the monarchy–nobility relationship, which in turn affected the ability of the various states to cope with the pressures.

When King Louis XII of France asked the Italian captain Gian-Giacomo Trivulzio (1448–1518) what it would take to conquer Milan, the reply was: 'It is necessary to prepare three things, Sir, money, money, and still more money.' The maxim could stand as an epigraph for the whole early modern period. The taxes established in various countries between 1300 and 1500 to finance war proved in the sixteenth century far and away inadequate for the original purpose. In 1523 the French Crown's income from taxes was just over 5 million *livres*. But in the period 1521–5 war cost King François I nearly 20 million *livres*. In the second half of 1521, fighting on three fronts devoured perhaps 700,000 *livres* every month. So in 1522 the Most Christian King sent his officials to Tours, where they tore down and melted the silver grill surrounding the shrine of St Martin. The act was as conducive to the liquidation of the king's deficit as it was to the salvation of his soul. And the most expensive conflict during this reign was yet to come: in 1542–6 more than 30 million *livres* went on war-making. On aggregate, François I's military outlays in his thirty-two years on the throne (1515–47) were 102 million *livres*. This amounted to more than half of the king's total expenditure throughout the reign, and to two-thirds of his intake from imposts. And yet by comparison with the next half century, both royal expenses and the burden of taxation were moderate. Under Henri II (1547–59) war was consuming every year only little less than the equivalent of the Crown's average annual revenue from taxation (13.5 million *livres*), which itself was almost double that of the period 1515–47.[2]

The Valois kings of France could perhaps take heart from the equal if not greater financial discomfiture of their arch-adversaries, the Spanish Habsburgs. A dynastic imperial conglomeration composed of widely scattered territories, the Habsburg bloc 'provides one of the greatest examples of strategical overstretch in history'. Inevitably, the Spanish Habsburgs overreached themselves financially as well, despite the American bullion bonanza. Central government deficit in the Habsburg Netherlands alone reached 7 million florins in 1555. In the kingdom of Naples, government income (1,330,241 ducats) was in 1550 outstripped by its expenses (1,376,363 ducats). Half of this sum was expended on the military, and a further third of it on debt charges. In 1574 expenditure exceeded income by 1,201,472 ducats (military expenses being larger than the deficit). Worse still was the situation at the empire's headquarters, Castile. In 1574 the estimated total debt and liabilities ran up to an overwhelming 81 million ducats – a sum nearly fifteen times the total annual revenue. The next year Philip II declared his third bankruptcy. It is easy to see why the Venetian ambassador to Charles V, having experienced from first hand the staggering magnitude of imperial military endeavour, exhorted the Senate in his concluding relation, 'Peace, Most Serene Prince, peace!'. Venice, however, like England, could fall back on its natural environment to keep foreign war at bay. But few land-based states could elude the escalating warfare and the attendant dramatic upward spiralling of expenses.[3]

The response of governments to this problem, and to that of the time lag between the urgent need for money in wartime and the protracted collection of taxes, was to resort to funded debt. There were various types, but they all rested on the principle of money being 'anticipated': the government raised loans on the systematic basis of earmarking specific sources of its revenue for the purpose of paying interest to creditors. Governments thus brought private finance into play, and on a vast scale. In Holland, where the first 'financial revolution' occurred, the system functioned so effectually that it became a source of strength, indeed an important factor in Holland's ability to stand up to Spain. The English ambassador to the Dutch Republic reported that 'when [the Dutch government] pay off any part of the principal, those it belongs to receive it with tears, not knowing how to dispose of it to interest with safety and ease'. But the Dutch were unique. Elsewhere, as Geoffrey Parker remarked, 'government creditors would have shed tears of joy to have their money safely returned'. In Spain, for instance, the government had by 1556 assigned to lenders all its future revenues up to 1560. In 1598, 62 per cent of the Crown's ordinary revenues went into servicing the consolidated debt. For the Kingdom of Naples in 1605, the figure is 50 per cent; this represented a sum that was higher than the actual military expenditure. Small wonder that the Spanish government was occasionally cut off from the financial circuit altogether, forced to surrender to its financiers control of the sources of income themselves.[4]

It would seem at first sight that the public debt must have been a cause of a chronic weakness of the warring states. That is true in some obvious respects. At the same time, it was also a source of political vigour. For its operation (unintentionally) helped the state to permeate, and embed itself in, society.[5] And it was a most powerful factor in bringing the nobility – or rather segments thereof – to identify its interests with those of the state. This presupposed, of course, an economic ability on the part of nobles to take part in the gestation of the public debt – a truism that needs to be stated in view of the resilience of the widespread notion of a 'crisis of the aristocracy' in that period. What perhaps is less self-evident is that the public debt not only reflected but also contributed to the economic vitality, success even, of sections of the nobility. In short, the organization of public debt was a central force shaping the structure of the nobility as well as that of the state.

In the first place, the financial system hit hardest those who were least able to pay, and benefited those who were most able to pay. This was typical, indeed constitutive, of an *ancien régime* economy of privilege. A classic example is provided by the city of Burgos. In 1591, when the Crown agents set about collecting the *millones* tax, the city numbered 3,319 citizens. The citizenry was made up of 1,722 *hidalgos*, 1,023 clergy, and 574 commoners. It was only the latter, comprising a mere 17.3 per cent of the population, that paid the amount the city was required to deliver. Now, as has been indicated, Crown revenues such as this tax were employed to pay the interest on loans made to the Crown. In this way, wealth was shunted up the social hierarchy.[6]

In some cases, notably early Habsburg Spain, wealth was siphoned off chiefly to merchant-bankers. But financial dominance of a 'rising bourgeoisie' was by no means the rule. Aristocratic wealth often made an impressive showing.[7] In the kingdom of Naples in 1563, the share of funded public debt held by nobles was 32 per cent. On the other hand, these nobles constituted only 8 per cent of all investors. In 1572, 67 nobles, or 5 per cent of all investors, controlled 34 per cent of the public debt, declining to 3 and 27 per cent respectively in 1596. At that date, a nobleman's average portfolio was worth nearly 42,000 ducats, as against 3,400 ducats of non-noble lenders.[8]

A similar pattern has emerged from research on the Grand-Duchy of Tuscany in the mid-eighteenth century.[9] Figure 4.1 displays the social distribution of investors in the public debt. It is also noteworthy that, among the noble investors, there was a striking distinction between families of recent origin and those of old stock. The latter held 93 per cent of the bonds in noble hands. The saying that nobility was ancient wealth was thus only half of the truth. There was another disequilibrium in the ranks of the nobility: a small group, some 13 per cent of all ancient Tuscan nobles, received 68 per cent of the interest flowing from the consolidated debt. The public debt in this way facilitated a twofold process of concentration: in society in general, reinforcing the nobility, and within the nobility itself, reinforcing a small coterie of the most illustrious old families. 'This kleptocracy', as it has been labelled, 'made of the monarchy the Peru of the aristocrats.'[10]

Noble finances, as Table 4.1 shows, dominated the public debt of German princely states too.[11] Nearly everywhere it was nobles who extended most of the credit princes required. When the Landgrave of Hesse planned a military expedition in 1534, he instructed his official to raise at least 282,550 Gulden in loans; alone the counts of Hanau promised him, and later advanced, 75,000 Gulden.[12] The loans made by German nobles were on average considerably higher than those advanced by commoners.

Public debt was a vehicle through which nobles could tap the wealth of their society in a way incomparably neater, more efficient, and less contested than direct feudal coercion. Yet this does not warrant the view put forward by Perry Anderson that the (absolutist)

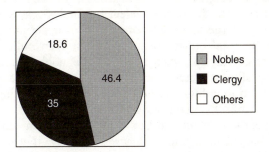

Figure 4.1 Social distributions of Tuscan investors in public debt.

Adapted from J.-C. Waquet, *Le Grand-Duché de Toscane sous les derniers Médicis: Essai sur le système des finances et la stabilité des institutions dans les anciens états italiens* (Paris, 1990), 360. The figure for nobles includes investments belonging to the Order of St Stephen (8 per cent), practically an arm of the nobility.

state 'was essentially just this: *a redeployed and recharged apparatus of feudal domination* . . . the new political carapace of a threatened nobility'. First, the state was not a machine blindly working in favour of the nobility as a whole. Not all nobles were well placed to profit from that inexorable motor of inequality that the state indeed was, for not all nobles were in a position to help satisfy the state's voracious appetite. The sire de Gouberville, that famously obscure gentleman, left us the tale of the travails he went through when, in 1555, he tried to procure a post in the *eaux et forêts*. He found no friend at Court, and the best he managed to achieve was glimpsing the king from a distance. Having frittered away forty-three days and one hundred *livres*, he returned to the *ennui* of his estates empty-handed. Gouberville was simply too small to make a difference and therefore to merit attention. And the only benefit his nobility brought him was his exemption from taxes, significant in itself, yet nothing new by the mid-sixteenth century.[13]

Table 4.1 Structure of debt of two German princes

Prince	Date	Debt (Gulden)	Proportion loaned by nobles (%)
Count of Württemberg	1483	213,358	82.6
Margrave of Brandenburg	1529	362,800	83.8

Sources: F. Ernst (1970, 74); U. Müller, (1984, 238).

Second, as the social complexion of the public debt shows, the state was to an appreciable degree dependent on nobles' capacity and readiness to invest large sums of money in it. But the public debt was only one financial outlet. In an age when even military operations had to be contracted out, the rich warrior noble was as valued a figure as the affluent merchant-banker. Nobles loomed large among those whose job description required an ability and willingness to risk their own ruin by 'replicating in miniature the costs of war to the royal treasury'. Antonio de Leyva met on his own some of his expenses in Italy as a captain in Charles V's pay, if that is what it was: 101,452 *escudos* in the period 1523–9, or 9.2 per cent of the amount raised in *asientos* for the Milan and Naples campaigns. In 1525 he was rewarded with the governorship of Milan. Another example is offered by Anne de Montmorency, *grand maître* of France. In 1537 he supplied King François I with 75,000 *livres*, partly in direct loan, partly in funding the army in Picardy, resorting in the process to melting down his gold plate. His nomination in 1538 as Constable of France was most likely in recognition of this service. It was also a handsome recompense. Until then the Crown paid Montmorency between 32,450 and 44,450 *livres* annually in emoluments and pensions. Already this sum was some four times greater than his revenues from his property. In 1538, the Constableship raised his pensions by a further 24,000 *livres*. But these were minor boons compared with those accruing to him from the political clout his position hard by the centre of power allowed him to exert: it enabled him to influence legal decisions and gave him access to ready money as well as to valuable property market information. It was a winning formula that earned him an immense landed fortune.[14]

The expanding purview of the state, then, intensified social stratification not only in society in general, but also among the nobility itself. It created a cleavage between those nobles who failed to gain a foothold in it and those who succeeded. The difference was clearly reflected in the income structure of nobles. Nobles enjoying proximity to the state relied on it for the better part of their livelihood.[15] But economic success on a scale otherwise inconceivable necessarily implied dependence of nobles on monarchs. And the grander the noble was, the deeper was his dependence. That is what lies behind the spectacle of leading nobles taking pains to provide their monarchs with credit of all kinds. Nobles were practically forced to invest in the state, for this was the most effective way of obtaining those means which enabled them to invest in the state. This circulation of political and financial capital between government and top nobles suggests that the state had come to generate something of a self-sustaining momentum. A powerful sector of society had become implicated in its functioning. And the rulers could harness their private wealth and political energies by giving them access to public resources, many of which the rulers were anyway scarcely able to exploit themselves. As one historian has observed, 'however these devices may be judged in terms of public morals or civic spirit, they allowed interests and consensus to crystallise around the state'.[16] The fisco-military exigencies of the age brought monarchy and nobility into close interdependence and interpenetration.

Nowhere were the substance and spirit and difficulties of this relationship more manifest, or of greater moment, than in the case of the noble high functionaries of the state, especially the provincial governors. Provincial governors were themselves created by the expansion of the state. In Germany, governorships burgeoned from around 1300 in all of the principalities. They were the jurisdictional building-blocks of territorial rule, the units on whose basis taxation was levied. Each provincial governorship therefore had a definite financial value. Together they underlay the princes' public debt: they were transferred, in the form of contractual liens, to noble creditors in return for sizeable loans. The noble creditor thus acted also as a governor, the highest military and judicial officer in the territorial administration. The lien transaction, however, was 'contaminated' by compelling political motives. It was a way, first, of recruiting to local government men trained to exercise leadership and military command in their own right. Second, it was a means of drawing local noblemen and their clients into closer association and identification with their territories. By the same token, the lien transaction led to a blending of public authority and private power to the point of dissolving the distinction, all the more so as many governors had their family estates in the very districts they headed. Their seigneurial power over their subjects was in this manner backed up by the state. An example is provided by the Franconian noble Georg von Guttenberg: governor of Marktleugast in the diocese of Bamberg, he used his public capacity to have one of his own 'private' tenants executed there.

But the lien arrangement was more than a state-sponsored apparatus of seigneurial exploitation. It gave the governors substantial power also relative to the princes themselves, especially since they could not be relieved of office until the principal was reimbursed. Given the continuation, let alone aggravation, of the financial predicament that constrained princes to pledge governorships in the first place, the clause allowing their redemption was effectively a dead letter. In fact, their very alienation reduced the income reaching the princes from the demesne and hence the chances of recovering them. It is not surprising, therefore, that numerous governorships ran in the same noble families for generations, or that some governorships were definitively lost to the princely fisc. Thus, while the German princely states were expanding in terms of their expenditure and income (including credit), they were being internally 'colonized' by their wealthier nobles.[17]

Some German princes, however, when acting as governors in the Habsburgs' service in The Netherlands, were the authors of the same loss of political control and abuses of power over which they presided in their own domains. But proportionate to their lofty rank and to the dimensions and importance of the governorships they directed, the inconveniences they caused were more difficult to overcome than those they experienced as rulers. The most notorious case of local empire-building involved the margraves of Baden. Margrave Christoph acquired in 1488 under a lien agreement the governorship of Luxemburg from Emperor Maximilian I. It devolved in hereditary tenure upon Bernhard of Baden who, in the 1520s, ruled Luxemburg with contumacious disregard for the central government in Brussels. He went so far as to set up tolls at the gates of towns, lining his pockets with the proceeds. He also farmed out the public domain of his own accord. Only in 1531 did Emperor Charles V and his regent rid themselves of him by repurchasing the office against a heavy indemnity.[18]

The situation in the other stadholderates was only slightly better during the first decades of the sixteenth century. Though in theory it was the sovereign's prerogative to appoint governors, Charles V mostly deferred to the natural desires of the stadholders to bequeath their office to their descendants. There were several reasons for Charles V's willingness to oblige. He grew up amid the Netherlandish aristocracy and shared their values. His relationship with some of them was veritably fraternal. 'If you could be in two places [at one time]', he wrote to Charles de Lannoy, his viceroy in Naples, 'it would be my wish often to have you in my presence.' In 1544, having witnessed the death in battle of René de Châlons, the emperor 'retired to his chamber . . . [and] gave evident signs of how much he loved him'. The magnates relished his attitude. Lannoy told Charles that his greatest wish was 'to be near Your Majesty, in your service . . . I have no other passion in this world'. Such effusive expressions of fidelity contrasted sharply with their forefathers' lack of affection towards the last of the Valois dukes of Burgundy, the Habsburgs' predecessors in the Low Countries. The suspicious and overbearing Charles the Bold never won the hearts of his nobles and was beset by a series of defections to the French camp. As Antoine de Croy summed it up with all the contempt he could summon up: 'I do not want to give up service to a French king for a count of Charolais [i.e. Charles the Bold].'[19]

But the love and loyalty towards Emperor Charles V rested on less flimsy a foundation than personal affinity. They were as much the consequence as the cause of royal rewards. And there was no grander reward with which to predispose a great Netherlandish noble than an appointment to one of the eleven governorships. Governors usually held the captaincy of a *bande d'ordonnance*. This was a matter of the utmost significance to the self-esteem of the grandees, imbued as they were with traditional martial ethos. It could also come in handy. Jean de Glymes, Marquis of Berghes and governor of Hainault, once sent his troops to his family estates 'in order to crush his peasants'.[20] In some provinces the governor also acted as the supreme judicial officer and occasionally enjoyed rights to grant pardons, privileges and immunities. Governors sometimes possessed the prerogative of appointing town magistrates and officers in the judicial and financial administration of their province. The extensive powers vested in the office made it the most coveted prize nobles could aspire to. Correspondingly, that office was the most important leverage the monarch had in ensuring the allegiance of the great aristocracy. And, indeed, half of the appointees between 1503 and 1572 came from a mere seven families: Croy, Nassau, Egmont, Lalaing, Berghes, Lannoy and Montmorency. There was thus a contradiction at work: the need to appropriate the governorships for the prominent families in order to tie them to the ruling dynasty resulted in these governorships becoming to all intents and purposes hereditary and therefore less and less fit to serve the purpose of keeping the great families in line.

All the same, a continuous reliance on the nobility was an ineluctable course of action, the more so since The Netherlands was only one of the Spanish Habsburgs' numerous and far-flung dominions. The Habsburgs were thrown upon an unmitigated form of exercising rule through intermediaries. It was vital to effective government to secure the willing co-operation of the most influential nobles; indeed, they needed to bolster these nobles' status and private power so as to enhance their performance as agents of central government. The Count of Hoorne did have a point when, in 1555,

he demanded to have in his gift all offices and benefices in his governorship of Gelderland 'in order to possess greater intelligence in the
province, for His Majesty's service'. This was also the argument of
Charles de Brimeu, Count of Meghen, who in 1560 asked to be
permitted a broad latitude in dispensing patronage 'in order to gain
greater respect in his governorship'. The regents shared this view
that patronage could work miracles for the governors' ability to elicit
local compliance. In 1560 Margaret of Parma recommended that
Berghes be installed as governor of Hainault because of his weight
there, which she hoped would help her to counterbalance that of the
provincial Estates and the Bishop of Cambrai.

Yet the regent was equally realistic about the other side of
patronage. Granted that the nobles' agenda overlapped only partially
with the regent's, patronage exposed the central government to
dangers. The gravest peril was that a governor would transgress the
thin line between representing the sovereign authority and arrogating
it to himself. Given the grandees' penchant to treat governorships
as ancestral fiefdoms, an irreversible loss of control over them was
a prospect never too remote. The dilemma was that a policy to
weaken the governors was as liable to have nasty consequences for
the central government as was a policy to strengthen them. Until the
Dutch Revolt, no satisfactory solution was found. The regent Mary
of Hungary (r. 1530–55), reputed to have had 'enough of a man in
her', instigated a campaign to check the expansion of gubernatorial
pretensions. For a while it worked. But under Margaret of Parma
the strain grew intolerable and led to a spectacularly self-defeating
rupture with the magnates.[21]

The Habsburgs' troubles with their Netherlandish grandees would
have struck a familiar chord in French monarchs. They were in the
same cleft stick: they had to keep the governors simultaneously
powerful and dependent. A poignant token of this quandary was the
entrées of major governors into towns of their provinces. Guillaume
Gouffier entered Grenoble in 1520 under a canopy of red damask,
thereby assuming a potent symbol of royalty. Another governor, entering Dijon, was hailed as 'the image of God and one of his ministers
on earth'.[22] This identification of royal and aristocratic authority was
not in itself damaging so long as it enhanced primarily the prestige of
the office rather than that of its incumbent. In fact, it could be useful,
for it enabled the king to manipulate governorships as the most
valuable recompense or incentive for distinguished services rendered
or expected. And this indeed was the overriding criterion for the
nominations made during the first half of the sixteenth century.

A change occurred in the second half of the century. More and more governors were permitted to designate their successors in office. In 1515–37, 23 per cent of the governors were heirs of their predecessor; in 1560–82 the figure mounted to 42 per cent. Governorships were becoming patrimonial. Gaspard de Saulx-Tavanes made in 1572 his governorship of Provence over to Albert de Gondi, on condition that Gondi make the government of the town of Metz over to Saulx-Tavanes's son. This pact and many others like it were endorsed by the king. Small wonder that governors were taking on attributes of caste and that governorships were increasingly getting out of reach for all bar the grandest personages of the realm. While nine of the thirty governors appointed in 1515–37 were barons or seigneurs, the humblest appointee in 1605–27 was a count.[23]

Some contemporaries inveighed against this development. One argued that hereditary transmission of governorships 'led to much evil . . . because [the governors] do not hold themselves beholden to the king'. But if there was a grain of truth in this assertion, it was the result of the king's effort to secure the loyalty of great nobles and thereby maintain public order. By countenancing the 'privatization' of governorships the monarchy actively encouraged the upper nobility to identify the future interest of their families with the well-being of the state. And the social basis the monarchy thus created for itself was actually broader than the group of the *Grands*, because it included the hundreds of lesser families which were associated with them through ties of clientage. The French monarchical state, as Robert Harding has pointed out, 'was built on the confusion of the public domain and the private. Fundamentally, the system of governors was a way of coopting the private power and resources of the aristocracy into the framework of the state.'[24]

The analysis of the system of governors in various early modern states suggests that, for all the inherent conflicts, a strong monarchy and a strong nobility were not mutually exclusive. In fact, their power grew in tandem during the first half of the sixteenth century. One particularly pertinent conclusion Harding has drawn is that 'instead of dissolving the confusion between social pre-eminence and administrative authority the rise of absolutism coincided with a closer identification of these two things in the corps of governors'.[25] Leaving aside for the moment the question of what it implies for the term 'absolutism',[26] this closer identification, as the discussion of noble creditors has also shown, was already happening in the first half of the sixteenth century if not earlier. The very opportunities, then, which the expansion of the state opened up for nobles to consolidate their hold on power, also enmeshed them in the structure and operation of the state. As has been intimated in the previous chapter, this coalescence for a while lent the sociopolitical order a good deal of coherence at the top. But in the second half the century the pact suffered a severe setback. Indeed, the period witnessed some of the most spectacular conflicts ever between monarchs and their nobles. Conflicts, of course, were nothing new, except that now they acquired a dimension that radically altered their character and gave aristocratic opposition an extremely dangerous edge. This dimension was ideology.

The years around the mid-sixteenth century, as those around 1400, saw nearly everywhere in Western Europe a certain spurt in the fashioning of noble collective identity, in the development by them of self-awareness of what they shared *qua* nobles and what distinguished them from non-nobles.[27] This ideological movement, though, was not unitary. The elements of which it consisted and their permutations varied from one country to the next. Most significantly, they interacted with the political and social environment in different ways to produce different outcomes. In some cases the uprush in nobles' group consciousness came from conflict with the monarchical state. In other, social considerations predominated, revealing little if any trace of political battle. The Italian states are a case in point. Around mid-century nobiliary ideology was in full bloom, and under its influence the dominant classes grew ever more uniform. This development, however, did not run counter to the simultaneous advance of the absolutist theory. The relation between the two, it has been held, was marked by a search after reciprocal integration and compromise. In Spain, too, the second half of the sixteenth century marked a formative phase in the crystallization of noble self-perception. The relative openness that was the bequest of the Reconquest was giving way to a more stringent concept of nobility. Ancient lineage, newly coupled with the notion of purity of blood (*limpieza de sangre*) and wedded to a genteel way of life, became the decisive tests of nobility. Unlike Italy, however, the emphasis on nobility of blood seems to have been a reaction to the rise of royal absolutism. Be that as it may, the ideological consolidation of nobility did not lead to open conflict with King Philip II (1556–98).[28]

In parts of Germany, by contrast, the aristocratic collective personality, more advanced than anywhere else in Western Europe, was forged on the anvil of political opposition to princely territorial and fiscal claims.[29] The nobles' resistance is interesting on two accounts in particular. First, while the creation of the Imperial Knightage (*Reichsritterschaft*) as an institutional counterpoise to the princes' ambitions involved a great deal of friction, the political heat it generated did not spark a violent flare-up. The so-called Knights' Revolt of 1522–3, whose driving force was allegedly the Franconian nobility, was not at all what the name denotes. It was a revolutionary venture all right, but of one man: the condottiere Franz von Sickingen. His was an extravagant plan: to take advantage of the Reformation, secularize the ecclesiastical principality of Trier and install himself as its ruler. Very few Franconian nobles proved reckless enough to cast in their lot with Sickingen. The fact that he chose to strike at an ecclesiastical principality and yet received so little support from nobles in a state of agitation is the second remarkable point. In these *Sturm und Drang* years of the Reformation, religion plainly was not allowed to outweigh what was essentially a constitutional and political struggle. Nor was it later in the century. This pragmatism was in no small part the product of weakness: in those geopolitically fragmented areas where the Imperial Knightage arose, the princes who clung to the old faith were too feeble even to contemplate forcing religious conformity on the numerous nobles who converted to Lutheranism. The nobles for their part had no reason to make of religion an issue of political authority.[30]

These were not the circumstances prevalent in neighbouring Bavaria. The duke was proverbially rich and one of the most powerful princes in Germany. His authority was institutionally a great deal more established than that of the prince-bishops in neighbouring Franconia. He therefore dared to be resolute. The counts and barons, on the other hand, had for some time been augmenting and cementing their lordships and seeking to bypass the prince's jurisdiction by placing themselves under the immediate authority of the empire. A collision became inevitable when they came out firmly for Lutheran tenets and flew in the teeth of the staunchly Catholic duke. In 1563 they demanded that the Confession of Augsburg be recognized in the duchy. The threat to the duke's rule was absolute: a nobility that had initially challenged him on political rights now came together fortified by a creed which they construed as legitimating their position. They had come to equate freedom of worship with noble privilege. This made for a non-negotiable stance. The duke had no remedy but to hazard the use of force. He carried all before him.[31]

Thus, in the stronger states the Reformation changed the rules of the political game. It contributed to the redefinition of princely power. This holds good not only for those states whose rulers abjured the ancestral faith to be followed by their subjects, but also in those states where the new faith failed to make headway. For in either case the ruler had to insist on the formula of *cuius regio eius religio* in order to keep the realm together. To do just this, alas, 'implied an extension of government power over all the individuals within the state'. Now this redefined power was perilously top-heavy. As J. H. Shennan explained, the prince was 'borne down by an authority too weighty now to be justified in personal or dynastic terms, increasingly vulnerable to domestic resentment and ultimately to rebellion in the absence of some other mutually acceptable justification'. If even a prince 'by the grace of God' was not secure, how much more so where disagreement raged over how that grace was to be secured. In such a situation, religion had a truly awesome potential for inflaming the ongoing low-intensity political struggles between prince and nobles over the balance of power. This potential was realized under specific conditions: where the growth in the rulers' authority beyond its traditional limits was matched by an ability and willingness on their part to try repression, and where this led to the questioning of their authority, the nobles resorted to active disobedience. They did this in France; they did this in The Netherlands; they did this in Austria and Bohemia.[32]

In 1559 King Henri II of France was killed in a jousting accident, the lance of his opponent, Count Montgomery, having penetrated his left eye. This was the thin end of the wedge. The new king, François II, was a boy of fifteen. The ensuing jockeying for power positions was won by Duke François of Guise and his brother Charles, Cardinal of Lorraine. Why other nobles had reasons for anxiety has been made plain by an analysis of *registres d'expéditions*, records of royal gifts and favours: while in 1553 28 per cent of the volume of royal patronage was distributed through the Guise, in 1560 the figure soared to 74 per cent. And as if this near-monopoly at the Court were not gall and wormwood enough to the other pretenders, the Guises were also militant Catholics. This added to the political contest an ingredient that transformed it almost beyond recognition. It was not accidental that the conspirators of the 'Tumult of Amboise' in 1560, a botched attempt to wrest control of the Court from the Guises, were nobles of Calvinist sympathies. Nor was it fortuitous that it was a Calvinist gentleman who in 1560 delivered a sensational disquisition on the topic of nobility before the Estates General. In his *Harangue de par la Noblesse de toute la France*, Jacques de Silly, Count of Rochefort, excoriated ennoblements and asserted emphatically that the only true nobility was nobility of blood. His 'predestinarian' nobility was, as a social quality, outside the remit of the monarch. This indeed harbingered a process which ended some fifty years later with the nobles articulating an ideology in which the once critical element of Virtue was pushed into the background and Birth to the foreground, accentuated as the overriding criterion of membership. But it was 'the first manifestation of an aristocratic reaction' in another, more immediate respect as well. Formidably cultivated and erudite, Rochefort mentioned in the *Harangue* Maternus and Cleander the Phrygian, who wanted to supplant their master, Emperor Commodus. This was not too abstruse an allusion to the brothers Guise.[33]

The problem that Rochefort raised and that engrossed other nobles was legitimacy. A good many of those out of grace and favour felt persecuted for their faith, not just excluded. It was natural that they would query whether the inequity they suffered had any legitimate basis and, if not, what the limits of obedience were. The conjuncture of political and religious circumstances gave the nobles furiously to think about the nature of monarchical polity and of their own place in it. The Wars of Religion (1562–98) served to stimulate further the political consciousness of nobles. Already by 1567 the idea was canvassed that the duty to protect the kingdom from tyranny did not fall solely to the princes. The *Avertissement sur la Protestation de Monseigneur le Prince de Condé* proclaimed: 'does not the entire nobility have a similar obligation and a special and solemn vow to preserve the public weal, the state of the kingdom, and the Crown?'

The events of 1568 polarized monarchy and nobility further. The execution in June at the behest of Philip II of Spain of Egmont and Hoorne, the latter a Montmorency, was perceived as an inter-monarchical plot to extirpate the nobility. In August that year, Prince Louis of Condé and Admiral Gaspard de Coligny concluded an agreement with Prince William of Orange. They railed against their kings' 'evil councillors' and their intention 'to exterminate the true Religion and also the nobility and other worthy people, without which the Kings cannot be maintained in their kingdoms, aspiring ... to establish their Tyrannies everywhere and enlarge their domination'. These suspicions seemed corroborated by the Saint Bartholomew Day Massacre in 1572. The response was a spate of pamphlets labouring the point that what these enormities really were about was annihilation of the nobility because the nobility was the natural guardian of those fundamental laws which prevented monarchy from degenerating into tyranny. In 1574, the fifth outburst of organized violence was less a religious war than an aristocratic revolt. It was led by the so-called Malcontents. The movement comprised noblemen of both confessions. Their common ground was a personal experience of exclusion from power and favour by the king or his entourage. But there was more to them than a cabal of disgruntled souls. They did apparently believe that their misfortune presaged the destruction that would sooner or later be inflicted on the nobility at large. And their platform was that for the nobility to foil this scheme they had to transcend their religious division and rally around their obligation to resist the establishment of a despotic regime. The nobiliary ideology behind this revolt was thus grounded also in the recognition that effective opposition presupposed religious toleration; only confessional indifference in the public sphere could allow the nobles to fulfil their *raison d'être* and safeguard the body politic.[34]

No one embodied this aristocratic public spirit better than William of Orange (1533–84). To begin with, Orange is rightly renowned for his tolerance. Indeed, had he been less latitudinarian and chosen to avenge himself on his wife's lover Jan, who was at his mercy, western civilization would have lost one of its icons: for Jan proceeded to father (intramaritally) Peter Paul Rubens. Like his cosmopolitan half-son, Orange lacked strong religious convictions. He was first and foremost a pragmatic aristocratic statesman. But like his French counterparts he was, under the pressures of political and religious strife, impelled to expound a 'theory' of the constitutional role of the nobility. The theory was predicated on the intermediate position that the magnates occupied between ruler and subjects. Until the troubles began in the 1560s Orange could be relied on to interpret this charge one-sidedly as the duty to relay to the people the commands of the king. But then the central government's ecclesiastical reform project and the campaign against heresy became entangled with its programme to curb the grandees and loosen their grip on the Council of State. Under the impression of these events Orange was gradually moved to explore other aspects of his function in society.

At first, still maintaining the fiction of the 'evil councillors', he propounded the position that if the monarch pursued a policy injurious to the commonwealth, the chief vassals were by definition obliged to put him right. If they neglected to do that, they would actually stand accused of disloyalty towards the monarch. This was how Orange, Egmont and Hoorne accounted for their vitriolic denunciation of Philip II's right-hand man in The Netherlands, Cardinal Granvelle, as the cause of 'the evident ruin of the country'. In a carefully crafted letter from 1563 they reasoned that the occasion to their remonstrance was no other than their 'ardour for Your Majesty's service and . . . our duty and oath of fealty'. From here, however, it was not too long a step to the standpoint that the only way to serve the prince was by safeguarding the public welfare. In 1568 Orange enunciated in a political manifesto thinly disguised as an instruction to his brother Louis of Nassau that, since he was beseeched by fellow countrymen

> to take action with the counsel of the Estates General of the country and for the service of His Majesty and to protect the freedom and liberty of everyone in his religion and conscience, we have asked our . . . brother . . . to contend against these conditions with such soldiers as he shall have need of . . . At our request, he has accepted this task out of love and affection for the King and for the Low Countries. We therefore call upon one and all to favour, help, and assist him in the performance of these tasks, as a duty in the service of His Majesty.

Orange thus appealed to a combination of the common interest, which included the king's, and his own status as high noble and great vassal in order to justify his struggle. And while a personal sense of the aggrieved honour of his House was a mainspring of his decision to take up arms, his invocation of a wider notion of nobility and of its public responsibilities was no mere rationalization. As late as 1580 he was thinking in terms of the nobility as a *corps intermédiaire* that served as a bulwark against arbitrary rule. As he had it written in his *Apologie*, the 'tyrannous affection and will' of the Spaniards were previously

> in some sorte restrained, by the good affection that the Emperour [Charles V] bare to the subiectes of this country: & because also, that these provinces were full of brave Lords, wise and valiaunt men, favoring of their auncient nobilitie (and would to God they had children like unto them) whiche served in steede of a bridle against their insolencie, and of a countermure against their pride & rashness.

Orange's revolt, however, turned out in one sense too successful: the provinces that broke away from Spain devised a republican regime. In the short and medium run the nobility adapted remarkably well to the new order. But in the long run the elimination of monarchical rule meant that the nobility, now more exclusive than ever, was divested of the only mechanism for replacing families that had died out. Unable to replenish its ranks, the nobility was doomed to distant demise.[35]

The Dutch naturally became the Counter-Reformers' bugbear. In Austria, a leading light of that camp, Cardinal Melchior Khlesl (1553–1631), imputed to the largely evangelical Estates the intention to set up a 'free Republic'. But though they did look up to the Dutch, there was nothing farther from the mind of the nobles who dominated the Estates than equality of whatever kind. Their well-read Calvinist leader, Georg Erasmus von Tschernembl, was a dyed-in-the-wool aristocratic lord who advocated an intensification of serfdom. The liberties he stood up for were those of the nobility. As in The Netherlands and France, religion transformed this issue into a crisis of authority. It may initially have been more acute in Habsburg Central Europe. For one thing, the number of nobles who had by the 1580s renounced the Catholic Church was alarmingly large: some 90 per cent in Lower Austria, and not much less in Bohemia and Moravia. For another, as has been indicated, these nobles called the tune at the Estates, and the governmental competence of the Estates in the Austrian Habsburgs' lands went wide. They controlled direct taxation and also handled military recruitment and other administrative tasks. So when their allegiance to the Habsburgs was qualified by religious variance, monarchical authority itself was qualified over again.

The Habsburgs reacted with a strategy designed to alter the composition of the Estates by tampering with the rules and definitions governing nobility. Utilizing the monarchical prerogative of ennoblement and somehow making service to the monarch a prerequisite for admission into the Estates, they packed these more and more with partisan Catholic nobles. Between 1580 and 1620 the proportion of Catholic families in the Estate of Lords grew from 25 to 39 per cent. A supplementary stratagem was to replace Protestant noble officials with Catholic ones. As Karin MacHardy has demonstrated, only 13 per cent (42 of 326) of Lower Austrian Protestant nobles were employed by the Crown in 1620. Among the numerically weaker Catholic nobles, 62 per cent (78 of 126) were engaged by the monarch. Excluded from positions in the state, extruded from the Court, losing ground in the Estates, the Protestants began to fear they were going down a path at the end of which awaited them social death. The perception of existential threat, provoked beyond endurance under Emperor Matthias, united many of these otherwise deeply divided nobles in an implacable opposition to the Habsburgs. So when Matthias died in 1619, the Protestant nobles refused to perform the customary oath of fealty to his successor, Ferdinand II, unless he first reconfirmed them in all the religious franchises accorded them by his predecessors. In 1620 the revolt broke out. The participants were a cross-section of the nobility: poor nobles and rich, old nobles and new – all joined in. But they did have one salient sociopolitical trait in common: none of them held office.[36]

The confrontations between monarchs and nobles (and other groups) in France, the Low Countries, and the Habsburg lands in Central Europe were the expressions of a general crisis. This arose, as Shennan described it, 'out of the burgeoning power of the princes which brought to a head the question of where ultimate power lay and what that sovereignty meant in terms of political action'. Various developments came together in the second half of the sixteenth century to cause the area of government intervention to widen so much beyond what was traditionally acceptable that it seemed massively to threaten the established rights of subjects and, most crucially, the position of social and political élites.[37] The revolts which nobles spearheaded in this period were therefore not primarily 'godly rebellions', though religion was certainly the ideological ingredient without which the crisis would not have turned out general: because rulers often took harsh measures to quash the religious dissidence which they felt jeopardized their authority, they raised the spectre of tyranny and, inadvertently, called their own legitimacy into question. But, second, because such measures barred nobles from access to the resources of the state, they quickly turned theoretical issues into bitterly concrete considerations. And this happened against the background of an already exceedingly tense situation created by protracted, large-scale wars which had bled whole societies white and at length tried the loyalty of the political classes.

In France, the enmity towards the Guises owed something to the fact that, faced with an exhausted treasury, they reduced the cascade of patronage emanating from the Court to a trickle. In turn this undermined the great nobles who depended on royal bounty to maintain their own patronage networks in good repair. Similar discontent, and for analogous reasons, simmered in Austria. The Habsburgs' wars against the Turks were a vast drain on the economy and aggravated intra-nobility competition over a contracting pool of resources. Their Spanish cousins, always fighting on one front too many, provoked similar disaffection in their Netherlands dominions. Charles V's and more so Philip II's demands for funds – perceived as serving military commitments largely unrelated to local needs – kept abreast of the stupendous growth of the Dutch economy. Accompanied by the centralizing efforts of the government, the trend provoked general ill-will and antagonized the magnates.[38]

Thus, the wars and the fiscal and social dynamic they set in motion had contradictory outcomes. In the first half of the sixteenth century they facilitated the incorporation of the nobility into the state, and hence the increase in the power of both. In the second half of the century they began to overtax and fray the relationship between monarchy and nobility on which that incorporation was delicately based. The resulting conflicts would likely have remained localized and diffuse had they not become intertwined and infused with religious dissension. The problem was that the Reformation tended both to reinforce monarchy in a novel, upsetting way and to galvanize aristocratic opposition. Large and significant sections of the nobility now came to confront the monarchical state equipped with an ideology that heightened their collective awareness of themselves as a separate body having autonomous sources of legitimacy and a responsibility to bound monarchical authority. This radically altered the nature of aristocratic recusancy. It is difficult to imagine that a scene such as the presentation on 5 July 1566 of the Request of the nobility in the Low Countries could have taken place prior to the Reformation: more than two hundred noblemen – claiming to represent some six thousand confederates – gatecrashed into the regent's palace in Brussels. Their leader, Baron Hendrik of Brederode, hands and voice trembling, read out to a shaken Margaret of Parma a petition demanding the moderation of the anti-heresy laws and an end to Inquisitorial activities. Then the nobles marched before her simulating a kind of a military manoeuvre known as *caracole*, making sure she noticed each and every one of them. The challenge to royal authority was of breathtaking starkness. So were some of the ideas expressed at and about the French General Estates of 1576 and 1588. Claude de Bauffremont, the speaker of the nobility, told Henri III that the nobility 'had this advantage over the other Estates ... that it was they (as our historians testify) who put the crown on the head of the first king'. And in Austria Tschernembl opined that the real sovereign of an hereditary land such as Austria was the people who 'make the [prince] and can also reject him'. In the political language of Austrian lords, 'the people' signified 'the nobility'.[39]

Monarchy under such or similar conditions was strictly speaking not fully worthy of the name. But towards the end of the sixteenth century such an arrangement seemed on the Continent not too unrealistic an option – surely less so than in the previous century or the next. Ideas gained currency which might in certain circumstances have turned the nobility from a practical limitation on monarchical government into a constitutional check. At any event, monarchs' and nobles' conceptions of the properly constituted polity had – except in England and Castile – drifted ominously apart. The consensus that had been building up over the previous hundred years all but collapsed. Absolutism was in large part a work of renovation.

5   Court, patronage and absolutist cohabitation

In the annals of the relationship between monarchs and nobles, the rise of the Court in the early modern period stands out as a pivotal development. The Court had had a long history. Its reputation for sophistication and splendour as well as sordidness and scandal was acquired early on. But despite these and other continuities, the early modern Court did represent a departure from earlier practices and functions. Unlike the medieval Court it was not itinerant, located 'on the back of the riding-horses, beasts of burden and wagons'; it was sedentary. A second distinguishing attribute of the early modern Court was its becoming a site suffused with the ruler's sovereignty, a stage for enacting the majesty of the monarch. The royal or princely Court thus set itself apart from even the largest aristocratic households. It became the focus of political authority in the realm.[1]

This important fact has underlain the until quite recently prevailing interpretative model of the Court. This model was constructed by the sociologist Norbert Elias, whose pioneering work helped to turn a once risqué subject into a highly respectable area of historical research. In Elias's view, the Court functioned to domesticate the nobility. Basing his explanation on Louis XIV's Versailles as described in the classic *Memoirs* of the Duke of Saint-Simon, Elias presented the Court as a gilded cage in which the unruly great nobles of France were once and for all tamed by the monarch. An extremely elaborate etiquette, a whole system of carefully orchestrated social rituals of deference, a finely gradated and strictly observed hierarchical order, an enormously lavish display – these features made the Court into a brilliant, distinct 'civilization' whose attraction was quite impossible to withstand. Permanent residence in the countryside was for the uncouth as well as the socially inferior. As the seigneur de Saint-Evremond wrote in the 1650s, those who come to Court from the cultural wasteland outside it 'come . . . like people from the other world; their dress, their manner, their language are no longer in style; they pass for foreigners in their own country, and for ridiculous among the young courtiers'. To be at Court was literally to be 'in'. The grandees flocked to it, vying for place under the Sun King. The effect was not unlike that which Adam Smith ascribed to trade and manufacture. As he disparagingly put it, 'having sold their birth-right ... for trinkets and baubles, fitter to be the play-things of children than the serious pursuits of men, they became as insignifi-cant as any substantial burgher or tradesman in a city'. The great nobles had to settle for the mystique of power. The real thing was monopolized by the master of ceremonies, the monarch. The Court was on this interpretation a royal Foppish Plot which served to enfeeble the nobility and impose absolutism on society.[2]

The impression of the Court as a dangerous, insalubrious venue for nobles is on the face of it corroborated by nobles' own reflec-tions on their world. What is particularly striking about these reflections is that they almost invariably exude a thick air of nostalgia for a simple, uncorrupted existence associated with country life. Thomas Wentworth, 1st Earl of Strafford, rhapsodized in 1623 in a letter to Secretary of State Calvert that he was

> where our Objects and Thoughts are limited in looking upon a Tulip, hearing a Bird sing, a Rivulet murmuring, or some such petty, yet innocent Pastime, which for my Part I begin to feed myself in, having, I praise God, recovered more in a Day by an open Country Air, than in a Fortnight's Time in that smothering one of *London*.

Nicolas Rapin (d. 1608) expressed a similar sentiment a little earlier in France. For him the atmosphere at Court was stultifying, that in the country liberating, in a political as well as cultural sense: one just did what one felt like doing, without worrying too much about having to please others, and one 'commande comme un petit roi'. Friedrich Rudolf von Canitz (1654–99) appreciated the same untram-melled dominance: 'I am above all a lord ... Here I live, as I should, my will is law, and am accountable to no one.' And in his famous *Georgica Curiosa Acta*, the Lower Austrian noble Wolf Helmhard von Hohberg (1612–88) described aristocratic bucolic life as an 'epitome and instance of the golden age and sweet freedom, which our forefathers enjoyed in a state of innocence in Paradise'.[3]

It would be rash, however, to conclude that this harking back to the traditional world of untouched manorial autonomy, as outside the constraints of the new power structures, reflected the loss of real power effected and symbolized by the Court. The first thing to be noted is that both anti-Court polemic and the praise of rural life were venerable topoi. Their appropriation by early modern nobles contained a strong element of *faux naïf* paradoxism: these nobles had to be well versed in literature and poetry in order to be able so eloquently to excoriate the place where high culture flourished, namely the Court, and to idealize the place where it was hard to come by, namely the country. One should be chary of taking these nobles' utterances at face value. The Duke of Strafford was anything but politically a marginal figure. And it was probably to this steadfast servant of the monarchy that Sir William Davenant alluded as 'Court-Sophister'. It has indeed been shown for Caroline England that pastoral was a courtly mode and that 'country' was an ideal embraced at Court. The Court was not an island unto itself; its culture formed part of the common values of society. This holds good for seventeenth-century France too. The trend there was not, as historians once used to argue, towards the formation of a Court nobility with a code of behaviour spurned by the rest of the nobility (and society), and hence towards a split between Court and country. What actually happened was that the nobility in general underwent a thorough and relatively rapid change, becoming more educated and civilized. If there was some incongruity between courtly culture and aristocratic self-perception in the sixteenth century, by the early seventeenth century it had all but disappeared. In other words, the Court could scarcely have been a cultural contrivance working sinisterly to enervate the high nobility. Elias's methodologically jejune thesis, resting on the account given by one disgruntled and surreptitiously tendentious noble, is misleadingly reductionist.[4]

An altogether different case from England and France was Austria, where there clearly existed a correspondence between political weakness and praise of rural life by nobles. On closer scrutiny, however, it turns out that here the theory does not apply at all that presents the nobles as facing a stark dilemma: either relocate to the Court and keep up the appearance of power but at the cost of forgoing any claim to independence; or stay in the country and keep up the appearance of independence but at the cost of forgoing any claim to power. For in truth those nobles who wrote lovingly about rural life did not even have the privilege of choice: they were nearly all Protestants who were denied access to the Habsburg Court on confessional grounds. The country was for them the ineluctable reality, not an escapist conceit. They therefore composed no diatribes against the

Court. On the other side, however, many of their Catholic fellows were apparently too successful both at Court and in the country to have the leisure and the urge to write for or against either. The Habsburg Court was not an instrument designed to hive the greater nobility off from its provincial power bases and discipline it under the controlling gaze of the monarch.[5]

The principal reason why nobles repaired to the Court is that they had an eye for the main chance. In the first place, a lot of money circulated at Court. It sometimes was the third largest area of state expenditure after warfare and debt service. The cost of the Bavarian Court represented 55 per cent of total government expenses in 1701, and 35 per cent in 1750. In France during the first third of the seventeenth century, the Court represented between 16.5 of annual expenditure (in 1625) and 44 per cent (in 1618). It was, in the words of David Parker, 'the ... focal point of a state apparatus dedicated to the redistribution of the wealth squeezed out of the labouring population'. It was also the point of contact *par excellence* for the political élites. With the expansion of the early modern monarchies, it became the apex of a vast patronage system that held the state together. It has been pointed out that 'the history of the origins of the modern state *is* the history of patronage; it is not the history of institutions in itself'. Cardinal Richelieu, for instance, owed his influence less to his position as *premier ministre* than to his position as patron. To be able to operate at the 'national' nerve centre of patronage was to take part in the exercise of political power in its highest manifestations.[6]

Paradoxical as it may seem, patronage grew so decisive in early modern Europe precisely because of the growth of the state. The official institutions that did develop were too rudimentary to be able to cope with the fast increasing volume and complexity of the business of government, with the need to mobilize ever larger human and material resources. It is noteworthy in this context that, looking at European history between 1500 and 1975, the seventeenth century stands out as far as the number, duration, and cost of wars are concerned. In terms of battle deaths per year it is exceeded only by the twentieth century. The rate at which expenses and the accompanying demand for taxes and credit mounted was correspondingly high. In fact, it represented a more dramatic break with previous levels than that which happened in the sixteenth century. In France in 1630, overall expenditure stood at 41.2 million *livres*. Then France became embroiled in the Thirty Years' War. In 1642 expenditure was 88.7 million. Revenues rose from 461,160 tons of silver-equivalent in 1630 to upwards of 1 million tons in 1642.[7]

This suggests that if the state was not yet strong enough to respond adequately to the overwhelming challenges of the time, it was already strong and intrusive enough to alienate its subjects and create for itself severe problems of legitimacy. Indeed, the 1640s and 1650s saw a rash of spectacular revolts: the Civil War in England, the insurrections of Portugal and Catalonia and Naples against the Spanish monarchy, the *Fronde* in France. As John Elliott has summed up, the financial demands of the state estranged important sections of the political nation; it was enough that these withheld their loyalty for the ruler to find himself isolated and vulnerable to rebellion. Under these conditions, the bonds created by ubiquitous patron–client relations were essential to the maintenance of order. With the state not yet able to enforce obedience on a regular basis, and with no nationalism to inculcate voluntary compliance in subjects, rulers had to act like patrons as well as sovereigns in order to secure the good-will of those who mattered. For the latter to be clients meant more say than otherwise in determining their own fate. From their perspective 'clienteles were needed ... in order to make [the judicial/administrative state] tolerable'.[8]

It was not accidental that the Court blossomed in these circumstances. As Ronald G. Asch has pointed out, one reason why the relationship between ruler and nobility came to revolve around the Court was that it was not governed by legal or institutional procedures. It was the perfect hinge of such a quintessentially informal, personalized system of power as patronage. Earlier chapters have argued that the extraction by the Crown of a growing share of the national wealth, which characterized the process of state formation, drew the nobility closer around the ruler; that in turn this facilitated the nobility's assimilation into the state, and hence the latter's emergence. The Court of the seventeenth century was in a sense the apogee of this trend. In accordance with the fact that patronage compensated for an inability to accomplish centralization by formal, institutional means, complementing weak bureaucratic structures, the magnates assumed the role of brokers. They acted as distributors of protection and advantages and opportunities. Their operational basis was the Court, the 'fountain of favours' offered by the monarch. The Court did not serve rulers to monopolize power, for it served them to share some of their power with some nobles in order to strengthen the state and their own hold on it.[9]

Once patronage is established as a sociopolitical system, rather than merely pervasive dyadic relations, clients become a resource too, and patrons come under competitive pressure to recruit them. A noble patron's position at Court, the central patronage agency, therefore becomes vital to his ability to gather a clientele and dominate an area of the country; and his ability to gather a clientele and use it to get things done for central government may prove vital to his position at Court. The career soldier Henri de Campion (1613–63) had to spend a month at Court in 1653 'soliciting payment for [the] winter wages' of his regiment. Conversely, when financial difficulties prevented Henri-Charles de La Trémoille (1620–72) from levying troops, he was quickly given to understand that he was about to lose favour with the Court. This points up nobles' dependence on the monarch. While the clients of noble patronage-brokers could choose among patrons, the latter did not have this luxury. For them only one patron was available, the ruler. The nearer one stood to the ruler, the greater the influence one had as a broker, but the narrower was one's room for manoeuvre. Proximity to power meant dependence. On the other side, these brokers were indispensable to the ruler. Rulers had evidently been unable to distribute patronage on their own, for otherwise they would by definition have destroyed the system of patronage and come each to embody a strong state; nor would they have needed favourites – a Buckingham, a Richelieu, an Olivares – to shield them from the overpowering importunacy of a multitude of aspirants.[10]

The Court evidently helped to modify the relationship between monarchy and nobility. The precise nature of the change depended on the pre-existing structure of relations. It has been argued for England that, by the early seventeenth century, it had grown quite difficult to exercise influence at both Court and country. The peers who managed to retain a modicum of authority in the shires were more often than not those who tended to stay away from the Court; the dominant courtiers, on the other hand, usually had little weight in the country. This is not surprising. The early and advanced centralization of England left no scope for the local or corporative privileges and immunities that were characteristic of Continental states. Furthermore, as an earlier chapter has suggested, the magnates had under the early Tudors lost their dominance over the shires. The net result was that there was no institution but Parliament that could serve to countervail the Court. This made for a volatile situation, all the more so as Parliament under Charles I risked falling into terminal disuse. The Court inadvertently magnified the importance of Parliament as the only political resort for those of the ruling élite who failed to protect and further their interests at Court – a telling example of how a successfully centralized government might engender dangerous central opposition.[11]

This was not the case in the mainland monarchies. Unlike the English, the nobles of some Continental states still had territorial and military power. No English magnate could match the forty-two pieces of artillery which the Duke of Medina Sidonia had in his castle of Santiago in 1639. The Court did not sever the links between great nobles and the provinces. Indeed, by giving rise to brokerage, it in a way reinforced them. But in so doing it did shift the concerns of the nobles more towards the centre. For France this is underscored by the fact that, while in 1515–37 only 4 per cent of the provincial governors were born in Paris and 8 per cent died there, in 1627–50 the figures were 64 and 68 per cent, respectively. This shift transformed the pattern of their patronage. Their clienteles were becoming of more civil than military orientation, degrading in the process their capacity to embark on revolts. To be sure, this involved a certain loss of autonomy, but not necessarily of power. For the nature of power had changed too. It now was more closely associated with the possibility of influencing decision-making at the centre and manipulating the redistribution mechanisms of the state. As one Dijon *parlementaire* wrote in 1650 of Henri II and Louis II de Condé, whom he had rarely seen in their governorship of Burgundy:

> No one had acquired any office in the parlement or any other jurisdiction except through [Louis II de] Condé's mediation or that of his father. No one had ever been provided with a benefice but by their nomination. All the officers of the towns, whether mayors, *échevins*, captains, lieutenants or *enseignes*, had acquired these honours only through the influence of the Condés. In short, Messieurs les Princes ... had governed Burgundy with total authority for more than twenty years.

The victory of one's faction in courtly infighting could be at least as effective as instigating a provincial uprising, and was certainly a less risky business. Aristocratic power was now subject to more control and presupposed a wider range of social and political skills, but it was no less imposing for that.[12]

If this interpretation is correct, then the Court intensified the interdependence between monarchy and nobility (or section thereof).

It was an arena for the deployment and representation of aristocratic as well as for royal power, and therefore also for the balancing of aristocratic and royal interests. A further, related implication is that, if the Court is taken as a measure of absolutism, then absolutism was not – as it has often been depicted – a royal, despotic and bureaucratic triumph over particularistic social groups, the nobility foremost among them. It was more like a re-adjustment of the political order to changing conditions or its restoration where one foundation – the relationship between monarchy and nobility – was badly damaged in the second half of the sixteenth century.[13]

The outstanding case is the France of Henri IV (1589–1610). It was under him that the French monarchy programmatically elevated itself to unchallenged heights above the warring confessions, forming the focus of national unity that religion had all but extinguished. The nobility, frightened by the popular tendencies associated with the Catholic League, again awoke to the advantages of a strong monarchy. But Henri IV had to be actively persuasive, especially when dealing with his hard-headed magnates. And he had to offer them more than his personal charm and panache. Provincial governorships, lucrative posts and liberal pensions proved highly effective in enticing the noble leaders of the League into the royal camp, or at least non-partisanship. According to the finance minister Sully, the campaign to placate these former foes cost the king the gargantuan sum of 32 million *livres*.[14] If, after Henri gained confidence and supposedly revealed his real 'absolutist' face, nobles became disenchanted with the monarchy, this is by no means apparent from an anonymous pamphlet composed by a nobleman in 1614. Published on the occasion of the convocation of the Estates General, it is a remarkably self-conscious, lucid statement of where aristocratic interests exactly lie. Representative assemblies, the author reminds his readers, had always sought to reduce the authority of the sovereign. This the nobility must oppose. For the nobility

> is tied to the interest of its King or Monarch, and obliged to maintain his authority and strive to augment his revenue and the foundation of his finance, instead of demanding their diminution: for the nobles (if the laws, ordinances and institutions of state are well kept) are or should be those who receive the most of the King's money ... The nobility should in its own interest desire a rich monarchy ... With regard to the authority of the Monarch, the Nobles ought to [help] preserve it as if it were their own life ... in order to maintain that which [royal authority]

gives them. It is certain that if France were to be governed by Oligarchy, Aristocracy, or Democracy, the Nobility would all be humbled and deprived of its dignity and authority, having nothing but the government of the Royal Monarchy that can conserve it.[15]

If a representative assembly was one of the most important checks on absolutism, then this noble welcomed absolutism. A potent monarchy was what he thought best suited the nobility. And yet the text betrays no sign of obsequiousness. Nobility and monarchy appear as partners, albeit unequal. The indispensability of the nobility to the monarchy is only just implicit. The author after all attempts to persuade fellow nobles to give their support to the monarchy. It is essentially a cold calculation that underlies this tractate on the community of interest binding noble and monarch.

Nobles in Spain and Habsburg Central Europe would presumably not have taken exception to such a view. In both monarchies absolutist grandeur went hand in hand with a resurgence of the nobility. In Spain, King Philip II's death gave the signal for an aristocratic comeback. Under Philip III (1598–1621) and Philip IV (1621–65), the magnates returned in force to the council of state: of seventeen councillors in 1623, ten were titled nobles; of twelve councillors in 1649, all but one were *Grandes* or *Títulos*. It is true that the grandees were excluded from holding domestic offices, but they made up for this deficiency by dominating the Court. Of the eleven major-domos in 1623, nine were of old noble families. All of the favourites (*validos*) up to the minority of Charles II (1665–1700) emerged from the royal household. And they all came from the upper nobility. The power they exercised was virtually regal. Francisco Gómez de Sandoval y Rojas, 1st Duke of Lerma, controlled not only the king's movement, so as to restrict access to him, but apparently also the king's will. In 1608 Philip III transferred to him the lordship over eleven towns in Old Castile. By 1618 his annual rents was 120,000 ducats, compared with 20,000 ducats in 1598.

The nobility also regained military weight lost under Philip II. At the end of 1632 the Secretary of War asked the Dukes of Cardona, Béjar, Osuna, Arcos, and Medina Sidonia, and the Marquis of Priego, to serve each with 4,000 men. In 1640 a request was made to the Dukes of Béjar, Medina Sidonia, and Maqueda, and the Marquis of Priego, to raise 4,000 troops at their own cost. Engaged in a costly war, the Crown grew increasingly dependent on the great nobles' ability to come to its military and financial aid. The king was forced to confer on them important fiscal and lordship rights in order to enable them the better to exploit their estates and tenants. In the same vein, Philip IV assigned private judges to the grandees to manage the payment of their debts, many of which were incurred in the service of the Crown. As a result, creditors lost their right to sue these nobles on a plea of debt. In either case, the financial burden was shifted on to the lower orders of society. The mutual reliance of Crown and nobility became deeply entrenched. Aristocratic power increased in tandem with dependence on the monarch.[16]

A more far-reaching consolidation of aristocratic power took place in the Habsburg lands in Central Europe after the defeat of the rebellion at the battle of White Mountain in 1620. Many Protestant nobles lost their lands, and their world. Some 800 Styrian, Carinthian and Carniolan nobles went into exile in 1628–30. In Bohemia and Moravia, between half to three-quarters of all noble estates changed hands. The winners were the loyalist Catholic magnates as well as the emperor. The failed revolt accelerated a process, which had been underway since around 1600, of concentration of property in their hands, with the active co-operation of the ruling dynasty. As R. J. W. Evans has noted, 'the heritage of shared power gave way to a more conscious political alliance'. It was based on the cementation of noble lordship to the point of precluding any possibility of royal intervention in noble local affairs. Huge blocks of lands came under the exclusive control of the great. And a vast chasm opened up within the nobility. In 1571, for instance, the Estate of Lords in the *Viertel unter dem Wienerwald*, making up 27 per cent of the nobility, collected 45.9 per cent of the income from rent; the Estate of Knights, comprising 73 per cent of the nobility, collected 54.1 per cent. In 1637, the Lords, now making up 51.6 per cent of the nobility, received 80.6 of the income from rents. With variations this was the general pattern in Upper Austria, Moravia, and Bohemia. The number of peasant households subject to the Dietrichsteins mounted from 1,652 in 1618 to 5,628 in the 1640s. And their gains were modest compared with those of the Liechtensteins. It was a small coterie of such prominent families which held sway over the provincial administration. They also colonized the Court, being the ones with the financial wherewithal to afford a prolonged presence in that bastion of the nobility. As one historian has remarked, the share in power which the nobility had failed to win through conflicts with the monarch over the competence of the Estates, it now acquired through occupation of all important offices in the Church, army, administration, and diplomatic corps under the aegis of the monarch.[17] Nobles, it seems, had never had it better than under absolutism.

One significant implication of the foregoing discussion is that the seventeenth-century monarchies were a great deal less mighty than the term 'absolutism' suggests. This has indeed been amply demonstrated by research. It has already been shown that the fiscal pressure generated by war escalated to such an extent that it began to 'irrationalize' the state, thereby reversing the trend of the fourteenth and fifteenth centuries.[18] The drift continued and even intensified in the seventeenth century. Venality of office, a pervasive phenomenon in the early modern monarchies, provides a prime example. It is estimated that there were some 46,000 *officiers* in France in 1665, a ratio of 1 to 380 inhabitants. In Castile the ratio was still higher: around 1650 there were some 30,000 officials, or 1 to 166 inhabitants. By selling offices and allowing them to become proprietary (e.g. the *paulette* in France) as a means of raising money to finance war, the state lost control over its own bureaucracy and judiciary. And the more offices were put up for sale, the greater the long-term financial liability that the state incurred in the form of salaries to officials (in effect, interest on loans). Moreover, since many offices entailed exemption from taxes, a vicious circle was set up: more and more people who were able to pay taxes did not, the tax basis contracted, and therefore more and more tax-exempt patrimonial offices had to be created and sold in order to make up for lost revenue. With such powerful vested interest ensconced in the state, reform was out of the question.[19]

The trajectory along which the Continental monarchies now travelled was one of increasing privatization and decentralization under the violent impact of international war. The privatization of Spain's armed forces, once the envy of Europe, has already been touched upon. In 1640 King Philip IV was advised by one official that 'the manner of raising troops ... must be to entrust it to the grandees and lords of Castile who are most influential in the provincial capitals'. In the same year the Marquis of Los Vélez was appointed to command the army dispatched to suppress the revolt of the Catalans, because he was 'the descendant and heir of the House of ... Don Luis de Requesens, and regarded as a son of Catalonia where, through his estate Martorell, he maintained ties of kinship, friendship and alliance with many illustrious Houses'. Aristocratic re-militarization, though, had its own dynamic, which made it difficult to confine their brief to recruitment. Responsibility for the defence of Spain's southwest corner, for instance, fell almost entirely to the Guzmán dukes of Medina Sidonia. The inability of the Castilian Crown to keep central control of the army was exacerbated by extensive alienation of Crown lands. Castile underwent a massive process of seigneurialization. Between 1625 and 1668 some 15 per cent of the population of the royal domain had been transferred to private jurisdiction. In Andalusia, the titled nobility acquired over 50 per cent of the jurisdictions and vassals sold by the Crown and over 70 per cent of the *alcabalas* and *tercias*. In Catalonia, too, the barons enlarged their jurisdictional share. It is true that the grandees paid a high price for their enhanced local domination, especially under the régime of the count-duke of Olivares, who relentlessly sought to harness their wealth to the Crown's fisco-military enterprise. But there is no question that, compared with the second half of the previous century, the grandees emerged strengthened from their trials in the seventeenth century. All this did not mean a simple handover of power from the monarchical state to the grandees. It was not only that the benefits they derived from it encouraged them to support it; the manner of derivation was such as to lead to an integration of the great nobility into the structure of the state. Yet this alliance, for all its advantages to the state, at the same time constricted royal power further, precisely because it entailed a close interdependence. A Venetian observer who took stock of the situation in 1683 commented that:

> power is entirely in the hands of the grandees . . . So much has their power increased, and so much has that of the king diminished, that if he wanted to rule in an absolute and despotic manner, I doubt if he would succeed.[20]

He would have used much the same language, and with greater credibility, had he visited the territories of the Austrian Habsburg. Financial straits forced the Habsburgs to pledge more and more royal estates to lords able to supply them with loans. This in its turn reduced the possibility of the Crown ever redeeming the alienated estates, so eventually they had to be definitively sold. Most of the royal domain in Lower Austria, with the exception of the Salzkammergut, was gone by 1650. So it was in Upper Austria: while in 1620–5 the Crown was the lord of some 24 per cent of the tenant households, by 1750 the proportion had plummeted to 2 per cent. Of the gross declared dominical revenue in 1750, 53.7 per cent fell to the lords, 39.3 to the Church, 6.2 to the knights, and a paltry 0.8 per cent to the Crown. And while around 1500 only two of the twelve towns in the Waldviertel were under noblemen's jurisdiction, by 1700 the number had risen to six. Albrecht von Wallenstein's duchy of Friedland was a monument to this process of devolution.[21]

In France, the monarchy's record on this issue was somewhat better mixed. Richelieu realized full well that the nobility was 'one of the principal organs of the state, capable of contributing much to its preservation and stability'. Accordingly, he set out to persuade the wavering among them to relinquish the Huguenot cause. Combining a barrage of material advantages with an ideological offensive, he achieved his end. This was a decisive step towards recovering royal authority. By 1630 the last enclaves of Huguenot resistance had been wiped out. But that was about as far as Richelieu went in centralizing France. In fact, there was also some backtracking on this score: under the immense fiscal strain created by war, this exponent of reason of state began to reverse Michel de Marillac's zealously centralist policies one by one. The *paulette*, to which Richelieu himself had initially objected, was left intact. The plan to establish a uniform administration in France's disparate provinces was abandoned. The provincial Estates, in return for financial contributions to the Crown, were left alone. And the military high command, for all the critical importance of the army to Richelieu's position, increasingly fell into the hands of the provincial governors. Institutional centralization was sacrificed on the altar of international ambition.[22]

More insidious developments occurred in the area of French royal finances. Vital to the operation of government and its ability to field unprecedently large armies was the system of credit. However, having irreparably undermined its own credibility as debtor, the Crown had to resort to private financiers as the main source of credit. Daniel Dessert's investigations have shown that the capital mobilized by the financiers came in very large measure from the upper ranks of the nobility, sword and robe alike, with a foothold at Court and in the administration. Closely interrelated, these nobles brought their familial and political connections to bear on the government to favour this financier or other, or to determine on this financial project or that. The arrangement was thus roundabout but all the more effective for that: the Crown's insatiable craving for ready cash led it to large-scale credit transactions with financiers; in exchange, the financiers were assigned on an infinite variety of sources of royal revenue; the financiers then shared the pickings with their sleeping partners, that is those distinguished nobles who – if they did not initiate the transaction in question – provided the necessary political protection and influence. They were the chief beneficiaries of the French fiscal system. And their activities conspired with incessant wars to reproduce it, foreclosing the option of reforming it. If the state had to combat those who exploited it, it could not do this without attacking those who financed it. The state was thus cornered by the nobility and other privileged élites. There was next to nothing the monarchy could do to extricate itself from its predicament without destabilizing itself to the point of breakdown. From this perspective, the resplendent spectacle of royalty put on at Versailles has dazzled and overawed modern historians more than it did contemporary nobles. The latter were very far from being an unwitting claque. The Court, Dessert has asserted, was above all an exercise in limiting the damage caused by aristocratic fiscal imperialism.[23]

Dessert has concluded that in light of these findings it is necessary to question the concept of 'absolutism'. A recent revision of the concept has in fact gone so far as to recommend discarding it altogether on the ground that it is largely devoid of historiographical value. France under Louis XIV has naturally been the crucial test case. It has been contended that close examination of the features which should ideal-typically have characterized an absolute régime corroborates the verdict that, contrary to appearance, Louis's reign fails to qualify. To give but a few examples, the *parlements* remained important, legislative sovereignty was relatively unimportant, and the judiciary retained its partial autonomy. With regard to the nobility, Louis did indeed try to practise what he preached to Philip V of Spain, namely to conserve the grandees 'in all the external prerogatives of their dignity, and at the same time to exclude them from all matters which, known by them, might increase their influence'. The French grandees were barred from the council of state. But they did not need it to make their presence felt, for informal mechanisms of power counted no less than institutional ones. These criticisms have been used to transcend the argument that the main problem seventeenth-century monarchs came up against was the hiatus between the absolutist promise and the practical inability to fulfil it. Absolutism was not incomplete, it simply did not exist, as Nicholas Henshall has put it. 'Traditional historiography rested "absolutism" on well advertised support systems fortifying it against society – standing armies and bureaucracy.' The new picture to have emerged portrays these institutions as actually the strongholds of those powerful social groups which absolutism was once believed to have subdued but which in reality it consciously buttressed in its own interest. They make mockery of any claim to autonomy of the state. 'The novelty,' Henshall summed up, 'was not absolute power but its media coverage.'[24]

As is often the case with revisionist polemic, this one too exhibits a certain proclivity to tilt against windmills set up by itself. Besides, breaking the tyranny of a concept, however useful a service it may be, one may expose oneself to the disorders of too great a freedom. There is a danger that dispensing with the semantically misleading notion of 'absolutism' in the name of the realities of power will actually result in obscuring those realities.[25] For even if Louis XIV may not fully fulfil the requirements of a theoretical model of absolute ruler, it is nonetheless idle to deny that he was extremely successful in baron-management, putting an end to the French aristocratic tradition of open opposition and rebellion, and that under him the polity enjoyed stability and tranquillity it had lacked before.

The secret of Louis's achievement was not Versailles in itself. It was rather that his initiative was more restorative than innovative. His genius lay in an uncanny knack for moulding and consolidating the social order in a manner that both increased his own authority and benefited the traditional élites. An example is the distribution of the wealth extracted in taxation. Of the 5,250,000 *livres* raised in direct taxes in Languedoc in 1677, the king received 62.2 per cent; the rest went to the provincial notables. Their share thus rose by some 8 per cent in comparison with the tax year 1647, i.e. before Louis acceded to the throne. This paragon of an absolutist ruler was more congenial to the provincial élite than his predecessors. And in its turn this both induced and enabled them to advance more money in loans to the king. The interest was collected from the local producers in taxes and imposts. As William Beik has put it, 'the king was granting his power of command in order to get immediate access to liquid resources that were otherwise shielded from his power of command'. The nobility and other élites profited also from Louis's fastidious emphasis on hierarchy and distinction. Under-scoring his supremacy, it reinforced their position as well. In return Louis asked and received compliance and willing co-operation. He was fifty-five years on the throne, and had no one executed for treason.

Louis did not rule through a faceless bureaucracy. His governance was strongly personal, founded on meticulous attention to social detail and on nearly impeccable direction and manipulation of human relations. The consequent effectiveness of the royal network of patronage earned it a popularity among clients that reduced other networks to unimportance or subordination. It became preponderant, unifying patronage in the king. This was arguably the most important sense in which Louis was a truly absolute monarch. But that is precisely why he could rule – in such an 'unabsolutist' fashion – in the interest of the aristocracy, provided they played their part in ensuring the smooth functioning of the sociopolitical order. And that, in the final analysis, is why they happily acquiesced.

> They had gotten what they wanted: a revalorisation of their status, a clearer and less ambiguous place in society . . . , a confirmation of privileges, and a share of the proceeds. The result was that a smaller, more concentrated ruling class enjoyed greater power, even while giving up independence of action and certain claims to social exclusivity.

While the period 1560–1660 abounded in revolts sparked off by a feeling of insecurity among the great, Louis XIV's able exercise of royal power removed that cause.[26]

Louis XIV was a monarch more proficient in the craft of kingship than his colleagues. His skills enabled him to control and direct forces that other monarchs were less capable of containing. It is indeed indicative of the nature of absolute monarchy that it so much hinged on the personal qualities and style of its head. It was Louis's unmatched success in making the system work for him that allows him to stand for what absolutism was about: regulation of the sociopolitical order along traditional lines. Bearing in mind that this is something of a contradiction in terms, the essence of the absolutist re-arrangement was a tighter collaboration between ruler and nobility; the reinforcement of the latter as a central conduit of government; an accompanying protection and enhancement of their elevated position in society; but all this at the price of a greater dependence on the Crown as the main source and guarantor of privilege and legitimacy. This amounted to a restoration of the equilibrium between monarchy and nobility, if on a quite different footing from that established around 1500. The tortuous process of alignment between monarchy and nobility that had begun in the fourteenth century culminated in the seventeenth with both state and society aristocratized to the core.[27]

It is against this background, finally, that the contrasting peculiarities of England become more evident. On the face of it, the English royal state suffered from even more structural weaknesses than the

Continental ones. Like his European rivals, the English monarch was beset by a chronic shortage of funds. Moreover, the Crown's income had been stagnating since Elizabeth I's reign. But because the English monarch's claim on the wealth of the nation was weak, there was little that could be done to remedy the situation. Involvement in international competition was only possible with full parliamentary support or else was likely to spell financial crisis and bring on domestic political difficulties, as happened in the 1620s. In the face of MPs ever unwilling to commit the resources of localities to meet royal demands, a prolonged war was unsustainable. On the other hand, England did not invite attack by European rivals: the vastly expanded size of European armies, a salient feature of the 'military revolution', militated against an invasion of England because of the almost insurmountable logistical difficulties. As a result of all this, England, unlike the European monarchies, 'experienced the military revolution negatively, as it were'. Uncompelled and unable to maintain a standing army, the Crown focused its military efforts on defending the coasts and dominating Scotland and Ireland.[28]

However, in view of the course of development described above of the mainland absolutist monarchies, England's weaknesses can be judged to have been blessings in disguise. The narrow seas and Parliament mitigated against exorbitant international military commitments. After the Hundred Years' War, England largely kept aloof from the European fray, precisely at the time when other monarchies, incapable of discovering any better way to pay for their conflicts, took literally to mortgaging their future. Their precocity was in the long run a hindrance: the early formation and consolidation of their fiscal systems, based on ingenious yet compromising expedients, were to prove inherently unsusceptible to reform. When they turned out to be inadequate to financing modern, unprecedently expensive forms of warfare, it was too late. In France, beyond a certain point, every new war only further weakened the state, leading in the end to the collapse of the ramshackle *ancien régime*.[29]

England, by contrast, was not encumbered with the legacy of an unwieldy state apparatus held down by formidable vested interests. This enabled a small group of reformers, backed politically by Parliament, to overhaul the bureaucracy and place public debt on a new and sound foundation. This was the inception of the famous 'financial revolution' of the late seventeenth century that transformed England, after more than two centuries on the margins, into a major European power. The story of this achievement need not be retold here. Suffice it to say that it was underpinned by the two institutional pillars of Parliament, which consensually raised the taxes that guaranteed the permanent funded debt, and the Bank of England, established in 1694, which managed it. But equally if not more important were the social and political pre-conditions. In the first place, the nobles contributed in taxes. It is true that the landed classes were normally underassessed. But in wartime their contributions could be hefty. This was dramatically the case during the Civil War, which was actually a turning point in the history of the English state, bringing about the fiscal growth which on the Continent was caused by international wars. It was similarly the case in the period 1688–1714, when direct taxation in the form of land tax preponderated over indirect taxation. On the other hand, the political representatives of the upper classes accepted the principle that the 'necessities of the poor' should be subject to moderate taxation or altogether exempted. The resulting relatively wide and ostensibly equitable tax base, which was conducive to general consent vital to the nearly frictionless operation of the funded debt, reflected the fact that neither the nobles, nor for that matter any other group, had captured the state. The 'financial revolution' did involve a political struggle to eradicate patrimonial elements in the bureaucracy. But these were incomparably less deeply rooted than they were in France, for instance. The fate of the struggle might have been quite different had the peers not lost so much of their clout in the wake of the Wars of the Roses, and had the long period of peace that followed not prevented them from recovering it, despite the marked improvement in their lot under Elizabeth I. And it is highly significant in this respect that the revival in the fortunes of the nobility after 1660, and in particular after the Glorious Revolution of 1688, was not of the sort that could lead to a recrudescence of privatized power, as happened in Spain, for example. For it was founded on the Lords' role as defenders of the commonwealth against autocracy and popery in co-operation with Parliament.[30]

The idea of mixed monarchy that some European aristocratic constitutionalists from time to time entertained was thus realized only in England. There is some historical irony in that: the English monarchy that under the first two Tudors was strong enough not to need persistently to placate the nobility into acquiescence in its policies found under the Stuarts that the nobles, having as a result little by way of financial interest in the state, had relatively few disincentives to oppose its policies if they saw fit to do so.[31] This is quite different from the attitude of contemporary French grandees, who over the seventeenth century became good 'absolutists'.[32] This suggests that the English outcome was in part made possible because the nobility was too weak to balance the monarchy on it own. To maintain their position they had to allow themselves, at some cost to their status, to be absorbed into a much wider interest than themselves. It also suggests that the Continental nobles were perhaps too successful for their own (long-term) good. With its remarkably favourable alliance with the absolutist monarchies, the nobility paved the way for its own political retreat in the eighteenth and nineteenth centuries.

6 Epilogue

A salient feature of the history of the relationship between monarchy and nobility in the period 1350–1700 was the ultimate weakness of the opposition that nobles every now and then sought to offer to the monarchical state. They instigated countless rebellions, and many of these yielded substantial tactical gains. But none produced anything approaching a restructuring of the constitutional arrangements such as occurred in England in the seventeenth century. Strictly speaking, this was not a failure: few aristocratic rebellions aimed for such an outcome; and it is revealing that the few that did miscarried, even when the balance of force did not favour the monarch. One reason was that – once again unlike England – revolts led by nobles were also for nobles. The attitude of rebelling great nobles towards their inferior co-rebels was for the most part coldly instrumental and, it has been noticed, 'could all too readily give way to a fearful disdain'.[1] This was not a sound basis for the sustained effort required to effect broad changes. Another reason is implicit in Machiavelli's thesis that a monarchical state like France was vulnerable to conquest because of the presence in it of malcontent barons willing to change the regime; implicit, because Machiavelli passed over the fact that for every malcontent baron there was always at least one other baron willing to support the regime.[2] Also, until the seventeenth century, it was not rare for nobles to shuttle between these two stances. This suggests a certain superficiality of conviction on their part. Nobles did not normally consider alternatives to monarchy as either viable or desirable. And if they entertained anything like a coherent idea of the polity, it was usually in terms of their own eminent place in a monarchically ruled society. They therefore condemned themselves to acting within narrow constitutional confines; they were forced to pursue their goals within limits imposed by their own need for a strong – if preferably not too strong – monarchy.

The need had several facets. One was cultural, a tradition which invested kingship with sacral qualities. Another was rational-functional: to borrow the words of Philippe de Commynes, 'it is almost impossible for many great people together and of like estate to agree among themselves for any length of time, unless there is someone over them all'. The need of potentates to avoid internecine strife over resources recommended an arrangement whereby one person was maintained at a position so much higher above themselves as to have a minimal or no personal stake in social competition and hence a presumed capacity to regulate conflicts with minimal or no partiality.[3] A dialectical relation indeed existed between the competence with which the monarch performed this task and the obedience and respect which he or she was able to elicit. Finally, there was a historical-political facet of decisive significance: the legacy of feudalism.

Jean-Philippe Genet has pointed out that feudalism provided the very matrix from which the modern state emerged. Feudo-vassalic institutions lay the foundations for later, state institutions: 'national taxation is the son of the feudal *auxilium*, just as representative assemblies are the daughters of the [feudal] *consilium*'. Necessary for the 'mutation' of these elements were the existence and dynamics of a military aristocracy. First, and quite unique to Europe, the military aristocracy developed concurrently with, and in fact assisted the growth of, vibrant urban classes. The resulting diversity enabled the creation of the fiction of common good which came to be embodied in the state. But, second, it was significantly the feudal aristocracy which was the more dominant component. Its values preponderated, and it was its essentially martial ethos which informed feudal society. It thus helped to feed that engine of state formation that was war.[4]

Feudalism had other, more specific traits which were favourable to the nascent state in that they strengthened the position of the monarch relative to the nobility. Feudo-vassalic ties, for all their inherent contractualism and the reality of frequent tergiversations, not only engendered an ideological idiom of loyal service to one's superior. In addition to being personal, the ties that bound nobles to the ruler were 'vertical'. This left only limited scope to associations based on 'horizontal' links. Assemblies and gatherings of nobles not at the behest of the ruler were held in profound suspicion. When some south German knights swore a union directed against the city of Nuremberg in 1500, Emperor Maximilian I hastened to brand it 'an alliance against us . . . a crimen conspiracionis and rebellionis'. And when Egmont visited Philip II on the eve of the Dutch Revolt, the king conveyed to him in no uncertain terms his dismay at the leagues of the Netherlandish nobles and told him 'Conde, no se haga más' – 'Let there be no more of this, count.'[5]

Nobles had institutionally little in common with each other but the way in which each of them related to the monarch. Unlike peasants or burghers, they were not forced by material circumstances to develop enduring communal structures. They might share a way of life, but if this was conducive to the fostering of common values and outlook, it actually compounded the difficulties of close political co-operation: what one saw from one's castle's windows was the houses of one's tenants, not those of one's fellow nobles.[6] Nobles had literally to go out of their way to collaborate politically. And indeed aristocratic collective ventures were typically sporadic and for *ad hoc* purposes. This desultoriness and inconstancy could not but facilitate the growth of the state: in its potentially most formidable opponent, the state encountered not a cohesive group, but a collection of individuals imbued with a competitive spirit who normally found it extraordinarily difficult to make common cause against it. It is true that the expansion of the state, having helped to shape the nobility in the first place, not only created a certain common ground between nobles, but also gave them just such a cause. Yet at the same time it intensified the intrinsic fragmentation of the nobility. From the moment of its inception, the state reinforced disparities and hierarchy in society in general and among the nobility in particular.[7] What German historians call 'proximity to rule' (*Herrschaftsnähe*) became a principal factor of social differentiation.[8] The state played a critical part in the tendency towards the concentration of power and wealth in the hands of an ever smaller number of prominent nobles.

The Court of the seventeenth and early eighteenth century was perhaps the clearest manifestation of this phenomenon. Those who enjoyed intimate proximity to the ruler could amass great wealth at a disturbing speed. Influence and prestige became the preserve of a restricted circle of men (and sometimes women), leaving a good many hopeless and resentful. The Court, at least in the late seventeenth and eighteenth centuries, was a force more divisive than integrative. Patronage, too, had disuniting effects on the nobility. It is almost axiomatic that the 'vertical', asymmetrical relationship which it creates between individuals tend to weaken the force of 'horizontal' ones and so the solidarity of the status groups in question. Moreover, historians found that, due in part to growing economic differences between great nobles and small, patron–client ties lost over the seventeenth century much of their former meaning. Already in 1614 locally prominent French nobles asked the king that he dispense his favours directly, bypassing the intermediary offices of the *Grands*.[9]

This points up the extent to which the monarchical state acted as a potent agent of social stratification – and as a solvent on aristocratic solidarity. The rules of the game which the state introduced determined that success was achieved primarily individually, not collectively. This fomented competition and discord among nobles and helped to reproduce or even boost state power. In 1641 the Duke of Nájera wrote to the Duke of Medina Sidonia, whose conspiracy has just been uncovered, that 'we grandees have ourselves to blame for what is done to us because some of us revel in the hardships caused to others. If we unite, as it is convenient that we should, this type of thing would not happen.' But this was easier said than done. When the Bourbons arrived in 1701 to replace the Habsburgs on the Spanish throne, they were no doubt delighted to discover that the grandees were considerably less powerful than they feared them to be, and one of the explanations their officials put forward was the disunity among the nobles.[10]

Looked at against this background, the nobility's 'finest hour' was during the second half of the sixteenth century and the early decades of the seventeenth – the period in which 'the political development in Europe reached a crucial stage'. To a large extent nobles rose to the occasion. The political developments, to which religious divisions gave a decisive impetus, modified habitual noble attitudes and priorities. While self-interest never quite lost its primacy, higher, more general motives were superimposed on it. Unity gained an unprecedented practical importance, overshadowing particularist considerations. The nobles worked out a political consciousness and wider vision of their role as a collective in the society they inhabited. The period was indeed characterized by the enthusiasm and earnestness with which nobles examined alternative arrangements of their relationship with the monarch; and this re-thinking was done in terms not solely of the obligations and rewards of service to the monarch, but sometimes also in terms of responsibility to the commonwealth, albeit from a decidedly aristocratic vantage point. Equally novel and significant was the fact that the concern with questions of this order was no longer restricted to the great nobles, who actually could not bring themselves to envisage any other way to limit monarchical power than control it themselves. It was nobles of somewhat lesser or middling rank – a Jean de Saulx-Tavanes in France, a Tschernembl in Austria, a Philips van Marnix van St Aldegonde in The Netherlands – who exhibited something like genuine public commitments. In fact, it was in large part this self-emancipation from magnate tutelage and the resulting wider nobiliary participation in high politics which gave the movement its thrust, distinguishing it from earlier attempts to impose limitations on the monarchy and share its power.[11]

But this period of political ferment was of relatively brief duration. For one thing, the confessional divisions produced tensions and dangers that dampened that political ardour and initiative which they originally stimulated among the nobles. In France, when Protestant nobles and the Malcontents challenged the monarchy, staunchly Catholic nobles rallied behind it. When later the Catholic League took the lead in contesting Henri IV's claim to succeed to the throne and evinced some disconcerting popular tendencies to boot, Huguenot and less zealous Catholic nobles scurried for safety under monarchical aegis. The deep rifts thus exposed within the nobility led to the withdrawal of many gentlemen from involvement in issues of high politics, an apathy that could not but assist the re-establishment of an authoritarian monarchy. The great nobles followed suit. The revolts on which they embarked in the first half of the seventeenth century became increasingly devoid of political content. But their abandonment of the cause of the public weal had different reasons from those of their lesser fellow nobles. They were driven by actual or anticipated exclusion from royal favour and the rational expectation that a demonstration of their tremendous nuisance value would effect their readmittance to royal grace.[12]

It was these characteristically aristocratic modes of thought and behaviour which made the *Fronde* virtually a forgone conclusion. This is the more notable as the *Fronde* witnessed a revival of *esprit de corps* among the middling and lesser nobles. The movement placed emphasis on equality, asserting the irrelevance of 'all distinctions of rank and quality'. As Jean-Marie Constant has stressed, this was a significant novelty in the aristocratic milieu and might have resulted in hitherto unexplored political forms. But they foundered on two accounts. First, their wish to see their spontaneous assemblies institutionalized and ratified by the government could not be reconciled with their wish to preserve the fiscal privileges of their order. For the government, noble assemblies were worth the trouble only if they voted taxes. When faced with the choice, the nobles opted for exemption. Second, the ideal of royal service and the desire to rise in the world through it ultimately overrode all other considerations and outweighed the attraction of an alternative conception of their relationship with the monarchy. The Frondeur princes for their part provided no leadership. For one thing, they were hostile to the lesser nobles' undertaking as much as this undertaking expressed the aspiration of the lesser nobles for independence from their betters. For another, their main objective was to wring for themselves further advantages from the monarch; by definition they could not strive to change the system.[13] Thus, personal motives, which the expanding state mightily abetted and satisfied, rendered other interests insignificant by comparison.

The more dramatic failure of aristocratic opposition in the Habsburg hereditary lands had generically similar causes. The royal victory was made possible because it meant a triumph for the Catholic nobility as well. Catholic nobles were certainly animated by sincerely held religious precepts. But no doubt the policies pursued by the Austrian Habsburgs in the decades leading up to 1620 encouraged them to believe that their own good lay in individual success achieved in and through the monarchical state, and not in a collective aristocratic enterprise designed to temper the monarchy. The post-1620 settlement vindicated their choice and laid to rest ideologically ambitious political programmes such as that espoused by Tschernembl. Here too, noble interest and engagement in politics in the strict – which is also the widest – sense of the term faded, leaving scope to mainly factional jockeying for power and pragmatic bargaining with the Crown.[14]

The emergence of the monarchical state, while contributing to the juridical and social formation of the nobility, could at the same time lead to its atomization. Such a process was at its most advanced in the great Continental monarchies. It was in the nature of the favourable alliance with the monarchy that it impeded the development by nobles of an institutionalized corporate structure that would likely have made it more difficult to incorporate them into the state. This impression is lent credence by those cases where the nobility did manage to construct an institutional framework for collective action on a long-term basis. The example of the south and southwest of Germany is particularly instructive: here those mechanisms failed to come to fruition that elsewhere drew nobles increasingly effectively into the state. Conversely, the political form of aristocratic unions gained increasing ballast and endowed the nobles with a capacity for concerted action. It was these fraternities that both kept the nobles out of the reach of the princely states until the very end of the Old Reich in 1806 and stood in the way of the full solid-ification of those states. As one might expect, these noble associations set much store by equality and unity among their companions.[15]

The configuration of these features – a politically founded aristo-cratic solidarity and a relatively weak monarchy – is readily apparent also in the case of the Polish nobility. The notorious constraint on royal authority exercised by the nobles through the *Sejm* was accom-panied by an accentuation of parity among the nobles to the point indeed of disabling the *Sejm*: all Polish nobles, high and low, rich and poor, were deemed legally equal, and any single nobleman had the right to veto any motion. By contrast, the nobilities in France, Spain and (to a somewhat lesser extent) Austria were ideologically and organizationally ill-equipped to resist the greater social and political penetrative power of their monarchical states. This, it has earlier been suggested, was at once a by-product of, and a contributing factor in, the formation of those states: it brought about a situation whereby, for the attainment of what they construed as success, nobles were much more dependent on their personal position in the state than on each other as a group.[16] Another comparison which may further illustrate the point is with England. Here the state, quite unlike the monarchy, was robust, and did not open up such great opportu-nities for nobles as did the Continental states. As Privy Councillor Lord Buckhurst reminded the Earl of Shrewsbury in 1592, 'in the policy of this commonwealth we are not ready to add increase of power and countenance to such great personages as you are'. And in truth, the subtle and complex machinery of the English state did not lend itself to monopolization by nobles. The latter were as a result forced to co-operate in a more abiding way both among them-selves and with other sections of society as a means of preserving their power. Ironically perhaps, the impracticability of success in a grand Continental manner seems to have been one of the guarantors of a more durable one.[17]

But the evolution of the state impinged not only on the internal structure of the nobility; it also shifted the nobility's place in society. Once the state becomes the most powerful factor of social stratifi-cation, then the traditional nobility must share more power with more people and/or other groups. It may become subsumed under a larger élite, even – or especially – if it reacts to this change by underlining its social exclusivity. The emergence of robe nobilities provides the prime example. This still did not imply that personal merit took precedence over all other criteria of selection; in truth, the insistence by these officers on their noble quality only serves to show the persistent charm of nobility. All the same, change there was: nobility was gradually becoming more one mark among others of membership in the élite and less a prerequisite for joining it. Those wealthy and/or talented nobles who made a brilliant career in the state now had more in common with commoners who rose to prominence in and through the state than with fellow nobles who lacked the financial and cultural resources necessary for such an accomplishment. This was another side of the stratification and atomization of the nobility by the state.[18]

All this was part of a wider and momentous transformation in which the state played a leading role: the creation of the national community. As has been seen, the continuous geopolitical competition in Europe and the steadily soaring costs of warfare forced monarchs to appeal to as wide a constituency as possible, to engage the 'political society', in order to secure consent to taxation and other contributions. The resulting multifaceted dialogue, revolving around the questions of public interest and individual liberties, was at the bottom of this transformation.[19] It was at its most pronounced and sophisticated in England. It is revealing in this regard that the public debt came in 1712 to be called *The Debts of the Nation* (by Robert Walpole), and in the 1730s the term 'national debt' appeared. Now a nation has no place for nobility as a constitutive principle and embodiment of the social order, for this by definition implies not only social and economic, but also legal inequality. This is incompatible with the doctrine that the state belongs to its people, the nation, which consists of individual citizens none of whom is legally worthier than his fellows and all of whom are immediate to the 'mortal God'.[20]

In 1765 Justus Möser wrote that 'we commoners have long enough suffered the oppressive imputation that we are of Helot origin. This should be no more.' He added that 'the nobility in Germany has in truth never belonged to the nation'. Möser was baying at the moon. In fragmented, multi-state Germany his view could evoke little more than literary resonance. Indeed, various regional nobilities were able, with the full backing of government, to preserve well into the nineteenth century not only their actual social predominance but also their exclusive legal status. *Mésalliances*, for instance, were proscribed in law. But Germany was, in this respect at least, an exception. Elsewhere, in western mainland Europe, the notion that the nobility was an alien in the body politic had better prospects of gaining currency. It was in France that it was turned into a political common property, by a younger contemporary of Möser. In *What Is the Third Estate?*, published in January 1789, Abbé Sieyès proclaimed that:

> it is impossible to find what place to assign to the caste of nobles among all the elements of a nation ... The nobility ... [is] a foreigner in our midst because of its *civil and political* prerogatives ... its private rights make it a people apart in the great nation.

The vision was acted out in 4 August 1789, when the National Assembly abrogated many noble privileges, and then in June 1790, when it abolished the status of nobility altogether. And while nobility was resuscitated by the Restoration, its privileges were not. Article 71 of the Charter of 1814 proclaimed that 'the former *noblesse* takes up its titles; the new [*scil.* Napoleonic] keeps its own. The King creates nobles at will, but he only accords them ranks and honours with no exemption from the burdens and duties of society.' The nobility survived as a pale shadow of its former self, a mere ornament or else a recognition of personal achievement or contribution, and thus part of a theoretically open élite. And where the principle of popular sovereignty was crowned, even this kind of artificial nobility was not tolerated: Article 1, Section 9.8 of the American Constitution reads:

> No Title of Nobility shall be granted by the United States; And no Person holding any Office of Profit or Trust under them, shall, without the Consent of the Congress, accept any present, Emolument, Office, or Title, of any kind whatever, from any King, Prince, or foreign State.[21]

In France and America it took a Revolution to create a new social order. Elsewhere nobility could not be cast out by summary acts of constitutional will. This was particularly the case in Central Europe, where the privileged legal position of the nobility proved more immune to criticism and challenge than in Western and southern Europe. But retreat there was even there, and before forces and ideas akin to those that propelled the French and American Revolutions. In Austria, as Otto Brunner observed long ago, a contradiction had arisen between the noble lordship and the requirements of the modern state and economy. The needs of security dictated increasing intervention in the sphere of noble lordship, and the demands for taxes and military service made on the peasant were turning him into a subject not only of his lord but also of the state. The more the state undermined aristocratic local authority, the wider became the circle of people immediately subordinate to it, or the other way around. The subject was at once politically individualized and socially univer-salized; his or her relation to the state was increasingly similar to that of fellow subjects. In 1787 and 1788 the concept of equality before the law was promulgated in the law codes of Joseph II. The lords' privileged position remained but its basis was now social rather than juridical; their public function *qua* lords was eroded. From lords of the land they were turned into landlords.[22]

The same shift occurred in Spain. The increasing 'nationalization' of the Spanish monarchy under the Bourbons produced an ideolog-ical assault on *señoríos*, the aristocratic lordships. These came to be deemed property of the nation, not of the monarch, and their alien-ation in the past came to be viewed as a diminution of national sovereignty which had to be remedied by their resumption. Such a demand was aired in the *Cortes* of Cadiz in 1811 which found it unacceptable 'that there should be partial states implanted within the national state; . . . [and] that there should be Spaniards who recog-nize and are subject to any other lordship than that of the nation of which they are an integral part'. As I. A. A. Thompson has observed, it is highly revealing of the change that had taken place that the lords did not resist the abolition of the *señorío* and instead sought to defend their 'property rights'. Like the Austrian lords, the Spanish ones were relegated to the private sphere; from primarily 'political' lords of the land defined by legal status and privilege they became predominantly 'economic' landowners defined by wealth. Of the Duke of Osuna, who by the mid-nineteenth century had collected over a fifth of all revenues accruing to nobles, a government offi-cial commented that 'His Excellency . . . is today, in truth, an ordinary property owner.' That the Spanish nobility, like other nobilities, proved remarkably successful in modernizing and adjusting to the new social, economic and political circumstances is a significant historical fact indeed, but must not be confounded with an effective continuation of the *ancien régime*. This was terminated in 1837 with the legislation that finally annulled the *señorío*. Nobility in the juridical sense, constitutive of the *ancien régime* social order, was disestablished.[23]

These far-reaching changes created for the Continental nobles political conditions reminiscent of those under which nobles in England had long been accustomed to operate. Here the domains of politics and economy had been hived off earlier than in any other monarchy. Political power, while it could certainly come in handy, was not a necessary condition for the acquisition of great personal wealth – quite the opposite of the situation in other monarchies. This is a feature demonstrative of the existence of civil society. It assumed, as Hobbes observed, a society whose basic units were individuals enjoying equality before the law; and this social order, as Locke later expounded, was underpinned by the rule of law as the safeguard of liberty and property rights. The role and character of the English state were indeed strikingly modern: reflecting a unique and felicitous balance between the producers of capital and wielders of coercion, it early came to act as an executive and impersonal 'watchman'. It belonged to all and to no-one at the same time.

> Behind the façade of king, lords and commons, and the related local infrastructure of squires and justices of the peace, lurked an authority which guarded the interests and therefore held the loyalty of all. Such a power, by the very nature of its universality, transcended the personal and therefore had no need to purchase loyalty.

By the same token, it could not be captured by any particular interest, aristocratic or other.[24]

An important precondition of this structural fitness of the English state in this period was its modest size in the sixteenth and early seventeenth centuries. This in turn was in no small measure due to the fact that England shunned the European geopolitical fray which caused the Continental states to swell exuberantly. There was little here which an already enfeebled aristocracy could live off. Just as important was the progressive enervation of the English monarchy. So when, in the late seventeenth century, England did get involved in large-scale conflict, the massive state machinery it consequently began to set up could be protected from appropriation by sectional interest. This, of course, perpetuated the relative weakness of the aristocracy's grip on the state. Hence, as David Parker noted:

> the remaining elements of the "feudal" aristocracy could only survive by becoming improving landlords and equipping themselves for government. From the mid-seventeenth century they did this with consummate success, re-establishing their social dominance within the framework of a capitalist mode of production and a system of parliamentary government.

Thus, if there was a certain resurgence in the power of the nobility in late seventeenth-century England, it is also true that this reinvigorated nobility had a different complexion from that of the distant past. It was an organic part of a flexible sociopolitical order that did not rest on the principle of institutionalized inequality. It is hard, for instance, to imagine a French grandee inviting, as the Duke of Norfolk did in 1764, 364 of his agricultural wage earners to dinner. Integral to the nation, the English nobles had of necessity to display leadership and public spirit; complementarily, in the absence of rigid privileges, they were characteristically thrown back on the subtler, informal mechanisms of snobbery to set themselves apart from the common run of wealthy compatriots. In other words, the English nobility was quite well prepared for the modern world. Its later decline was accordingly slow and gentle.[25]

In all these respects, early modern England diverged markedly from the pattern of the great Continental monarchies. There state and society remained intimately intertwined and the private and public spheres hopelessly intermingled until the latter part of the eighteenth century. The war-driven expansion of the state magnified rather than diminished that confusion.[26] It has been a central contention of this book that this development was largely responsible for three tightly interrelated phenomena: for the western Continental state becoming the chief means for nobles to acquire and exercise significant power, for the assimilation of the nobility into it, but also for its becoming virtually a preserve of the nobility. The European monarchical state was accordingly considerably less autonomous than the English one; it was in and around it that large areas of the relationship between the ruler and the nobility were arranged.[27]

All this underscores the interdependence of the monarchical state and the upper echelons of the nobility. But at this point both reached the limits of their evolution. For the nobility to go beyond it could only mean overtaking the state by either overthrowing the monarchy altogether or tempering it out of any substantive authority. As the historical record shows, however, neither option was viable. On the other hand, for the monarchy to rule without the nobility implied a redefinition of its rationale. 'No monarch, no nobility; no nobility, no monarch', went Montesquieu's famous aphorism. For, he expatiated, the nobility as an intermediary power was a bulwark against both a despotic state and a popular state. In the latter case, the monarchy would be made redundant; in the former, it would have to assume a different role and offer a different justification. All the more so as under the impact of the Enlightenment – sometimes aided by subversive ideas imported from England – the religious and traditional foundations of monarchy were disintegrating. Denuded of sacrality and confronting the subjects/citizens without having recourse to 'intermediate, subordinate and dependent powers', the monarch would perforce have, if he wished to be counted legitimate, either to concede some representative authority to the people or act as a servant of an impersonal state.[28]

Either way implied the dissolution of the fundamental bond between monarchy and nobility. To a far-sighted freethinker like the Marquis d'Argenson this was both clearly necessary and welcome. Montesquieu who, as one historian noted, was the true voice of the French political establishment, was fighting the previous war. As has been suggested above, over the eighteenth century forces gathered momentum that would in the fullness of time lead to the separation between state and society. It was by no means a coincidence that the word 'society', denoting an entity composed of individual subjects and distinct from the state, came into use from about mid-century. In these circumstances, Montesquieu's liaison of monarchy and nobility was growing untenable. The blurred line between the private and the public was drawn ever more sharply. The confusion of the two, which aristocratic domination helped to keep up, and which was one of its main foundations, was being cleared away. The state no longer represented the area where aristocratic 'private' and 'public' authority intersected and reinforced each other. The nobility consequently lost much of its power. If some nobles retained influence, this achievement had a different basis: many of them did after all remain rich and socially eminent. But these qualities were now, as they had long been in England, more the cause of positions in the state than their consequence. Moreover, commercialization and then industrialization opened up new sources of wealth, the tapping of which required no aristocratic credentials. In such a society nobility could only be justified by utilitarian argument, and that of course was also the weapon of its opponents. Edmund Burke's indubitably sincere claim to have done his best to support 'those old prejudices which buoy up the ponderous mass' of noble status, wealth and titles, suggests, by the sheer incongruity of its self-conscious rational advocacy of tradition, that the aristocratic world was coming to an end. To uphold nobility was plainly becoming increasingly necessary and therefore difficult. Indeed, in France, one fashionable legitimation of nobility was turned around against it. The French nobles, who took to grounding their privileged position in an alleged descent from the

Germanic conquerors, were told by Sieyès that the French nation was in fact eager to see them repatriated to the Teutonic woodland from which they pretended to have originated.[29]

The course of this transformation reveals the predicament of the European nobilities in the eighteenth century. Where, as in France, the state came to be the mainstay of the prominent among them, they were comparatively strong. The more the state expanded, the greater the power they could accumulate. But for that they depended not only on the monarch personally, but also on the working of financial system over which the monarch presided. As Arlette Jouanna has pointed out, they were simultaneously its masters and hostages. It is in this sense that the remarkable growth and consolidation of aristocratic power during the early modern period may be said to have constituted too great a success.[30] It left the nobility a house divided against itself, detached from the larger community, and highly vulnerable to change at the centre. As the state continued to develop its dynamics and began to transcend the traditional monarchical form, it turned into a source of aristocratic weakness. No longer props of monarchical polity, neither were the Continental nobilities pillars of their emergent nations. While this was not the end of their history, it was very much the end of their historical role.

Where, on the other hand, as in England, the nobles' power did not fundamentally repose on the state, they were less privileged and, as individuals, their judicial and political authority was comparatively weak. But in the same way as the constitutional polity of England proved more resilient than its absolutist rivals, so did the English nobility prove more resilient than the Continental ones. And it is telling that its growing dominance in the state after 1688 rested on a different, sounder basis which enabled it to maintain its place and enjoy society's respect for longer. Their enormous wealth was a crucial factor. It has been said that 'an observer entering a room full of Britain's 200 wealthiest men in 1825 might be forgiven for thinking that the Industrial Revolution had not occurred'. The concentration of property was indeed unique: around 1875, 400 peers held 17.4 per cent of the land in England and Wales. All in all, 4,217 people possessed 56.3 per cent of the land. And yet the English nobility provoked relatively little resentment. For one thing, its fortune did not derive predominantly from its position in the state. On the contrary, it was more because of their own economic power that English nobles were able to play an important political role. For another, the ascendancy of property as a criterion of membership in the nobility entailed that wealthy commoners could entertain – and not too infrequently realize – hopes of upward mobility. Combined with the lack of rigid formal barriers, this militated against social isolation and sheltered the nobility from the kind of corrosive criticism levelled at Continental nobilities. The twin foundations of the English nobility's long-lasting hegemony were thus private property and feeble privileges.[31]

Decline set in only as late as the 1880s. Not even the English nobility, for all its flexibility and adaptability, could withstand the kind of forces that were shaping the modern world. Walter Bagehot wrote in 1867:

> The aristocracy cannot lead the old life if they would, they are ruled by a stronger power. They suffer from the tendency of all modern society to raise the average, and to lower – comparatively, and perhaps absolutely, to lower – the summit.[32]

Notes

Introduction

1 P. Bracciolini, *On Nobility*, in *Knowledge, Goodness, and Power: The Debate over Nobility among Quattrocento Italian Humanists*, ed. A. Rabil, Jr (Binghamton, NY, 1991), 63–89, especially 67–71 (quotation p. 67). Niccoli later announces, though on different grounds, that 'Nobility . . . seems to be nothing' (p. 75). See also C. Donati, *L'idea di nobiltà in Italia: Secoli XIV–XVIII* (Bari, 1988), 11.

2 J. B. Wood, *The Nobility of the 'Election' of Bayeux, 1463–1666: Continuity through Change* (Princeton, 1980), 170.

3 A. Molho, 'The State and Public Finance: A Hypothesis Based on the History of Late Medieval Florence,' in *The Origins of the State in Italy 1300–1600*, ed. J. Kirshner (Chicago, 1996), 97–135, at 101.

4 Cf. J. Casey, *Early Modern Spain: A Social History* (London, 1999), 138–64; A. Molho, *Marriage Alliance in Late Medieval Florence* (Cambridge, MA, 1994), especially 334–5.

5 A first attempt has been made by J. Dewald, *The European Nobility, 1400–1800* (Cambridge, 1996).

6 A. J. Arriaza, 'Nobility in Renaissance Castile: The Formation of the Juristic Structure of Nobiliary Ideology' (University of Iowa PhD thesis, 1980), 5–6 (quotation p. 5); Wood, *The Nobility of the 'Election' of Bayeux*, 12–13.

7 See J. Casey, *The History of the Family* (Oxford, 1989), 19; H. Kaminsky, 'Estate, Nobility, and the Exhibition of Estate in the Later Middle Ages', *Speculum* 68 (1993), 684–709, at 691–2.

8 Cf. A. Jouanna, 'Recherches sur la notion d'honneur au xvième siècle,' *Revue d'histoire moderne et contemporaine* 15 (1968), 597–623, especially 603; Kaminsky, 'Estate, Nobility, and the Exhibition of Estate', 695.

9 Quotations respectively from O. Brunner, 'Die Freiheitsrechte in der altständischen Gesellschaft,' in his *Neue Wege der Verfassungs- und Sozialgeschichte*, 3rd edn (Göttingen, 1980), 187–98, at 187; K. B. McFarlane, 'The English Nobility, 1290–1536,' in his *The Nobility of Later Medieval England: The Ford Lectures for 1953 and Related Studies* (Oxford, 1973), 1–141, at 121.

10 Cf. H. Boldt, *Deutsche Verfassungsgeschichte*, vol. 1, *Von den Anfängen bis zum Ende des älteren deutschen Reiches 1806*, 2nd edn (Munich, 1990), 85; J. H. Shennan, *The Origins of the Modern European State,*

1450–1725 (London, 1974), 40, 50–1. An attempt has been made throughout the text to keep 'state' and 'monarchy' conceptually apart, though often implicitly rather than explicitly. It is expected that in each instance of using either or both terms the context would suffice to make the meaning clear.

11 J. H. Hexter, '*Il Principe* and *lo stato*', in his *The Vision of Politics on the Eve of the Reformation: More, Machiavelli, and Seyssel* (London, 1973), 150–78; 'The Loom of Language and the Fabric of Imperatives: The Case of *Il Principe* and *Utopia*', ibid., 179–203 (quotation p. 188). See also H. C. Mansfield, 'Machiavelli's *Stato* and the Impersonal State', in his *Machiavelli's Virtue* (Chicago, 1996), 281–94, especially 290.

12 D. Parker, *Class and State in Ancien Régime France: The Road to Modernity?* (London, 1996), 268.

13 Cf. W. G. Runciman, 'The Origins of the Modern State in Europe and as a Topic in the Theory of Social Selection', in *Visions sur le développement des états européens: Théories et historiographies de l'état moderne*, ed. W. Blockmans and J.-P. Genet (Rome, 1993), 45–60, at 53.

1   The dawn of modern times

1 J.-P. Genet, 'L'état moderne: Un modèle opératoire?', in *Genèse de l'état moderne: Bilans et perspectives*, ed. J.-P. Genet (Paris, 1990), 261–81; J.-P. Genet, 'Which State Rises?', *Historical Research* 65 (1992), 119–33; C. Tilly, *Coercion, Capital, and European States, AD 990–1992* (Oxford, 1992), 66–91; M. Mann, *The Sources of Social Power*, vol. 1, *A History of Power from the Beginning to A.D. 1760* (Cambridge, 1986), 416–49; M. Prestwich, 'War and Taxation in England in the XIIIth and XIVth Centuries', in *Genèse de l'état moderne: Prélèvement et redistribution*, ed. J.-P. Genet and M. Le Mené (Paris, 1987), 181–92. Quotation from S. E. Finer, *The History of Government from the Earliest Times*, 3 vols (Oxford, 1997), 1277.

2 H. Rothwell (ed.), *English Historical Documents, 1189–1327* (London, 1975), 472. See also ibid., 486 (Clause 5).

3 G. L. Harriss, *King, Parliament, and Public Finance in Medieval England to 1369* (Oxford, 1975); 'Political Society and the Growth of Government in Late Medieval England', *Past and Present* 138 (1993), 28–57. See also J.-P. Genet, 'Les débuts de l'impôt national en Angleterre,' *Annales: E.S.C.* (1979), 348–54.

4 J. B. Henneman, *Royal Taxation in Fourteenth-Century France: The Captivity and Ransom of John II, 1356–1370* (Philadelphia, 1976). See also C. Allmand, *The Hundred Years War: England and France at War c. 1300–c. 1450* (Cambridge, 1988), 148. Quotations from D. F. Secousse *et al.* (eds), *Ordonnances des roys de France de la troisième race recueillis par ordre chronologique*, 21 vols (Paris, 1723–1849), III, 433–9.

5 W. M. Ormrod, 'The West European Monarchies in the Later Middle Ages', in *Economic Systems and State Finance*, ed. R. Bonney (Oxford, 1995), 123–60, at 144, 152; M. A. Ladero Quesada, 'Ingresso, gasto y política fiscal de la Corona de Castilla: desde Alfonso X a Enrique III (1252–1406)', in his *El siglo XV en Castilla: Fuenetes de renta y política fiscal* (Barcelona, 1982), 13–57, especially 45–7, 56–7; 'La genèse de

l'état dans les royaumes hispaniques médiévaux (1250–1450)', in *Le premier âge de l'état en Espagne (1450–1700)*, ed. C. Hermann (Paris, 1989), 9–65, at 41, 47; D. Menjot, 'L'établissement du système fiscal étatique en Castilla (1268–1342),' in *Génesis medieval del estado moderno: Castilla y Navarra (1250–1370)* (Valladolid, 1987), 149–72; A. MacKay, *Spain in the Middle Ages: From Frontier to Empire, 1000–1500* (London, 1977), 145–6; J. H. Elliott, *Imperial Spain 1469–1716* (London, 1963), 194.

6 J. A. Hall and G. J. Ikenberry, *The State* (Milton Keynes, 1989), 37–9; Genet, 'Which State Rises?'.

7 N. Machiavelli, *The Prince*, ed. Q. Skinner and R. Price (Cambridge, 1988), 43.

8 *Die Goldene Bulle: Nach König Wenzels Prachthandschrift*, ed. K. Müller (Dortmund, 1978); N. Bulst, 'Impôts et finances publiques en Allemagne au XVe siècle', in *Genèse de l'état moderne: Prélèvement et redistribution*, 65–76; P. Schmid, *Der Gemeine Pfennig von 1495: Vorgeschichte und Entstehung, verfassungsgeschichtliche, politische und finanzielle Bedeutung* (Göttingen, 1989); W. Reinhard, 'Kriegsstaat – Steuerstaat – Machtstaat', in *Der Absolutismus – ein Mythos?: Strukturwandel monarchischer Herrschaft in West- und Mitteleuropa (ca. 1550–1700)*, ed. R. G. Asch and H. Durchhardt (Cologne, 1996), 277–310, at 298; T. A. Brady Jr, *Turning Swiss: Cities and Empire, 1450–1550* (Cambridge, 1985); P. Moraw, 'Fürstentum, Königtum und "Reichsreform" im deutschen Spätmittelalter', *Blätter für deutsche Landesgeschichte* 122 (1986), 117–36; 'Bestehende, fehlende und heranwachsende Voraussetzungen des deutschen Nationalbewußtseins im späten Mittelalter,' in *Ansätze und Diskontinuität deutscher Nationsbildung im Mittelalter*, ed. J. Ehlers (Sigmaringen, 1989), 99–120.

9 M. Weber, 'Politics as a Vocation', in *From Max Weber: Essays in Sociology*, ed. and trans. H. H. Gerth and C. W. Mills (London, 1947), 77–128, at 78. See also ibid., 334.

10 O. Brunner, *'Land' and Lordship: Structures of Governance in Medieval Austria*, trans. H. Kaminsky and J. van Horn Melton (Philadelphia, 1992). Quotation from O. Brunner, 'Moderner Verfassungsbegriff und mittelalterliche Verfassungsgeschichte', *Mitteilungen des österreichischen Instituts für Geschichtsforschung. Erg.-Band* 14 (1939), 513–28, at 527.

11 J. B. Henneman, *Olivier de Clisson and Political Society in France under Charles V and Charles VI* (Philadelphia, 1996), 1; R. Vaughan, *Philip the Bold: The Formation of the Burgundian State* (London, 1962), 42.

12 M.-T. Caron, *Noblesse et pouvoir royal en France: XIIIe–XVIe siècle* (Paris, 1994), 103–4. For other examples see ibid., 85, 102, 109, 122, 132.

13 For a systematic case study see L. V. Díaz Martín, 'El preludio de la guerra civil: la traición nobiliaria en Castilla', in *Genèse médiévale de l'Espagne moderne: Du refus à la révolte: Les résistances*, ed. A. Rucquoi (Nice, 1991), 31–49.

14 P. de Commynes, *Memoirs: The Reign of Louis XI, 1461–83*, trans. M. Jones (Harmondsworth, 1972), 97; A. Walther, *Die Anfänge Karls V.* (Leipzig, 1911), 51–65. Quotations respectively from L. P. Gachard (ed.), *Collection des voyages des souverains des Pays-Bas*, vol. 1 (Brussels,

1876), 434, and F. Walser, *Die spanischen Zentralbehörden und der Staatsrat Karls V.: Grundlagen und Aufbau bis zum Tode Gattinaras*, ed. R. Wolhlfeil (Göttingen, 1959), 58, n. 90.

15 See the illuminating remarks by G. Chittolini, 'The "Private," the "Public," the State', in *The Origins of the State in Italy 1300–1600*, ed. J. Kirshner (Chicago, 1996), 34–61, at 45–8.

16 N. Machiavelli, *The Discourses*, ed. B. Crick (Harmondsworth, 1970), 243–8.

17 Machiavelli, *The Prince*, 15–16.

18 K. B. McFarlane, 'The English Nobility, 1290–1536', in his *The Nobility of Later Medieval England: The Ford Lectures for 1953 and Related Studies* (Oxford, 1973), 1–141, at 120. Quotation from M. Greengrass, 'Noble Affinities in Early Modern France: The Case of Henri I de Montmorency, Constable of France', *European History Quarterly* 16 (1986), 275–311, at 276.

19 W. Abel, *Agricultural Fluctuations in Europe: From the Thirteenth to the Twentieth Centuries*, trans. O. Ordish (London, 1980), 35–95; D. Herlihy, *The Black Death and the Transformation of the West*, ed. S. K. Cohn, Jr (Cambridge, MA, 1997), 39–57.

20 G. Bois, 'Noblesse et crise des revenues seigneuriaux en France aux XIVᵉ et XVᵉ siècles: Essai d'interprétation,' in *La noblesse au moyen âge, XIᵉ–XVᵉ siècles: Essais à la mémoire de Robert Boutruche*, ed. P. Contamine (Paris, 1976), 219–33. See also W. Paravicini, 'Die Krise der französischen Gesellschaft im Zeitalter des Hundertjährigen Krieges,' in *Europa 1400: Die Krise des Spätmittelalters*, ed. F. Seibt and W. Eberhard (1984), 210–20, at 215–16.

21 Henneman, *Olivier de Clisson*, 10–13; Ladero Quesada, 'Ingresso, gasto y política fiscal de la Corona de Castilla', 37. See also Genet, 'L'état moderne: Un modèl opératoire?', 266–7.

22 Robert C. Palmer, *English Law in the Age of the Black Death, 1348–1381: A Transformation of Government and Law* (Chapel Hill, 1993), 14–27; Harriss, *King, Parliament, and Public Finance*, 333–4, 340–6. Quotation from *The Peasants' Revolt of 1381*, ed. R. B. Dobson (London, 1970), 64.

23 R. Cazelles, 'The *Jacquerie*', in *The English Rising of 1381*, ed. R. H. Hilton and T. H. Aston (Cambridge, 1984), 74–83; J. B. Henneman, *Royal Taxation in Fourteenth Century France: The Development of War Financing, 1322–1356* (Princeton, 1971), especially 316–20; J. B. Henneman, 'The Military Class and the French Monarchy in the Late Middle Ages', *The American Historical Review* 83, 4 (1978), 946–65; J. B. Henneman, 'Nobility, Privilege and Fiscal Politics in Late Medieval France', *French Historical Studies* 13, 1 (1983), 1–17, especially 12–13; J. B. Henneman, *Olivier de Clisson*, 19 (quotation from p. 240 n. 102). See also P. Contamine, *La noblesse au royaume de France de Philippe le Bel à Louis XII: Essai de synthèse* (Paris, 1997), 318–20.

24 C. Estow, *Pedro the Cruel of Castile, 1350–1369* (Leiden, 1995), 40–77; H. Nader, *The Mendoza Family in the Spanish Renaissance, 1350 to 1550* (New Brunswick, 1979), 38–45; S. de Moxó, 'Los orígines de la percepción de alcabalas por particulares', *Hispania* 18 (1958), 307–39; MacKay, *Spain in the Middle Ages*, 133–5, 179–80. Quotation from J. Valdeón

Baruque, 'Las crisis del siglo XIV en la Corona de Castilla', in *La historia en el contexto de las ciencias humanas y sociales: Homenaje a Marcelo Vigil Pascual*, ed. M. J. Hidalgo de la Vega (Salamanca, 1989), 217–35, at 235.

25 Harriss, *King, Parliament, and Public Finance*, 334; Nader, *The Mendoza Family in the Spanish Renaissance*, 38–41; Henneman, *Olivier de Clisson*, 131–4 and *passim*; Henneman, 'The Military Class'.

26 O. Engels, 'Die Krise in Kastilien während des 14. Jahrhunderts', in *Europa 1400*, 257–66, at 265.

27 J. Froissart, *Chronicles*, ed. G. Brereton (Harmondsworth, 1978), 153–5, 243–51; N. Saul, *Richard II* (New Haven and London, 1997), 77–8. For an analytical overview of the revolts see R. Comba, 'Rivolte e ribellioni fra tre e quattrocento,' in *La Storia: I grandi problemi dal Medioevo all'Età Contemporanea*, vol. 2, *Il Medioevo*, ii, *Popoli et strutture politiche*, ed. N. Tranfaglia and M. Firpo (Turin, 1986), 673–91. For the bulk of the commanders of the French armed forces in 1360–1415 being nobles, see Henneman, *Olivier de Clisson*, 4.

28 Henneman, *Royal Taxation in Fourteenth Century France: The Development of War Financing*, 317; *Olivier de Clisson*, 98, 105, 230–2, 236 n. 14. Quotations respectively from Herlihy, *The Black Death*, 47–8 and Dobson (ed.), *The Peasants' Revolt*, 73.

29 These issues will be taken up in the next chapters.

2 The changing face of nobility

1 M. Solomon, 'The Nobility Pretense', in his *Beethoven Essays* (Cambridge, MA, 1988), 43–55.

2 J. Mourier, 'Nobilitas, quid est?: Un procès à Tain-l'Hermitage en 1408', *Bibliothèque de l'École des Chartes* 142 (1984), 255–69; M. Bloch, *Feudal Society*, trans. L. A. Manyon, 2 vols (Chicago, 1964), 283, 285.

3 Notably L. Genicot, 'La noblesse au moyen âge dans l'ancienne "Francie": Continuité, rupture ou évolution', *Comparative Studies in Society and History* 5 (1962–3), 52–9; L. Genicot, 'La noblesse médiévale: Encore!', *Revue d'histoire ecclésiastique* 88 (1993), 173–201. See also J. B. Freed, 'The Origins of the European Nobility: The Problem of the Ministerials', *Viator* 7 (1976), 211–41. Overviews of the debate by R. Bordone, 'L'aristocrazia: Ricambi e convergenze ai vertici della scala sociale', in *La Storia: I grandi problemi dal Medioevo all'Età Contemporanea*, vol. 1, *Il Medioevo*, i, *I quadri generali*, ed. N. Tranfaglia and M. Firpo (Turin, 1988), 145–75; T. N. Bisson, 'Nobility and Family in Medieval France: A Review Essay', *French Historical Studies* 16, 3 (1990), 597–613.

4 C. B. Bouchard, *'Strong of Body, Brave and Noble': Chivalry and Society in Medieval France* (Ithaca, 1998), 1–27; A. Murray, *Reason and Society in the Middle Ages* (Oxford, 1978), 90–4. R. W. Southern, *The Making of the Middle Ages* (London, 1953), 107–8, argued that 'by the beginning of the eleventh century [the] ancient distinction of blood had ceased to have any significance', and that between 'the eleventh and the thirteenth centuries there is no nobility of blood'.

5 O. Brunner, *Adeliges Landleben und europäischer Geist: Leben und Werk*

Wolf Helmhards von Hohberg 1612–1688 (Salzburg, 1949); C. Donati, *L'idea di nobiltà in Italia: Secoli XIV–XVIII* (Bari, 1988); C. Lansing, *The Florentine Magnates: Lineage and Faction in a Medieval Commune* (Princeton, 1991), 212–4l; M. Keen, *Chivalry* (New Haven, 1984), 156–61; Aristotle, *The Politics*, ed. S. Everson (Cambridge, 1988), 94 (1294ª, lines 21–2); H. Kaminsky, 'Estate, Nobility, and the Exhibition of Estate in the Later Middle Ages', *Speculum* 68 (1993), 684–709, at 699; K. B. McFarlane, 'The English Nobility, 1290–1536', in his *The Nobility of Later Medieval England: The Ford Lectures for 1953 and Related Studies* (Oxford, 1973), 1–141, at 8; J. R. Lander, 'Introduction: Aspects of Fifteenth-Century Studies', in his *Crown and Nobility, 1450–1509* (London, 1976), 1–56, at 13.

6 C. C. Willard, 'The Concept of True Nobility at the Burgundian Court', *Studies in the Renaissance* 14 (1967), 33–48; Donati, *L'idea di nobiltà in Italia*, 10–11; D. F. Strauß (ed.), *Gespräche von Ulrich von Hutten* (Leipzig, 1860), 318–19.

7 Exponents of the 'blood' school indeed denied *dérogeance* any validity. Cf. A. J. Arriaza, 'Nobility in Renaissance Castile: The Formation of the Juristic Structure of Nobiliary Ideology' (University of Iowa PhD thesis, 1980), 203–16.

8 Keen, *Chivalry*, 157, 161, (quotation, 177); R. Favreau, 'La preuve de noblesse en Poitou au XVᵉ siècle', *Bulletin de la société des antiquaires de l'Ouest et des musées de Poitiers*, 4th ser., 5 (1959–60), 618–22; G. Giordanengo, 'Enquête sur la noblesse de quelques habitants de Chabeuil au XIVᵉ siècle', *Provence historique* 23 (1973), 99–107; E. Dravasa, '"Vivre noblement": Recherches sur la dérogeance de noblesse du XIVᵉ au XVIᵉ siècles', parts 1 and 2, *Revue juridique et économique du Sud-Ouest, série juridique* 16 (1965), 135–93; 17 (1966), 23–129: pt 1, 147–8; Mourier, 'Nobilitas, quid est?,' 267; Kaminsky, 'Estate, Nobility, and the Exhibition of Estate', 699, 701–2; Willard, 'The Concept of True Nobility', 43; Arriaza, 'Nobility in Renaissance Castile, 124–31. For extinction rates see A. Grant, 'Extinction of Direct Male Lines Among Scottish Noble Families in the Fourteenth and Fifteenth Centuries', in *Essays on the Nobility of Medieval Scotland*, ed. K. J. Stinger (Edinburgh, 1985), 210–31; H. K. F. van Nierop, *The Nobility of Holland: From Knights to Regents, 1500–1650*, trans. M. Ultee (Cambridge, 1993), 47; P. de Win, 'The Lesser Nobility of the Burgundian Netherlands', in *Gentry and Lesser Nobility in Late Medieval Europe*, ed. M. Jones (Gloucester, 1986), 95–118, at 116 n. 79. See also works cited in note 25 below.

9 Kaminsky, 'Estate, Nobility, and the Exhibition of Estate', 699.

10 O. Engels, 'Die Krise in Kastilien während des 14. Jahrhunderts', in *Europa 1400: Die Krise des Spätmittelalters*, ed. F. Seibt and W. Eberhard (Stuttgart, 1984), 257–66, at 261; A. MacKay, 'The Lesser Nobility in the Kingdom of Castile', in *Gentry and Lesser Nobility*, 159–80, at 162; Arriaza, 'Nobility in Renaissance Castile', 66–70; J. Fayard and M.-C. Gerbet, 'Fermeture de la noblesse et pureté de sang en Castille: À travers les procès de *hidalguía* au XVIème siècle', *Histoire, économie et société* (1982), 51–75. See also A. Rucquoi, 'Être noble en Espagne aux XIVᵉ–XVIᵉ siècles', in *Nobilitas: Funktion und Repräsentation des Adels in Alteuropa*, ed. O. G. Oexle and W. Paravicini (Göttingen, 1997), 273–98;

H. R. Guggisberg, 'Zur sozialen Stellung und Funktion des Adels im früh-neuzeitlichen Spanien', in *Ständische Gesellschaft und soziale Mobilität*, ed. W. Schulze (Munich, 1988), 205–20, at 208–9.

11 J. B. Henneman, 'Nobility, Privilege and Fiscal Politics in Late Medieval France', *French Historical Studies* 13, 1 (1983), 1–17; P. Salvadori, *La chasse sous l'Ancien Régime* (Paris, 1996), 18. For the exclusivity of hunting rights elsewhere see Nierop, *The Nobility of Holland*, 37; H. W. Eckardt, *Herrschaftliche Jagd, bäuerliche Not und Bürgerliche Kritik: Zur Geschichte der fürstlichen und adligen Jagdprivilegien vornehmlich im südwestdeutschen Raum* (Göttingen, 1976). Quotation from D. F. Secousse *et al.* (eds), *Ordonnances des roys de France de la troisième race recueillis par ordre chronologique*, 21 vols (Paris, 1723–1849), VII, 188.

12 P. B. Munsche, *Gentlemen and Poachers: The English Game Laws 1671–1831* (Cambridge, 1981), 11.

13 P. Geyl, 'Shakespeare as a Historian: A Fragment', in his *Encounters in History* (London, 1963), 7–105, at 25; C. Carpenter, *Locality and Polity: A Study of Warwickshire Landed Society, 1401–1499* (Cambridge, 1992), 42–6; McFarlane, 'The English Nobility, 1290–1536', 122–5; McFarlane, 'Extinction and Recruitment', in his *The Nobility of Later Medieval England*, 142–76, at 142–3; 'The English Nobility in the Later Middle Ages', ibid., 268–78, at 275 (quotation pp. 268–9); S. Clark, *State and Status: The Rise of the State and Aristocratic Power in Western Europe* (Cardiff, 1995), 196–7. See also C. Given-Wilson, *The English Nobility in the Late Middle Ages: The Fourteenth Century Political Community* (London, 1987), 55–68. Generally speaking, what is meant by 'nobility' in England, i.e. earls, dukes, etc., corresponds to the 'higher' or titled nobility in Continental Europe. I therefore use the term 'titled nobility' to avoid terminological confusion between this group and the gentry, which some may wish to consider as having been 'lower nobility'.

14 H.-P. Baum, 'Der Lehenhof des Hochstifts Würzburg im Spätmittelalter (1303–1519): Eine rechts- und sozialgeschichtliche Studie', 3 vols (unpub. *Habilitationsschrift*, University of Würzburg, 1990), I, 18–22; C. Ulrichs, *Vom Lehnhof zur Reichsritterschaft: Strukturen des fränkischen Nieder-adels am Übergang vom späten Mittelalter zur frühen Neuzeit* (Stuttgart, 1997), 41–3, 86–8, 90, 108; J. Morsel, 'Die Erfindung des Adels: zur Soziogenese des Adels am Ende des Mittelalters – das Beispiel Frankens', in *Nobilitas: Funktion und Repräsentation des Adels in Alteuropa*, ed. O. G. Oexle and W. Paravicini, (Göttingen, 1997), 312–75; G. Fouquet, *Das Speyerer Domkapitel im späten Mittelalter (ca. 1350–1450): Adlige Freundschaft, fürstliche Patronage und päpstliche Klientel*, 2 vols (Mainz, 1987), 43. Quotation from H.-M. Decker-Hauff (ed.), *Die Chronik der Grafen von Zimmern*, vol. 3 (Sigmaringen, 1972), 72.

15 Lansing, *The Florentine Magnates*, 13–17, 163, 195–211.

16 N. Machiavelli, *The Discourses*, ed. B. Crick (Harmondsworth, 1970), 247.

17 O. Brunner, 'Zwei Studien zum Verhältnis von Bürgertum und Adel', in his *Neue Wege der Verfassungs- und Sozialgeschichte*, 3rd edn (Göttingen, 1980), 242–80, at 274; Nierop, *The Nobility of Holland*, 27; M. Jones, 'The Late Medieval State and Social Change: A View from the Duchy

of Brittany', in *L'état ou le roi: Les fondations de la modernité monar-chique en France (XIVe–XVIIe siècles)*, ed. N. Bulst, R. Descimon and A. Guerreau (Paris, 1996), 117–44, at 130 n. 53; Fayard and Gerbet, 'Fermeture de la noblesse et pureté de sang en Castille'; Baum, 'Der Lehenhof des Hochstifts Würzburg', I, 198–9; J. Mezník, 'Der böhmische und mährische Adel im 14. und 15. Jahrhundert', *Bohemia* 28 (1987), 69–91, especially 78–9. For the relative ease of advancement into the nobility during the Middle Ages see the classic study by E. Perroy, 'Social Mobility among the French *Noblesse* in the Later Middle Ages', *Past and Present* 21 (1962), 25–38.

18 See Chapter 1. For an alliance between the Danish Crown and nobility that produced a similar result in the sixteenth century, see R. Braun, 'Staying on Top: Socio-Cultural Reproduction of European Power Elites', in *Power Elites and State Building*, ed. W. Reinhard (Oxford, 1996), 235–59, at 241.

19 Seyssel quoted in P. Contamine, 'France at the End of the Middle Ages: Who Was Then the Gentleman?', in *Gentry and Lesser Nobility* 201–16, at 211.

20 This is a central argument of J. Dewald, *The European Nobility, 1400–1800* (Cambridge, 1996). See also Fayard and Gerbet, 'Fermeture de la noblesse et pureté de sang en Castille'. For Gouberville see E. Le Roy Ladurie, 'In Normandy's Woods and Fields', in his *The Territory of the Historian*, trans. B. and S. Reynolds (Chicago, 1979), 133–71, especially 155.

21 J. B. Wood, *The Nobility of the 'Election' of Bayeux, 1463–1666: Contin-uity through Change* (Princeton, 1980), 12–13. See also Nierop, *The Nobility of Holland*, 23; K. Bleeck and J. Garber, 'Nobilitas: Standes-und Privilegienlegitimation in deutschen Adelstheorien des 16. und 17. Jahrhunderts', in *Hof, Staat und Gesellschaft in der Literatur des 17. Jahrhunderts*, ed. E. Blühm, J. Garber and K. Garber (Amsterdam, 1982), 49–114, at 63.

22 G. Simmel, *Soziologie: Untersuchungen über die Formen der Vergesell-schaftung* (Leipzig, 1908), 732–3.

23 Kaminsky, 'Estate, Nobility, and the Exhibition of Estate', 695, has described the difference in terms of a transformation of 'an original nobility of lordship' into 'a territorial aristocracy, its rights, powers, and privi-leges publicly established in the polity'.

24 Cf. ibid., 695–7.

25 McFarlane, 'Extinction and Recruitment', 144, 173; K.-H. Spieß, *Familie und Verwandtschaft im deutschen Hochadel des Spätmittelalters: 13. bis Anfang des 16. Jahrhundert* (Stuttgart, 1993), 445; S. de Moxó, 'De la nobleza vieja a la nobleza nueva: La transformación nobiliaria castellana en la Baja Edad Media', *Cuadernos de Historia* 3 (1969), 1–210. Moxó's method and interpretation have been questioned by N. Binayán Carmona, 'De la nobleza vieja . . . a la nobleza vieja', in *Estudios en Homenaje a Don Claudio Sanchez Albornoz en sus 90 Años*, IV (Buenos Aires, 1986), 103–37, who has argued for more genealogical continuity than Moxó allowed but does not deny that the nobility was socially and politically restructured. M.-C. Gerbet, *Les noblesses espagnoles au moyen âge: XIe–XVe siècle* (Paris, 1995), 100–4 discusses this debate and suggests that the change be conceived as accelerated social mobility. For France

see K. F. Werner, 'Adel', in *Lexikon des Mittelalters*, vol. 1 (Munich, 1980), 118–26, at 125. See also Dewald, *The European Nobility*, 17.

26 H. Nader, *The Mendoza Family in the Spanish Renaissance, 1350 to 1550* (New Brunswick, NJ, 1979), 36–45; Gerbet, *Les noblesses espagnoles au moyen âge*, 99–120; M. A. Ladero Quesada, 'La genèse de l'état dans les royaumes hispaniques médiévaux (1250–1450)', in *Le premier âge de l'état en Espagne (1450–1700)*, ed. C. Hermann (Paris, 1989), 9–65, at 51, 53; W. S. Maltby, *Alba: A Biography of Fernando Alvarez de Toledo, Third Duke of Alba, 1507–1582* (Berkeley, 1983). Figures for wealth of grandees in H. Kellenbenz (ed.), *Die Fugger in Spanien und Portugal bis 1560: Dokumente* (Munich, 1990), 264–9; H. Nader, 'Noble Income in Sixteenth-Century Castile: The Case of the Marquises of Mondéjar, 1480–1580', *The Economic History Review*, 2nd ser., 30 (1977), 411–28, at 426.

27 F. A. F. T. de Reiffenberg, *Histoire de l'Ordre de la Toison d'Or depuis son institution jusqu'à la cessation des chapitres généraux* (Brussels, 1830), xxxiii–xxxiv, 499–500, 508–12; *The Apologie of Prince William of Orange against the Proclamation of the King of Spaine*, ed. H. Wansink (Leiden, 1969), 40.

28 W. Paravicini, *Guy de Brimeu: Der burgundische Staat und seine adlige Führungsschicht unter Karl dem Kühnen* (Bonn, 1975), 539, 545–6; M. R. Thielemans, 'Les Croÿ, conseillers des ducs de Bourgogne: Documents extraits de leurs archives familiales, 1357–1487', *Bulletin de la Commission Royale d'Histoire* 124 (1959), 1–141; C. A. J. Armstrong, 'Had the Burgundian Government a Policy for the Nobility?', in *Britain and the Netherlands*, vol. 1, ed. J. S. Bromley and E. H. Kossmann (Groningen, 1964), 9–32. Quotations from F. Walser, *Die spanischen Zentralbehörden und der Staatsrat Karls V.: Grundlagen und Aufbau bis zum Tode Gattinaras*, ed. R. Wohlhfeil (Göttingen, 1959), 122 nn. 3–4.

29 C. R. Young, *The Making of the Neville Family in England, 1166–1400* (Woodbridge, 1996); L. Stone, *The Crisis of the Aristocracy, 1558–1641* (Oxford, 1965), 191–2; W. K. Jordan, *Edward VI: The Young King: The Protectorship of the Duke of Somerset* (London, 1968), 89–103. Quotations from *The Dictionary of National Biography*, III (1917), 1315; R. Lockyer, *Buckingham: The Life and Political Career of George Villiers, First Duke of Buckingham 1592–1628* (London, 1981), 3.

30 E. Oberhammer (ed.), *Der ganzen Welt ein Lob und Spiegel: Das Fürstenhaus Liechtenstein in der frühen Neuzeit* (Munich, 1990); R. J. W. Evans, *The Making of the Habsburg Monarchy 1550–1700: An Interpretation* (Oxford, 1979), 204 n. 19; L. Arcangeli, 'Chronik der Familie Farnese', in *Der Glanz der Farnese: Kunst und Sammelleidenschaft in der Renaissance* (Munich, 1995), 21–46. See also W. Reinhard, 'Ämterlaufbahn und Familienstatus: Der Aufstieg des Hauses Borghese', *Quellen und Forschungen aus italienischen Archiven und Bibliotheken* 54 (1974), 328–427; G. Klingenstein, *Der Aufstieg des Hauses Kaunitz: Studien zur Herkunft und Bildung des Staatskanzlers Wenzel Anton* (Göttingen, 1975); P. Moraw, *Von offener Verfassung zu gestalteter Verdichtung: Das Reich im späten Mittelalter 1250 bis 1490* (Frankfurt am Main, 1985), 390 (for Thurn und Taxis).

31 Given-Wilson, *The English Nobility in the Late Middle Ages*, 47,50; Nader,

The Mendoza Family in the Spanish Renaissance, 48; R. Griffiths [and R. S. Thomas], *The Making of the Tudor Dynasty* (Gloucester, 1985). According to Ladero Quesada, 'La genèse de l'état,' 51, the Guzmán were the first to receive the title of count outside the royal family, in 1369.

32 J. M. Calderón Ortega, *Álvaro de Luna: Riqueza y poder en la Castilla del siglo XV* (Madrid, 1998), 251–4; N. Round, *The Greatest Man Uncrowned: A Study of the Fall of Don Alvaro de Luna* (London, 1986), 52 n. 29; Paravicini, *Guy de Brimeu*, 424 n. 111; P.-R. Gaussin, 'Les conseillers de Louis XI (1461–1483)', in *La France de la fin du XVe siècle: Renouveau et apogée*, ed. B. Chevalier and P. Contamine (Paris, 1985), 105–34, at 128; S. J. Gunn, *Early Tudor Government, 1485–1558* (Basingstoke, 1995), 36; S. A. Eurich, *The Economics of Power: The Private Finances of the House of Foix-Navarre-Albret during the Religious Wars* (Kirksville, Missouri, 1994), 57–8; M. Greengrass, 'Noble Affinities in Early Modern France: The Case of Henri I de Montmorency, Constable of France,' *European History Quarterly* 16 (1986), 275–311, at 308, n. 115; D. García Hernán, *La nobleza en la España moderna* (Madrid, 1992), 151; C. J. Jago, 'The "Crisis of the Aristocracy" in Seventeenth-Century Castile', *Past and Present* 84 (1979), 60–90, at 65; J. Bergin, *Cardinal Richelieu: Power and the Pursuit of Wealth* (New Haven, 1985), 255; D. Parker, *Class and State in Ancien Régime France: The Road to Modernity?* (London, 1996), 183. Quotation from Round, *The Greatest Man Uncrowned*, 218, n. 11.

33 S. Kinser (ed.), *The Memoirs of Philippe de Commynes*, trans. I. Cazeaux, 2 vols (Columbia, South Carolina, 1969–73), I, 336; Maltby, *Alba*, 344, n. 19.

34 See, for example, G. W. Bernard, 'Introduction: The Tudor Nobility in Perspective', in *The Tudor Nobility*, ed. G. W. Bernard (Manchester, 1992), 1–48; G. W. Bernard, 'La noblesse anglaise sous Henri VIII,' in *Pouvoir et institutions en Europe au XVIème siècle*, ed. A. Stegmann (Paris, 1987), 153–62.

35 A superb case study is by M. Roberts, *On Aristocratic Constitutionalism in Swedish History, 1520–1720* (London, 1966).

3 A question of definition: state power and aristocratic authority

1 D. F. Secousse et al. (eds), *Ordonnances des roys de France de la troisième race recueillis par ordre chronologiques*, 21 vols (Paris, 1723–1849), XIII, 306–13. See also G. du Fresne de Beaucourt, *Histoire de Charles VII*, 6 vols (1881–91), III, 384–416.

2 M. G. A. Vale, *Charles VII* (London, 1974), 70–86.

3 P. Contamine, *Guerre, état et société à la fin du moyen âge: Études sur les armées des rois de France 1337–1494* (Paris, 1972), 277–319; Beaucourt, *Histoire de Charles VII*, IV, 387–404; Vale, *Charles VII*, 104; M. Wolfe, *The Fiscal System of Renaissance France* (New Haven, 1972), 36.

4 T. Basin, *Histoire de Charles VII*, ed. C. Samaran, vol. 2 (Paris, 1965), 27–9. For the coercion–extraction cycle see S. E. Finer, *The History of Government from the Earliest Times*, 3 vols (Oxford, 1997), 15, 1266,

1281–2. See also C. Tilly, 'War Making and State Making as Organized Crime', in *Bringing the State Back In*, ed. P. B. Evans, D. Rueschemeyer and T. Skocpol (Cambridge, 1985), 169–91; A. Guéry, 'Le roi dépensier: Le don, la contrainte, et l'origine du système financier de la monarchie française d'Ancien Régime,' *Annales: E.S.C.* 39 (1984), 1241–69, especially 1258–60.

5 Contamine, *Guerre, état et société*, 282, 314.

6 For the staggering growth of fiscal burden under Louis XI see P. Chaunu, 'L'état', in *Histoire économique et sociale de la France*, ed. F. Braudel and E. Labrousse, vol. 1, *L'état et la ville* (Paris, 1977), 9–228, at 147, 150–1. The annual revenue of the king, between 1480 and 1483, ranged from 100 to 140 tons of silver-equivalent, as against 40 to 50 tons in 1430 and 65 to 75 tons at the end of Charles VII's reign, and 60 to 63 tons in 1484–1515 (*sic*).

7 Unsurpassed reconstruction of the War of the Public Weal by K. Bittmann, *Ludwig XI und Karl der Kühne: Die Memoiren des Philippe de Commynes als historische Quelle*, 2 vols (Göttingen, 1964–70), I, 23–192. See also A. Grunzweig, 'Namur et le début de la Guerre du Bien Public', in *Études d'histoire et d'archéologie namuroises dédiées à Ferdinand Courtoy*, vol. 2 (Namur, 1952), 531–64; J. M. Tyrrell, *Louis XI* (Boston, 1980), 74–108. Quotations respectively from Bittmann, *Ludwig XI*, 143–4 n. 74; P. de Commynes, *Memoirs: The Reign of Louis XI, 1461–83*, trans. M. Jones (Harmondsworth, 1972), 104.

8 A. MacKay, 'Ritual and Propaganda in Fifteenth-Century Castile', *Past and Present* 107 (1985), 3–43 (p. 10 for differences between chronicles as to who played what role in the 'deposition').

9 W. D. Phillips, Jr, *Enrique IV and the Crisis of Fifteenth-Century Castile, 1425–1480* (Cambridge, MA, 1978), 63–79; I. Beceiro Pita, 'Doléances et ligues de la noblesse dans la Castille de la fin du moyen âge (1420–1464)', in *Genèse médiévale de l'Espagne moderne: Du refus à la révolte: Les résistances*, ed. A. Rucquoi (Nice, 1991), 107–26.

10 G. E. Aylmer, 'Centre and Locality: The Nature of Power Elites', in *Power Elites and State Building*, ed. W. Reinhard (Oxford, 1996), 59–77; Finer, *The History of Government*, 66–8; R. Bendix, *Kings or People: Power and the Mandate to Rule* (Berkeley, 1978), 222. See also I. A. A. Thompson, *War and Government in Habsburg Spain 1560–1620* (London, 1976), 148–51. Quotations from H. Nader, *The Mendoza Family in the Spanish Renaissance, 1350 to 1550* (New Brunswick, NJ, 1979), 166; W. A. Weary, 'La maison de La Trémoille pendant la Renaissance: Une seigneurie agrandie,' in *La France de la fin du XVe siècle: Renouveau et apogée*, ed. B. Chevalier and P. Contamine (Paris, 1985), 197–212, at 210. Chinese proverb from P. Crone, *Pre-Industrial Societies* (Oxford, 1989), 45.

11 K. B. McFarlane, 'The English Nobility, 1290–1536', in his *The Nobility of Later Medieval England: The Ford Lectures for 1953 and Related Studies* (Oxford, 1973), 1–141, at 121; C. Carpenter, *The Wars of the Roses: Politics and the Constitution in England, c.1437–1509* (Cambridge, 1997), especially 39, 64–5.

12 S. de Dios, *El Consejo Real de Castilla (1385–1522)* (Madrid, 1982), 109–10; Vale, *Charles VII*, 86–7.

13 Phillips, *Enrique IV*, 72–3, 100 n. 11, 102–3, 130. Quotation from A.

MacKay, *Spain in the Middle Ages: From Frontier to Empire, 1000–1500* (London,1977), 181.

14 P. D. Lagomarsino, 'Court Faction and the Formulation of Spanish Policy towards the Netherlands (1559–67)', (Cambridge University PhD thesis, 1973), 91–119; G. Parker, *The Dutch Revolt*, rev. edn (Harmondsworth, 1985), 64–5. Orange's remark in G. Bentivoglio, *Della guerra di Fiandria*, pt 1 (Cologne, 1635), 65–6. The deepening implication of nobles in the process of state building will be discussed in Chapter 4.

15 G. L. Harriss, 'Theory and Practice in Royal Taxation: Some Observations', *The English Historical Review* 97 (1982), 811–19.

16 S. Walker, 'Autorité des magnats et pouvoir de la *gentry* en Angleterre à la fin du moyen âge', in *L'état et les aristocraties (France, Angleterre, Ecosse): XIIe–XVIIe siècle*, ed. P. Contamine (Paris, 1989), 189–211; A. J. Pollard, 'New Monarchy Renovated?: England, 1461–1509', *Medieval History* 2, 1 (1992), 78–82; Carpenter, *The Wars of the Roses*, 155, 227–8, 240–1, 263–5; S. J. Gunn, *Early Tudor Government, 1485–1558* (Basingstoke, 1995), 23–58, 204; S. J. Gunn, 'The Courtiers of Henry VII', *The English Historical Review* 108 (1993), 23–49. See also W. G. Runciman, 'The Origins of the Modern State in Europe and as a Topic in the Theory of Social Selection', in *Visions sur le développement des états européens: Théories et historiographies de l'état moderne*, ed. W. Blockmans and J.-P. Genet (Rome, 1993), 45–60, at 55; S. Clark, *State and Status: The Rise of the State and Aristocratic Power in Western Europe* (Cardiff, 1995), 194–5. For Richard II's royal affinity see N. Saul, *Richard II* (New Haven and London, 1997), 265–8. Quotations respectively from Gunn, *Early Tudor Government*, 28 and G. W. Bernard, 'Introduction: The Tudor Nobility in Perspective', in *The Tudor Nobility*, ed. G. W. Bernard (Manchester, 1992), 1–48, at 11.

17 L. Stone, *The Crisis of the Aristocracy, 1558–1641* (Oxford, 1965), 752.

18 S. Haliczer, 'The Castilian Aristocracy and the Mercedes Reform of 1478–1482', *The Hispanic American Historical Review* 55 (1975), 449–67; P. Toboso Sánchez, *La deuda pública castellana durante el Antiguo Régimen (juros) y su liquidación en el siglo XIX* (Madrid, 1987), 48–55; M. Lunenfeld, *The Council of the Santa Hermandad: A Study of the Pacification Forces of Ferdinand and Isabella* (Miami, 1970), 53–60; de Dios, *El Consejo Real*, 143–5, 151, 161–4; M. A. Ladero Quesada, 'La couronne et la noblesse au temps des Rois Catholiques,' in *Pouvoir et institutions en Europe au XVIe siècle*, ed. A. Stegmann (Paris, 1987), 75–87; Phillips, *Enrique IV*, 50–2, 127.

19 P.-R. Gaussin, *Louis XI: Un roi entre deux mondes* (Paris, 1976), 178 (slightly different figures in P. S. Lewis, *Later Medieval France: The Polity* [London, 1968], 109–10. See also his 'Les pensionnaires de Louis XI,' in *La France de la fin du XVe siècle*, 167–81); F. J. Baumgartner, *Louis XII* (Stroud, 1994), 101–2.

20 P.-R. Gaussin, 'Les conseillers de Louis XI (1461–1483)', in *La France de la fin du XVe siècle*, 105–34; J. A. Guy, 'The French King's Council, 1483–1526', in *Kings and Nobles in the Later Middle Ages: A Tribute to Charles Ross*, ed. R. A. Griffiths and J. Sherborne (Gloucester, 1986), 274–94; M. Harsgor, 'Maîtres d'un royaume: Le groupe dirigeant français

à la fin du XVe siècle', in *La France de la fin du XVe siècle*, 135–46.
For the French royal council under Charles VII see P.-R. Gaussin, 'Les
conseillers de Charles VII (1418–1461): Essai de politologie historique',
Francia 10 (1982), 67–130, especially 87–91. For the provincial governors see Chapter 4.

21 P. Moraw, *Von offener Verfassung zu gestalteter Verdichtung: Das Reich
im späten Mittelalter 1250 bis 1490* (Frankfurt am Main, 1985), 355–421;
P. Moraw, 'Fürstentum, Königtum und "Reichsreform" im deutschen
Spätmittelalter', *Blätter für deutsche Landesgeschichte* 122 (1986),
117–36; P. Moraw, 'Bestehende, fehlende und heranwachsende Voraussetzungen des deutschen Nationalbewußtseins im späten Mittelalter', in
Ansätze und Diskontinuität deutscher Nationsbildung im Mittelalter, ed.
J. Ehlers (Sigmaringen, 1989), 99–120; K.-F. Krieger, 'Fürstliche Standes-
vorrechte im Spätmittelalter', *Blätter für deutsche Landesgeschichte* 122
(1986), 91–116; E. Schubert, *Fürstliche Herrschaft und Territorium im
späten Mittelalter* (Munich, 1996).

22 S. Riezler, *Geschichte Baierns*, vol. 3 (Gotha, 1889), 536–64; G. Greindl,
'Der alte Adel in der bayerischen Landschaft des 16. Jahrhunderts', in
*Aus Bayerns Geschichte: Forschungen als Festgabe zum 70. Geburtstag
von Andreas Kraus*, ed. E. J. Greipl *et al.* (St Ottilien, 1992), 217–43;
W. Störmer, 'Der Adel im herzoglichen und kurfürstlichen Bayern der
Neuzeit: Fragen der adeligen Grundherrschaft und Ständemacht', in *Adel
im Wandel* (Vienna, 1991), 47–73. The protestations of the rebellious
lords in F. von Krenner (ed.), *Baierische Landtags-Handlungen in den
Jahren 1429 bis 1513*, vol. 11 (Munich, 1804), 72–115. For the recur-
rence of the conflict in the 1560s see Chapter 4.

23 P. Moraw, 'Franken als königsnahe Landschaft im späten Mittelalter',
Blätter für deutsche Landesgeschichte 112 (1976), 123–38; J.-M. Moeglin,
'Toi, Burgrave de Nuremberg, misérable gentilhomme dont la grandeur
est si récent: Essai sur la conscience dynastique des Hohenzollern de
Franconie au xve siècle', *Journal des Savants* (1991), 91–131.

24 E. Schubert, *Die Landstände des Hochstifts Würzburg* (Würzburg, 1967),
93–100; K. Rupprecht, *Ritterschaftliche Herrschaftswahrung in Franken:
Die Geschichte der Guttenberg im Spätmittelalter und zu Beginn der
Frühen Neuzeit* (Neustadt a.d. Aisch, 1994), *passim*. Quotation from
W. Vogel (ed.), *Des Ritters Ludwig von Eyb des Aelteren Aufzeichnung
über das kaiserliche Landgericht des Burggrafthums Nürnberg* (Erlangen,
1967), 62.

25 *Deutsche Reichstagsakten, mittlere Reihe*, vol. 5, *Reichstag von Worms
1495*, ed. H. Angermeier (Göttingen, 1981), 359–73; P. Schmid, *Der
Gemeine Pfennig von 1495: Vorgeschichte und Entstehung, verfassungs-
geschichtliche, politische und finanzielle Bedeutung* (Göttingen, 1989),
235–6, 242–3, 403, 450–3; C. Ulrichs, *Vom Lehnhof zur Reichsritterschaft:
Strukturen des fränkischen Niederadels am Übergang vom späten
Mittelalter zur frühen Neuzeit* (Stuttgart, 1997), 175–83. Quotation from
A. von Keller (ed.), *Die Geschichten und Taten Wilwolts von Schaumburg*
(Stuttgart, 1859), 156.

26 Ulrichs, *Vom Lehnhof zur Reichsritterschaft*, 190–4; V. Press, *Kaiser Karl
V., König Ferdinand und die Entstehung der Reichsritterschaft*, 2nd edn
(Wiesbaden, 1980); V. Press, 'Kaiser und Reichsritterschaft', in *Adel in*

124   *Notes*

der Frühneuzeit: Ein regionaler Vergleich, ed. R. Endres (Cologne, 1991), 165–94; A. Kulenkampff, 'Einungen und Reichsstandschaft fränkischer Grafen und Herren 1402–1641', *Württembergisch Franken* 55 (1971), 16–41; M. LeGates, 'The Knights and the State in Sixteenth-Century Germany' (Yale University PhD thesis, 1970); Rupprecht, *Ritterschaftliche Herrschaftswahrung in Franken*, 383–443; E. Böhme, *Das fränkische Reichsgrafenkollegium im 16. und 17. Jahrhundert: Untersuchungen zu den Möglichkeiten und Grenzen der korporativen Politik mindermächtiger Reichsstände* (Stuttgart, 1989), 77–130; G. Schmidt, *Der Wetterauer Grafenverein: Organisation und Politik einer Reichskorporation zwischen Reformation und Westfälischen Frieden* (Marburg, 1989), 17–55. Quotations respectively from J. C. Lünig, *Des Teutschen Reichs-Archiv partis specialis continuatio III*, pt 2 (Leipzig, 1713), no. 142; R. Schmitt, *Frankenberg: Besitz- und Wirtschaftsgeschichte einer reichsritterlichen Herrschaft in Franken, 1528–1806 (1848)* (Ansbach, 1986), 67 n. 3.

27 For the importance of this core zone see T. A. Brady, Jr, *Turning Swiss: Cities and Empire, 1450–1550* (Cambridge, 1985), 222–30; T. A. Brady, Jr, 'Review Article: Imperial Destinies: A New Biography of the Emperor Maximilian I', *Journal of Modern History* 62 (1990), 298–314. See further T. A. Brady, Jr, 'Some Peculiarities of German Histories in the Early Modern Era', in *Germania Illustrata: Essays on Early Modern Germany Presented to Gerald Strauss*, ed. A. C. Fix and S. C. Karant-Nunn (1992), 197–216.

28 R. Harding, 'Corruption and the Moral Boundaries of Patronage in the Renaissance', in *Patronage in the Renaissance*, ed. G. F. Lytle and S. Orgel (Princeton, 1981), 47–64, at 60; Carpenter, *The Wars of the Roses*, 41–4, 71; W. K. Jordan, *Edward VI: The Young King: The Protectorship of the Duke of Somerset* (London, 1968), 78–89. For the proportion of nobles in the council of Edward IV see J. R. Lander, 'Council, Administration and Councillors, 1461–85', in his *Crown and Nobility, 1450–1509* (London, 1976), 191–219, at 205.

29 J. Guy, *Tudor England* (Oxford, 1988), 65–6; J. R. Lander, 'Introduction: Aspects of Fifteenth-Century Studies', in his *Crown and Nobility*, 1–56, at 16 and 35; P. Anderson, *Lineages of the Absolutist State* (London, 1974), 124–5; D. H. Sacks, 'The Paradox of Taxation: Fiscal Crises, Parliament, and Liberty in England, 1450–1640', in *Fiscal Crises, Liberty, and Representative Government, 1450–1789*, ed. P. T. Hoffman and K. Norberg (Stanford, CA, 1994), 7–66, at 39; Gunn, *Early Tudor Government*, 111, 143; R. Hoyle, 'War and Public Finance', in *The Reign of Henry VIII: Politics, Policy and Piety*, ed. D. MacCulloch (Basingstoke, 1995), 75–99, at 84–92, 96; P. K. O'Brien and P. A. Hunt, 'The Rise of a Fiscal State in England, 1485–1815', *Historical Research* 66 (1993), 129–76, at 153.

30 Stone, *The Crisis of the Aristocracy*, 266; Anderson, *Lineages of the Absolutist State*, 125–6; Gunn, *Early Tudor Government*, 162.

31 See Chapters 4 and 5.

4 From consensus to conflict: monarchy and nobility between war and religion

1 C. Tilly, *Coercion, Capital, and European States, AD 990–1992* (Oxford, 1992), 162. See also J. H. Shennan, *The Origins of the Modern European State, 1450–1725* (London, 1974), 32.
2 P. Hamon, *L'argent du roi: Les finances sous François Ier* (Paris, 1994), 46, 76, 246–7, 558; R. J. Knecht, *Renaissance Warrior and Patron: The Reign of Francis I* (Cambridge, 1994), 195–6; F. J. Baumgartner, *Henry II: King of France 1547–1559* (Durham, NC, 1988), 87; P. Chaunu, 'L'état', in *Histoire économique et sociale de la France*, ed. F. Braudel and E. Labrousse, vol. 1, *L'état et la ville* (Paris, 1977), 162–6; J. R. Hale, *War and Society in Renaissance Europe, 1450–1620* (London, 1985), 233. Quotation from M. Stolleis, *Pecunia nervus rerum: Zur Staatsfinanzierung der frühen Neuzeit* (Frankfurt am Main, 1983), 65.
3 M. J. Rodríguez-Salgado, *The Changing Face of Empire: Charles V, Philip II and Habsburg Authority, 1551–1559* (Cambridge, 1988), 55, 59, 64–5; A. Calabria, *The Cost of Empire: The Finances of the Kingdom of Naples in the Time of Spanish Rule* (Cambridge, 1991), 59–60, 83–4; G. Parker, *The Grand Strategy of Philip II* (New Haven, 1998), 87–8; A. W. Lovett, 'The Castilan Bankruptcy of 1575', *The Historical Journal* 23, 4 (1980), 899–911. Quotations respectively from P. Kennedy, *The Rise and Fall of the Great Powers: Economic Change and Military Conflicts from 1500 to 2000* (London, 1988), 48; *Relazione di Bernardo Navagero ritornato ambasciatore da Carlo V. nel luglio 1546*, in *Le relazioni di ambasciatori veneti al Senato*, ser. I, vol. 1 (Florence, 1839), 289–368, at 340.
4 J. D. Tracy, *A Financial Revolution in the Habsburg Netherlands: 'Renten' and 'Renteniers' in the County of Holland, 1515–1565* (Berkeley, 1985), especially 71–107; G. Parker, 'The Emergence of Modern Finance in Europe, 1500–1700', in *The Fontana Economic History of Europe*, vol. 2, *The Sixteenth and Seventeenth Centuries*, ed. C. M. Cipolla (Glasgow, 1974), 527–94, at 563, 574; A. Castillo Pintado, 'Dette flottante et dette consolidée en Espagne de 1557 à 1600,' *Annales E.S.C.* 18 (1963), 745–59; P. Toboso Sánchez, *La deuda pública castellana durante el Antiguo Régimen (juros) y su liquidación en el siglo XIX* (Madrid, 1987), 95, 115, 120, 149; Calabria, *The Cost of Empire*, 85; Rodríguez-Salgado, *The Changing Face of Empire*, 61.
5 Cf. J. Cornette, 'Le "point d'Archimède": Le renouveau de la recherche sur l'État des Finances,' *Revue d'histoire moderne et contemporaine* 35 (1988), 614–29, at 628.
6 Castillo Pintado, 'Dette flottante et dette consolidée en Espagne', 750–1; J.-C. Waquet, 'Who Profited from the Alienation of Public Revenues in Ancien Régime Societies?: Some Reflections on the Examples of France, Piedmont and Naples in the XVIIth and XVIIIth Centuries', *Journal of European Economic History* 11, 3 (1982), 665–73; J.-C. Waquet, 'Notes sur les caractères originaux du système financier toscan sous les Médicis', in *Genèse de l'état moderne: Prélèvement et redistribution*, ed. J.-P. Genet and M. Le Mené (Paris, 1987), 111–14; W. Blockmans, 'Finances publiques et inégalité sociale dans les Pays-Bas aux XIVe–XVIe siècles', in ibid., 77–90; A. Molho, 'The State and Public Finance: A Hypothesis

Based on the History of Late Medieval Florence', in *The Origins of the State in Italy 1300–1600*, ed. J. Kirshner (Chicago, 1996), 97–135, especially 106.

7 As far as I know there are no detailed analyses of the social structure of the public debt in sixteenth-century France and Castile. The fragmentary evidence suggests that great nobles either invested heavily in government bonds or received bonds as rewards or in recompense for services. See B. Schnapper, *Les rentes au XVIe siècle: Histoire d'un instrument de crédit* (Paris, 1957), 160–1; B. Bennassar, *Valladolid au Siècle d'Or: Une ville de Castille et sa campagne au XVIe siècle* (Paris, 1967), 257; Toboso Sánchez, *La deuda pública castellana durante el Antiguo Régimen*, 51 n. 7, 144.

8 Calabria, *The Cost of Empire*, 115–18.

9 The reason for adducing here evidence from the eighteenth century is twofold: the evidence for the sixteenth century is less complete yet sufficient to show that the social structure of the public debt in Florence had remained much the same. In fact, the continuity was not only social but also biological, the same families dominating the public debt over centuries. See A. Molho, *Marriage Alliance in Late Medieval Florence* (Cambridge, MA, 1994), especially 209–10, 336–8; Molho, 'The State and Public Finance'.

10 J.-C. Waquet, *Le Grand-Duché de Toscane sous les derniers Médicis: Essai sur le système des finances et la stabilité des institutions dans les anciens états italiens* (Paris, 1990), 356, 360, 369 (335–7 for definition of noble status). For concentration of wealth in the kingdom of Naples, see Calabria, *The Cost of Empire*, 121, 124. An Italian exception to the pattern of aristocratic domination of public debt was Piedmont. See E. Stumpo, 'La distribuzione sociale degli acquirenti dei titoli del debito pubblico in Piemonte nella seconda metà del seicento', in *La fiscalité et ses implications sociales en Italie et en France au XVIIe et XVIIIe siècles* (Rome, 1980), 113–24. Quotation from Waquet, 'Notes sur les caractères originaux du système financier toscan', 114.

11 For similar findings for other principalities than those in Table 4.1, see H. J. Cohn, *The Government of the Rhine Palatinate in the Fifteenth Century* (Oxford, 1965), 163; P.-M. Hahn, *Struktur und Funktion des brandenburgischen Adels im 16. Jahrhundert* (Berlin, 1979), 194; K. Andermann, 'Zu den Einkommensverhältnissen des Kraichgauer Adels an der Wende vom Mittelalter zur Neuzeit', in *Die Kraichgauer Ritterschaft in der frühen Neuzeit*, ed. S. Rhein (Sigmaringen, 1993), 65–121, at 103–8. K. Krüger, *Finanzstaat Hessen 1500–1567: Staatsbildung im Übergang vom Domänenstaat zum Steuerstaat* (Marburg, 1980), 228–40.

12 Ibid., 228.

13 P. Anderson, *Lineages of the Absolutist State* (London, 1974), 18; J. R. Major, *From Renaissance Monarchy to Absolute Monarchy: French Kings, Nobles and Estates* (Baltimore, 1994), 96. See also E. Le Roy Ladurie, 'In Normandy's Woods and Fields', in his *The Territory of the Historian*, trans. B. and S. Reynolds (Chicago, 1979), 133–71.

14 R. Carande, *Carlos V y sus banqueros*, vol. 3 (Madrid, 1967), 72, 77; Hamon, *L'argent du roi*, 176–7; M. Greengrass, 'Property and Politics in Sixteenth-Century France: The Landed Fortune of Constable Anne de

Montmorency', *French History* (1988), 371–98. Quotation from H. Nader, *Liberty in Absolutist Spain: The Habsburg Sale of Towns, 1516–1700* (Baltimore, 1990), 192.

15 Cf. Chapter 2.

16 G. Chittolini, 'The "Private," the "Public," the State', in *The Origins of the State in Italy 1300–1600*, 34–61, at 51. See also Hamon, *L'argent du roi*, 398–9, 404; Molho, *Marriage Alliance*, 336; A. Jouanna, *Le devoir de révolte: La noblesse française et la gestation de l'État moderne, 1559–1661* (Paris, 1989), 221–2; A. J. Arriaza, 'Nobility in Renaissance Castile: The Formation of the Juristic Structure of Nobiliary Ideology', (University of Iowa PhD thesis, 1980), 179–86, 406–7.

17 E. Schubert, *Fürstliche Herrschaft und Territorium im späten Mittelalter* (Munich, 1996), 15–16; K. Rupprecht, *Ritterschaftliche Herrschafts- wahrung in Franken: Die Geschichte der Guttenberg im Spätmittelalter und zu Beginn der Frühen Neuzeit* (Neustadt a.d. Aisch, 1994), 262–3, 292; K. Krüger, 'Public Finance and Modernisation: The Change from Domain State to Tax State in Hesse in the Sixteenth and Seventeenth Centuries – A Case Study', in *Wealth and Taxation in Central Europe: The History and Sociology of Public Finance*, ed. P.-C. Witt (Leamington Spa, 1987), 49–62. A more detailed analysis of the systems of pledges in H. Zmora, 'Princely State-Making and the "Crisis of the Aristocracy" in Late Medieval Germany', *Past and Present* 153 (1996), 37–63, at 41–7.

18 The preceding and following on The Netherlands is based on P. Rosenfeld, 'The Provincial Governors of the Netherlands from the Minority of Charles V to the Revolt', *Anciens pays et assemblées d'états – Standen en landen* 17 (1959), 1–63.

19 Quotations respectively from ibid., 6 and 12; M. R. Thielemans, 'Les Croÿ, conseillers des ducs de Bourgogne: Documents extraits de leurs archives familiales, 1357–1487', *Bulletin de la Commission Royale d'Histoire* 124 (1959), 1–141, at 17.

20 Rosenfeld, 'The Provincial Governors of the Netherlands', 51.

21 H. G. Koenigsberger, 'Orange, Granvelle and Philip II', in *Politics and Society in Reformation Europe: Essays for Sir Geoffrey Elton on his Sixty-Fifth Birthday*, ed. E. I. Kouri and T. Scott (1987), 353–78; Rodríguez-Salgado, *The Changing Face of Empire*, 349–50. For similar contradictions in the Spanish viceregal government in Sicily, see H. G. Koenigsberger, *The Government of Sicily under Philip II of Spain: A Study in the Practice of Empire* (London, 1951), 171–95. For a sceptical view of the patronage power of the great nobles, see H. F. K. Nierop, 'Willem van Oranje als hoog edelman: Patronage in de Habsburgse Nederlanden?', *Bijdragen en mededelingen betreffende de geschiedenis der Nederlanden* 99 (1984), 651–76. Quotations respectively from Rosenfeld, 'The Provincial Governors of the Netherlands', 42–3, 53; *Relazione di Bernardo Navagero*, 299.

22 R. R. Harding, *Anatomy of a Power Elite: The Provincial Governors of Early Modern France* (New Haven, 1978), 12–13.

23 Ibid., 126–7, 133.

24 Ibid., 122, 131. Quotations pp. 130, 167.

25 Ibid., 216.

26 See Chapter 5.

27 It is noteworthy in this respect that the first full-length treatise on nobility apeared in in 1549 in France. The first in Spain appeared in 1553. See Arriaza, 'Nobility in Renaissance Castile', 187.

28 C. Donati, *L'idea di nobiltà in Italia: Secoli XIV–XVIII* (Bari, 1988), 93, 152; I. A. A. Thompson, 'The Nobility in Spain, 1600–1800', in *The European Nobilities in the Seventeenth and Eighteenth Centuries*, ed. H. M. Scott (London, 1995), I, 174–236, at 185, 233–4; J. Fayard and M.-C. Gerbet, 'Fermeture de la noblesse et pureté de sang en Castille: À travers les procès de *hidalguía* au XVIème siècle', *Histoire, économie et société* (1982), 51–75. See also J. P. Cooper, 'General Introduction', in *The New Cambridge Modern History*, vol. 4, *The Decline of Spain and the Thirty Years War, 1609–48/59*, ed. J. P. Cooper (Cambridge, 1970), 1–66, at 23 (I owe this reference to the kindness of Professor Sir J. H. Elliott); F. Billacois, 'La crise de la noblesse européene (1550–1650): Une mise au point', *Revue d'histoire moderne et contemporaine* 23 (1976), 258–77, especially 275; O. Di Simplicio, 'La nobiltà europea', in *La storia: I grandi problemi dal Medioevo all'Età contemporanea*, vol. 3, *L'Età moderna*, i, *I quadri generali*, ed. N. Tranfaglia and M. Firpo (Turin, 1987), 487–526, at 506–7.

29 See Chapter 3.

30 H. H. Kehrer, 'The von Sickingen and the German Princes 1262–1523', (Boston University PhD thesis, 1977), 274–9; V. Press, 'Adel, Reich und Reformation', in *Stadtbürgertum und Adel in der Reformation: Studien zur Sozialgeschichte der Reformation in England und Deutschland*, ed. W. J. Mommsen *et al.* (Stuttgart, 1979), 330–83.

31 S. Weinfurter, 'Herzog, Adel und Reformation: Bayern im Übergang vom Mittelalter zur Neuzeit', *Zeitschrift für Historische Forschung* 10 (1983), 1–39.

32 Quotations from Shennan, *The Origins of the Modern European State*, 66, 69. Cf. E. Cameron, *The European Reformation* (Oxford, 1991), 354–6.

33 Harding, *Anatomy of a Power Elite*, 33–5; A. Devyver, *Le sang épuré: Les préjugés de race chez les gentilshommes français de l'Ancien Régime, 1560–1720* (Brussels, 1973), 7, 63–7 (quotation p. 67); E. Schalk, *From Valor to Pedigree: Ideas of Nobility in France in the Sixteenth and Seventeenth Centuries* (Princeton, 1986), 89–116; A. Jouanna, 'Die Legitimierung des Adels und die Erhebung in den Adelsstand in Frankreich (16.-18. Jahrhundert)', in *Ständische Gesellschaft und soziale Mobilität*, ed. W. Schulze (Munich, 1988), 165–77, especially 170. Maternus was 'a private soldier, of a daring boldness above his station', in Gibbon's words. He conceived an ambition to murder Commodus and 'ascend the vacant throne'. Cleander was a freedman who rose to become a praetorian prefect and effectively the ruler in Rome.

34 This paragraph is based on the superb analysis by Jouanna, *Le devoir de révolte*, 116, 119–79. See also A. Jouanna, 'La noblesse gardienne des lois du royaume: Un modèle politique proposé pendant les Guerres de Religion en France', in *Nobilitas: Funktion und Repräsentation des Adels in Alteuropa*, ed. O. G. Oexle and W. Paravicini (Göttingen, 1996), 177–92, at 183. Quotation from G. Groen van Prinsterer (ed.), *Archives ou correspondance inédites de la maison d'Orange-Nassau*, ser. I, vol. 3 (Leiden, 1836), no. 321, pp. 284–5.

35 J. I. Israel, *The Dutch Republic: Its Rise, Greatness, and Fall, 1477–1806* (Oxford, 1995), 138–46, 338; J. K. Oudendijk, 'Den coninck van Hispaengien heb ick altijt gheeert', in *Dancwerc: Opstellen aangeboden aan Prof. Dr D. Th. Enklaar* (Groningen, 1959), 264–78; K. W. Swart, 'Wat bewoog Willem van Oranje de strijd tegen de Spaanse overheersing aan te binden', *Bijdragen en mededelingen betreffende de geschiedenis der Nederlanden* 99 (1984), 554–72, at 563–4, 568–70, 572; H. K. F. van Nierop, *The Nobility of Holland: From Knights to Regents, 1500–1650*, trans. M. Ultee (Cambridge, 1993), 199–226; J. L. Price, 'The Dutch Nobility in the Seventeenth and Eighteenth Centuries', in *The European Nobilities in the Seventeenth and Eighteenth Centuries*, I, 82–113, at 85, 87, 112–13. Quotations from L. P. Gachard (ed.), *Correspondance de Guillaume le Taciturne, Prince d'Orange*, vol. 2 (Brussels, 1850), 35–9; H. H. Rowen (ed.), *The Low Countries in Early Modern Times* (New York, 1972), 39; *The Apologie of Prince William of Orange against the Proclamation of the King of Spaine*, ed. H. Wansink (Leiden, 1969), 53.

36 O. Brunner, *Adeliges Landleben und europäischer Geist: Leben und Werk Wolf Helmhards von Hohberg 1612–1688* (Salzburg, 1949), 29–35; H. Rebel, *Peasant Classes: The Bureaycratization of Property and Family Relations under Early Habsburg Absolutism, 1511–1636* (Princeton, 1983), 130–1; W. Schulze, 'Estates and the Problem of Resistance in Theory and Practice in the Sixteenth and Seventeenth Centuries', in *Crown, Church and Estates: Central European Politics in the Sixteenth and Seventeenth Centuries*, ed. R. J. W. Evans and T. V. Thomas (New York, 1991), 158–75, at 172–3; K. J. MacHardy, 'The Rise of Absolutism and Noble Rebellion in Early Modern Habsburg Austria, 1570–1620', *Comparative Studies in Society and History* 34 (1992), 407–38; K. J. MacHardy, 'Cultural Capital, Family Strategies and Noble Identity in Early Modern Habsburg Austria 1579–1620', *Past and Present* 163 (1999), 36–75; R. J. W. Evans, *The Making of the Habsburg Monarchy 1550–1700: An Interpretation* (Oxford, 1979), 52–68. For Tschernembl's well-stocked library, which contained books by Calvin and Hotman, see H. Sturmberger, *Georg Erasmus Tschernembl: Religion, Libertät und Widerstand. Ein Beitrag zur Geschichte der Gegenreformation und des Landes ob der Enns* (Linz, 1953), 253–9.

37 Shennan, *The Origins of the Modern European State*, 69–70, 72, 100–1, 112 (quotation p. 100).

38 Jouanna, *Le devoir de révolte*, 123, 152–3; Harding, *Anatomy of a Power Elite*, 31–7, 47–9 (but see M. Greengrass, 'Functions and Limits of Political Clientilism in France before Cardinal Richelieu', in *L'état ou le roi: Les fondations de la modernité monarchique en France (xive–xviie siècles)*, ed. N. Bulst, R. Descimon and A. Guerreau [Paris, 1996], 69–82, at 80); MacHardy, 'The Rise of Absolutism'; Israel, *The Dutch Republic*, 129–41; G. Parker, *The Dutch Revolt*, rev. edn (Harmondsworth, 1985), 37–55. Cf. J. H. Elliott, 'Revolution and Continuity in Early Modern Europe', *Past and Present* 42 (1969), 35–56, repr. in his *Spain and its World 1500–1700: Selected Essays* (New Haven, 1989), 92–113, especially 110.

39 P. L. Gachard, *Correspondance de Marguerite d'Autriche, Duchesse de Parme, avec Philippe II*, vol. 3 (Brussels, 1881), xii; W. S. Maltby, *Alba:*

A Biography of Fernando Alvarez de Toledo, Third Duke of Alba,
1507–1582 (Berkeley, 1983), 130; M. Orlea, *La noblesse aux États*
généraux de 1576 et de 1588: Étude politique et sociale (Paris, 1980),
156–7 (quotation p. 156); J.-M. Constant, *La noblesse française aux XVIe*
et XVIIe siècles (Paris, 1985), 238–9; Sturmberger, *Georg Erasmus*
Tschernembl, 78, 106, 288–9, 343–4 (quotation p. 344).

5   Court, patronage and absolutist cohabitation

1 R. A. Müller, *Der Fürstenhof in der Frühen Neuzeit* (Munich, 1995), 3–4,
   32; R. G. Asch, 'Introduction: Court and Household from the Fifteenth
   to the Seventeenth Centuries', in *Princes, Patronage, and the Nobility:*
   The Court at the Beginning of the Modern Age c. 1450–1650, ed. R. G.
   Asch and A. M. Birke (Oxford, 1991), 1–38; J. H. Elliott, 'The Court of
   the Spanish Habsburgs: A Peculiar Institution', in his *Spain and its World*
   1500–1700: Selected Essays (New Haven, 1989), 142–61, especially
   146–7; R. Chartier, 'Construction de l'état moderne et formes culturelles:
   Perspectives et questions,' in *Culture et idéologie dans la genèse de l'état*
   moderne (Rome, 1985), 491–503, at 501. Quotation from E. Schubert,
   Fürstliche Herrschaft und Territorium im späten Mittelalter (Munich,
   1996), 77.
2 N. Elias, *The Court Society*, trans, E. Jephcott (Oxford, 1983). Cf. Müller,
   Der Fürstenhof in der Frühen Neuzeit, 32–5, 94–7. Quotations from J.
   Dewald, *Aristocratic Experience and the Origins of Modern Culture:*
   France, 1570–1715 (Berkeley, 1993), 27; Adam Smith, *An Inquiry into*
   the Nature and Causes of the Wealth of Nations, ed. R. H. Campbell, A.
   S. Skinner and W. B. Todd, vol. 1 (The Glasgow Edition of the Works
   and Correspondence of Adam Smith, vol. 2; Oxford, 1976), 421.
3 D. Howarth, *Images of Rule: Art and Politics in the English Renaissance,*
   1485–1649 (Berkeley, 1997), 192; E. Schalk, 'The Court as "Civilizer"
   of the Nobility: Noble Attitudes and the Court in France in the Late
   Sixteenth and Early Seventeenth Centuries', in *Princes, Patronage, and*
   the Nobility, (Oxford, 1991) 245–63, at 254; A.-M. Lohmeier, 'Das Lob
   des adligen Landlebens in der deutschen Literatur des 17. Jahrhunderts',
   in *Arte et Marte: Studien zur Adelskultur des Barockzeitalters in Schweden,*
   Dänemark und Schleswig-Holstein, ed. D. Lohmeier (Neumünster, 1978),
   173–91, at 189; W. Neuber, 'Adeliges Landleben in Österreich und die
   Literatur im 16. und im 17. Jahrhundert', in *Adel im Wandel: Politik,*
   Kultur, Konfession 1500–1700, ed. H. Knittler, G. Stangler and R.
   Zedlinger (Vienna, 1990), 543–53, at 544.
4 K. Sharpe, *Criticism and Compliment: The Politics of Literature in the*
   England of Charles I (Cambridge, 1987), 9, 14, 20, 42, 52–3, 99; R. G.
   Asch, *Der Hof Karls I. von England: Politik, Provinz und Patronage,*
   1625–1640 (Cologne, 1993), 7, 17, 24–5; Schalk, 'The Court as "Civilizer"
   of the Nobility'; J. Swann, 'The French Nobility, 1715–1789', in *The*
   European Nobilities in the Seventeenth and Eighteenth Centuries, ed. H.
   M. Scott, 2 vols (London, 1995), I, 142–73, at 169–70. A. Jouanna, *Le*
   devoir de révolte: La noblesse française et la gestation de l'État moderne,
   1559–1661 (Paris, 1989), 246, has argued for a divorce between Court
   and country, which was, alas, more imaginary than real.

5 Neuber, 'Adeliges Landleben in Österreich', 546–7; R. J. W. Evans, *The Making of the Habsburg Monarchy 1550–1700: An Interpretation* (Oxford, 1979), 174–9.

6 Müller, *Der Fürstenhof in der Frühen Neuzeit*, 31; F. Bayard, *Le monde des financiers au XVIIe siècle* (Paris, 1988), 35; R. J. W. Evans, 'The Court: A Protean Institution and an Elusive Subject', in *Princes, Patronage, and the Nobility*, 481–91, at 488–9; J. R. Major, *From Renaissance Monarchy to Absolute Monarchy: French Kings, Nobles and Estates* (Baltimore, 1994), 290–2; S. Kettering, *Patrons, Brokers, and Clients in Seventeenth-Century France* (Oxford, 1986), 142; D. Parker, *Class and State in Ancien Régime France: The Road to Modernity?* (London, 1996), 182 (quotation p. 193); S. E. Finer, *The History of Government from the Earliest Times*, 3 vols (Oxford, 1997), 1317. Quotation from R. Bonney, 'Guerre, fiscalité et activité d'état en France (1500–1660): Quelques remarques préliminaires sur les possibilités de recherche', in *Genèse de l'état moderne: Prélèvement et redistribution*, ed. J.-P. Genet and M. Le Mené (Paris, 1987), 193–201, at 199.

7 C. Tilly, *Coercion, Capital, and European States, AD 990–1992* (Oxford, 1992), 73; Bayard, *Le monde des financiers au XVIIe siècle*, 29; R. Bonney, 'The Secret Expenses of Richelieu and Mazarin, 1624–1661', *The English Historical Review* 91 (1976), 825–36; Parker, *Class and State in Ancien Régime France*, 196.

8 Asch, *Der Hof Karls I. von England*, 292–3; J. H. Elliott, 'Revolution and Continuity in Early Modern Europe', *Past and Present* 42 (1969), 35–56, reprinted in his *Spain and its World 1500–1700*, 92–113, at 110. Quotation from M. Greengrass, 'Functions and Limits of Political Clientilism in France before Cardinal Richelieu,' in *L'état ou le roi: Les fondations de la modernité monarchique en France (xive–xviie siècles)*, ed. N. Bulst, R. Descimon and A. Guerreau (Paris, 1996), 69–82, at 72.

9 Asch, *Der Hof Karls I. von England*, 15–16, 293–5; Kettering, *Patrons, Brokers, and Clients in Seventeenth-Century France*, 5; R. Mettam, 'The French Nobility, 1610–1715', in *The European Nobilities in the Seventeenth and Eighteenth Centuries*, I, 114–41, especially 121–2, 138–9; T. Dean, 'The Courts', in *The Origins of the State in Italy 1300–1600*, ed. J. Kirshner (Chicago, 1996), 136–51. The metaphor of 'fountain of favours' was coined in 1623 by John Webster. See R. Descimon, 'Power Elites and the Prince: The State as Enterprise', in *Power Elites and State Building*, ed. W. Reinhard (Oxford, 1996), 101–21, at 115.

10 Kettering, *Patrons, Brokers, and Clients in Seventeenth-Century France*, 5; Dewald, *Aristocratic Experience and the Origins of Modern Culture*, 61–2; Asch, *Der Hof Karls I. von England*, 304–7. An excellent sociological treatment of patronage is by T. Johnson and C. Dandeker, 'Patronage: Relation and System', in *Patronage in Ancient Society*, ed. A. Wallace-Hadrill (London, 1989), 219–42. On the fluidity of the system see H. F. K. Nierop, 'Willem van Oranje als hoog edelman: Patronage in de Habsburgse Nederlanden?', *Bijdragen en mededelingen betreffende de geschiedenis der Nederlanden* 99 (1984), 651–76, especially 675; K. B. Neuschel, *Word of Honor: Interpreting Noble Culture in Sixteenth-Century France* (Ithaca, 1989).

11 R. G. Asch, 'Krone, Hof und Adel in den Ländern der Stuart Dynastie im frühen 17. Jahrhundert', *Zeitschrift für Historische Forschung* 16 (1989), 183–220, at 212–13; Asch, *Der Hof Karls I. von England*, 395, 399–400.

12 Ibid.; I. A. A. Thompson, *War and Government in Habsburg Spain 1560–1620* (London,1976), 155; V. Press, 'Adel im Reich um 1600: Zur Einführung', in *Spezialforschung und 'Gesamtgeschichte': Beispiele und Methodenfragen zur Geschichte der frühen Neuzeit*, ed. G. Klingenstein and H. Lutz (Vienna, 1981), 15–47, at 39, 47; Greengrass, 'Functions and Limits of Political Clientilism in France before Cardinal Richelieu', 82; Harding, *Anatomy of a Power Elite*, 172, 201–4, 216 (quotation p. 202). See also S. Kettering, 'The Decline of Great Noble Clientage during the Reign of Louis XIV', *Canadian Journal of History* 24 (1989), 157–77, for a comprehensive analysis but too one-sided interpretation. D. Parrott, 'Richelieu, the *Grands*, and the French Army', in *Richelieu and his Age*, ed. J. Bergin and L. Brockliss (Oxford, 1992), 135–73, at 145 n. 33, has argued, against Harding, for continued military patronage of the provincial governors.

13 Asch, *Der Hof Karls I. von England*, 34. For the historiographical connotations of 'absolutism' see N. Henshall, *The Myth of Absolutism: Change and Continuity in Early Modern European Monarchy* (London, 1992), 1–2.

14 E. Hinrichs, 'Abschied vom Absolutismus?: Eine Antwort auf Nicholas Henshall', in *Der Absolutismus – ein Mythos?: Strukturwandel monarchischer Herrschaft in West- und Mitteleuropa (ca. 1550–1700)*, ed. R. G. Asch and H. Durchhardt (Cologne, 1996), 353–71, at 366–9; Jouanna, *Le devoir de révolte*, 200–11; J. B. Collins, *Fiscal Limits of Absolutism: Direct Taxation in Early Seventeenth-Century France* (Berkeley, 1988), 64; M. Greengrass, *France in the Age of Henri IV: The Struggle for Stability* (London, 1984), 172–84. For the years immediately after Henri IV's death see K. Malettke, 'The Crown, *Ministériat*, and Nobility at the Court of Louis XIII', in *Princes, Patronage, and the Nobility*, 415–39, especially 420–1.

15 *Discours d'un genti-homme François à la Noblesse de France, sur l'ouverture de l'assemblee des Estats generaux dans la ville de Paris en ceste annee 1614. Avec deux advertissemens particuliers à M^{rs} les Deputez du Clergé & de la Nobleße* (1614), 12–14.

16 C. J. Jago, 'Aristocracy, War, and Finance in Castile, 1621–1665: The Titled Nobility and the House of Béjar during the Reign of Philip IV' (Cambridge University PhD thesis, 1969), 32, 34, 42, 44–6, 73, 173, 238, 282–3, 341–7; C. J. Jago, 'The Influence of Debt on the Relations between Crown and Aristocracy in Seventeenth-Century Castile', *The Economic History Review* 26 (1973), 218–36; Elliott, 'The Court of the Spanish Habsburgs', 156; B. Yun Casalilla, 'The Castilian Aristocracy in the Seventeenth Century: Crisis, Refeudalisation, or Political Offensive?', in *The Castilian Crisis of the Seventeenth Century*, ed. I. A. A. Thompson and B. Yun Casalilla (Cambridge, 1994), 277–300, especially 287–9. See also Thompson, *War and Government in Habsburg Spain*, 146–59; J. Casey, *Early Modern Spain: A Social History* (London, 1999), 156–7. Figures for Lerma from H. Nader, *Liberty in Absolutist Spain: The*

Habsburg Sale of Towns, 1516–1700 (Baltimore, 1990), 121; Antonio Feros, letter to author, 2 September 1999.

17 Evans, *The Making of the Habsburg Monarchy*, 71, 167–8, 177–8, 197, 211 (quotation pp. 167–8); J. Van Horn Melton, 'The Nobility in the Bohemian and Austrian Lands, 1620–1780', in *The European Nobilities in the Seventeenth and Eighteenth Centuries*, II, 110–43, at 113–14, 117–18; T. Winkelbauer, 'Krise der Aristokratie?: Zum Strukturwandel des Adels in den böhmischen und niederösterreichischen Ländern im 16. und 17. Jahrhundert', *Mitteilungen des Instituts für österreichische Geschichte* 100 (1992), 328–53, at 337, 347–8, 352; P. G. M. Dickson, *Finance and Government under Maria Theresia, 1740–1780*, 2 vols (Oxford, 1987), I, 91–3, 113; G. Klingenstein, *Der Aufstieg des Hauses Kaunitz: Studien zur Herkunft und Bildung des Staatskanzlers Wenzel Anton* (Göttingen, 1975), 26–74.

18 Cf. Chapter 4. For a thorough discussion see T. Ertman, *Birth of the Leviathan: Building States and Regimes in Medieval and Early Modern Europe* (Cambridge, 1997), especially 90–155.

19 Ibid., 119; Parker, *Class and State in Ancien Régime France*, 187, 198; J. Brewer, *The Sinews of Power: War, Money and the English State, 1688–1783* (Cambridge, MA, 1988), 15–16; W. Reinhard, 'Staatsmacht als Kreditproblem: Zur Struktur und Funktion des frühneuzeitlichen Ämterhandels', *Vierteljahrschrift für Sozial- und Wirtschaftsgeschichte* 61 (1974), 289–319.

20 Thompson, *War and Government in Habsburg Spain*, 150–6; I. A. A. Thompson, 'The Nobility in Spain, 1600–1800', in *The European Nobilities in the Seventeenth and Eighteenth Centuries*, I, 174–236, especially 196, 215–17; Jago, 'Aristocracy, War, and Finance in Castile, 1621–1665', 60–5, 79–80, 243, 388; Yun Casalilla, 'The Castilian Aristocracy in the Seventeenth Century', 284–5, 296–8; J. H. Elliott, 'A Provincial Aristocracy: The Catalan Ruling Class in the Sixteenth and Seventeenth Centuries', in his *Spain and its World 1500–1700*, 71–91, at 85; R. A. Stradling, *Philip IV and the Government of Spain* (Cambridge, 1988), 151–71; M. J. Rodríguez-Salgado, 'The Court of Philip II of Spain', in *Princes, Patronage, and the Nobility*, 205–44, at 233; Ertman, *Birth of the Leviathan*, 119–21; R. G. Asch, 'Kriegsfinanzierung, Staatsbildung und ständische Ordnung in Westeuropa im 17. und 18. Jahrhundert', *Historische Zeitschrift* 268 (1999), 635–71, at 651–3. Quotations respectively from Thompson, *War and Government in Habsburg Spain*, 151, 149–50, and 'The Nobility in Spain', 218.

21 H. Knittler, 'Adelige Grundherrschaft im Übergang: Überlegungen zum Verhältnis von Adel und Wirtschaft in Niederösterreich um 1600', in *Spezialforschung und 'Gesamtgeschichte'*, 84–111, at 97; Evans, *The Making of the Habsburg Monarchy*, 168; Winkelbauer, 'Krise der Aristokratie?', 334–5; Dickson, *Finance and Government under Maria Theresia*, I, 95.

22 D. Parker, 'The Social Foundation of French Absolutism 1610–1630', *Past and Present* 53 (1971), 67–89; Major, *From Renaissance Monarchy to Absolute Monarchy*, 267–76; Bonney, *The European Dynastic States, 1494–1660* (Oxford, 1991), 232; Parrott, 'Richelieu, the *Grands*, and the

French Army', especially 166. Quotation from *The Political Testament of Cardinal Richelieu*, trans. H. B. Hill (Madison, WI, 1961), 20.

23 D. Dessert, 'Le rôle de la noblesse dans le finances royales sous le règne de Louis XIV,' in *La fiscalité et ses implications sociales en Italie et en France au XVIIe et XVIIIe siècles* (Rome, 1980), 175–90; D. Dessert, *Argent, pouvoir et société au Grand Siècle* (Paris, 1984), 341–78; H. L. Root, *The Fountain of Privilege: Political Foundations of Markets in Old Regime France and England* (Berkeley, 1994), 163–78; Parker, *Class and State in Ancien Régime France*, 187.

24 D. Parker, 'Sovereignty, Absolutism and the Function of the Law in Seventeenth-Century France', *Past and Present* 122 (1989), 36–74; Henshall, *The Myth of Absolutism*, 35–60. Quotations from Jago, 'Aristocracy, War, and Finance in Castile, 1621–1665', 29; N. Henshall, 'Early Modern Absolutism 1550–1700: Political Reality or Propaganda?', in *Der Absolutismus – ein Mythos?*, 25–53, at 40, 45.

25 For criticism of revisionist argument, see Parker, *Class and State in Ancien Régime France*, 159, 161, 163–5, 204. See also Asch, 'Kriegsfinanzierung, Staatsbildung und ständische Ordnung', 640–1; Hinrichs, 'Abschied vom Absolutismus?', in *Der Absolutismus – ein Mythos?*.

26 W. Beik, *Absolutism and Society in Seventeenth-Century France: State Power and Provincial Aristocracy in Languedoc* (Cambridge, 1985), 31, 244, 260–9, 277, 281, 304, 331; W. Beik, 'A Social Interpretation of the Reign of Louis XIV', in *L'état ou le roi*, 145–60 (quotations pp. 156, 160); Jouanna, *Le devoir de révolte*, 222, 244. See also Major, *From Renaissance Monarchy to Absolute Monarchy*, 314, 363–4, 375 and Parker, *Class and State in Ancien Régime France*, 144, 181, 187, 205–6.

27 It may be noted that 76.2 per cent of the 130 French bishops in 1789 came from *noblesse de race* families whose origins went back to before 1400. Only one bishop was non-noble, and two were of uncertain origins. By contrast, after the Wars of Religion, the proportion of non-nobles and persons of uncertain origins was 25 per cent. The change towards social exclusivity occurred in the seventeenth century. See O. Di Simplicio, 'Istituzioni e classi sociali: L'egemonia nobiliare', in *La storia: I grandi problemi dal Medioevo all'Età contemporanea*, vol. 3, *L'Età Moderna*, i, *I quadri generali*, ed. N. Tranfaglia and M. Firpo (Turin, 1987), 527–51, at 532–4.

28 D. H. Sacks, 'The Paradox of Taxation: Fiscal Crises, Parliament, and Liberty in England, 1450–1640', in *Fiscal Crises, Liberty, and Representative Government, 1450–1789*, ed. P. T. Hoffman and K. Norberg (Stanford, CA, 1994), 7–66, at 39, 51–3 (quotation p. 52); Brewer, *The Sinews of Power*, 7–13; Asch, *Der Hof Karls I. von England*, 302.

29 W. Reinhard, 'Kriegsstaat – Steuerstaat – Machtstaat', in *Der Absolutismus – ein Mythos?*, 277–310, at 286–7, 293, 306, 310; Brewer, *The Sinews of Power*, 21, 23–4; Ertman, *Birth of the Leviathan*, passim.

30 G. Parker, 'The Emergence of Modern Finance in Europe, 1500–1700,' in *The Fontana Economic History of Europe*, vol. 2, *The Sixteenth and Seventeenth Centuries*, ed. C. M. Cipolla (Glasgow, 1974), 527–94, at 577–89; Ertman, *Birth of the Leviathan*, 185–223; P. Kennedy, *The Rise and Fall of the Great Powers: Economic Change and Military Conflicts from 1500 to 2000* (London, 1988), 76–86; Asch, 'Kriegsfinanzierung,

Staatsbildung und ständische Ordnung', 659–66; Root, *The Fountain of Privilege*, 187–94; P. K. O'Brien, 'The Political Economy of British Taxation, 1660–1815', *Economic History Review*, 2nd ser., 41, no. 1 (1988), 1–32, at 12–17; Brewer, *The Sinews of Power*, 15, 24, 95–101, 129–34; C. Haigh, *Elizabeth I* (London, 1988), 61–2, 64; W. T. MacCaffrey, 'England: The Crown and the New Aristocracy', *Past and Present* 30 (1965), 52–64; J. H. Hexter, 'Lawrence Stone and the English Aristocracy', in his *On Historians: Reappraisals of Some of the Makers of Modern History* (London, 1979), 149–226, at 221–2; J. Cannon, 'The British Nobility, 1660–1800', in *The European Nobilities in the Seventeenth and Eighteenth Centuries*, I, 53–81, at 60–4. See also J. S. A. Adamson, 'The Baronial Context of the English Civil War,' *Transactions of the Royal Historical Society*, 5th ser., 40 (1990), 93–120, especially 115–20.

31 Asch, 'Kriegsfinanzierung, Staatsbildung und ständische Ordnung', 659 and n. 67.

32 Jouanna, *Le devoir de révolte*, 218–22.

6 Epilogue

1 D. Parker, *Class and State in Ancien Régime France: The Road to Modernity?* (London, 1996), 99.

2 See Chapter 1, n. 17, and Chapter 3.

3 See Chapter 3. Cf. Parker, *Class and State in Ancien Régime France*, 181–2, 267. For an eloquent articulation by a great noble of the need for a powerful, independent monarch, see A. Jouanna, *Le devoir de révolte: La noblesse française et la gestation de l'État moderne, 1559–1661* (Paris, 1989), 220. Quotation from P. de Commynes, *Memoirs: The Reign of Louis XI, 1461–83*, trans. M. Jones (Harmondsworth, 1972), 113.

4 J.-P. Genet, 'Féodalisme et naissance de l'état moderne: À propos des thèses de Charles Tilly', in *Villes, bonnes villes, cités et capitales: Études d'histoire urbaine (XIIe–XVIIIe siècles) offertes à Bernard Chevalier*, ed. M. Bourin, 2nd edn (Caen, 1993), 239–46 (quotation p. 243). See also O. Brunner, 'Europäisches Bauerntum', in his *Neue Wege der Verfassungs- und Sozialgeschichte*, 3rd edn (Göttingen, 1980), 199–212.

5 F. L. Ganshof, *Feudalism*, trans. P. Grierson, 3rd edn (New York, 1964), 169–70. Quotations from R. Seyboth, *Die Markgraftümer Ansbach und Kulmbach unter der Regierung Markgraf Friedrichs des Älteren (1486– 1515)* (Göttingen, 1985), 248; P. D. Lagomarsino, 'Court Faction and the Formulation of Spanish Policy towards the Netherlands (1559–67)' (Cambridge University Ph.D. thesis, 1973), 119.

6 Cf. C. J. Jago, 'The "Crisis of the Aristocracy" in Seventeenth-Century Castile', *Past and Present* 84 (1979), 60–90, at 86; J.-M. Constant, *La noblesse française aux XVIe et XVIIe siècles* (Paris, 1985), 260.

7 See examples given in Chapters 2, 3, 4, and 5. Cf. C. J. Jago, 'Aristocracy, War, and Finance in Castile, 1621–1665: The Titled Nobility and the House of Béjar during the Reign of Philip IV'. (Cambridge University PhD thesis, 1969), 378. For the some of the difficulties facing nobles' joint political ventures see M. Jahss LeGates, 'The Knights and the Problem of Political Organizing in Sixteenth-Century Germany', *Central European History* 7 (1974), 99–136.

8 Cf. W. Hörsch, 'Adel im Bannkreis Österreichs: Strukturen der Herr-schaftsnähe im Raum Aargau-Luzern', in G. P. Marchal, *Sempach 1386: Von den Anfängen des Territorialstaates Luzern: Beitrag zur Früh-geschichte des Kantons Luzern* (Basel, 1986), 353–402. See also Genet, 'Féodalisme et naissance de l'état moderne', 242.

9 J. Dewald, *The European Nobility, 1400–1800* (Cambridge, 1996), 145–6; J. Swann, 'The French Nobility, 1715–1789', in *The European Nobilities in the Seventeenth and Eighteenth Centuries*, ed. H. M. Scott, 2 vols (London, 1995), I, 142–73, at 168–9; H. M. Scott and C. Storrs, 'Introduction: The Consolidation of Noble Power in Europe, c.1600–1800', in ibid., 1–52, at 49; Parker, *Class and State in Ancien Régime France*, 206; T. Johnson and C. Dandeker, 'Patronage: Relation and System', in *Patronage in Ancient Society*, ed. A. Wallace-Hadrill (London, 1989), 219–42, at 229–30; S. Kettering, 'The Decline of Great Noble Clientage during the Reign of Louis XIV', *Canadian Journal of History* 24 (1989), 157–77, at 168–9; J. R. Major, *From Renaissance Monarchy to Absolute Monarchy: French Kings, Nobles and Estates* (Baltimore, 1994), 305, 330–1, 335, 374–5.

10 I. A. A. Thompson, 'The Nobility in Spain, 1600–1800', in *The European Nobilities in the Seventeenth and Eighteenth Centuries*, I, 174–236, at 219; C. J. Jago, 'La Corona y la aristocracia durante el régimen de Olivares: Un representante de la aristocracia en la Corte', in *La España del Conde Duque de Olivares*, ed. J. H. Elliott and A. García Sanz (Valladolid, 1990), 373–97, at 377–8, 397. Quotation from Jago, 'The "Crisis of the Aristo-cracy" in Seventeenth-Century Castile', 86.

11 See Chapter 4; Jouanna, *Le devoir de révolte*, 196, 199, 237, 262–70; Major, *From Renaissance Monarchy to Absolute Monarchy*, 306. Quotation from J. H. Shennan, *The Origins of the Modern European State, 1450–1725* (London, 1974), 69.

12 Jouanna, *Le devoir de révolte*, 199–200, 212–44, especially 218, 236; A. Jouanna, 'La noblesse gardienne des lois du royaume: Un modèle politique proposé pendant les Guerres de Religion en France', in *Nobilitas: Funktion und Repräsentation des Adels in Alteuropa*, ed. O. G. Oexle and W. Paravicini (Göttingen, 1996), 177–92, at 191–2.

13 J.-M. Constant, 'La troisième Fronde: Les gentilshommes et les libertés nobiliares', *XVIIe siècle* 145 (1984), 341–54; J.-M. Constant, *La noblesse française aux XVIe et XVIIe siècles*, 251–60; Jouanna, *Le devoir de révolte*, 263–70.

14 See Chapter 4; T. Winkelbauer, 'Krise der Aristokratie?: Zum Struktur-wandel des Adels in den böhmischen und niederösterreichischen Ländern im 16. und 17. Jahrhundert', *Mitteilungen des Instituts für österreichische Geschichte* 100 (1992), 328–53, at 352–3; G. Heilingsetzer, 'The Austrian Nobility, 1600–1650: Between Court and Estates', in *Crown, Church and Estates: Central European Politics in the Sixteenth and Seventeenth Centuries*, ed. R. J. W. Evans and T. V. Thomas (New York, 1991), 245–60, at 247; K. J. MacHardy, 'The Rise of Absolutism and Noble Rebellion in Early Modern Habsburg Austria, 1570–1620', *Comparative Studies in Society and History* 34 (1992), 407–38.

15 See Chapter 3. Cf. Jahss LeGates, 'The Knights and the Problem of Political Organizing', especially 134.

16 J. P. Cooper, 'General Introduction', in *The New Cambridge Modern History*, vol. 4, *The Decline of Spain and the Thirty Years War, 1609–48/59*, ed. J. P. Cooper (Cambridge, 1970), 1–66, at 18; S. E. Finer, *The History of Government from the Earliest Times*, 3 vols (Oxford, 1997), 47; O. Brunner, *Adeliges Landleben und europäischer Geist: Leben und Werk Wolf Helmhards von Hohberg 1612–1688* (Salzburg, 1949), 325; Jago, 'Aristocracy, War, and Finance in Castile, 1621–1665', 378.

17 Cf. Parker, *Class and State in Ancien Régime France*, 266. Quotation from C. Haigh, *Elizabeth I* (London, 1988), 61.

18 Dewald, *The European Nobility*, 193, 199–200; E. Schalk, *From Valor to Pedigree: Ideas of Nobility in France in the Sixteenth and Seventeenth Centuries* (Princeton, 1986), 211–12; Swann, 'The French Nobility, 1715–1789,' 147; J. Casey, *Early Modern Spain: A Social History* (London, 1999), 144; O. Di Simplicio, 'Istituzioni e classi sociali: L'egemonia nobiliare', in *La storia: I grandi problemi dal Medioevo all'Età contemporanea*, vol. 3, *L'Età Moderna*, i, *I quadri generali*, ed. N. Tranfaglia and M. Firpo (Turin, 1987), 527–51, at 546. See also J. Casey, *The History of the Family* (Oxford, 1989), 39.

19 J.-P. Genet, 'L'état moderne: Un modèle opératoire?', in *Genèse de l'état moderne: Bilans et perspectives*, ed. J.-P. Genet (Paris, 1990), 261–81, at 278; J.-P. Genet, 'Which State Rises?', *Historical Research* 65 (1992), 119–33, especially 128, 132; T. A. Brady, Jr, 'The Rise of Merchant Empires, 1400–1700: A European Counterpoint', in *The Political Economy of Merchant Empires*, ed. J. D. Tracy (Cambridge, 1997 [1991]), 117–60, at 147–8; Shennan, *The Origins of the Modern European State*, 10. See also Chapter 1.

20 J. H. Shennan, *Liberty and Order in Early Modern Europe: The Subject and the State 1650–1800* (London, 1986), 35; O. Brunner, 'Die Freiheitsrechte in der altständischen Gesellschaft', in his *Neue Wege der Verfassungs- und Sozialgeschichte*, 187–98, especially 197–8. See also G. Stourzh, 'The Modern State: Equal Rights. Equalizing the Individual's Status and the Breakthrough of the Modern Liberal State', in *The Individual in Political Theory and Practice*, ed. J. Coleman (Oxford, 1996), 303–27. 'Mortal God', from T. Hobbes, *Leviathan*, ed. R. Tuck, rev. edn. (Cambridge, 1996), 120.

21 C. Dipper, 'La noblesse allemande à l'époque de la bourgeoisie: Adaptation et continuité', in *Les noblesses européennes au xixᵉ siècle*, ed. G. Delille (Rome, 1988), 165–97; G. Delille, 'Introduction', in ibid., 1–12, at 10; Dewald, *The European Nobility*, 191; Finer, *The History of Government*, 1478. Quotations respectively from H. Möller, 'Aufklärung und Adel', in *Adel und Bürgertum in Deutschland, 1770–1850*, ed. E. Fehrenbach (Munich, 1994), 1–9, at 6 and n. 20; E. J. Sieyès, *What is the Third Estate?*, ed. S. E. Finer, trans. M. Blondel (London, 1963), 57–8; H. M. Scott, 'Conclusion: The Continuity of Aristocratic Power', in *The European Nobilities in the Seventeenth and Eighteenth Centuries*, II, 274–91, at 280.

22 Scott, 'Conclusion: The Continuity of Aristocratic Power', 289–91; Brunner, *Adeliges Landleben und europäischer Geist*, 316–17, 321, 336–7; O. Brunner, 'Das Zeitalter der Ideologien: Anfang und Ende', in his *Neue Wege der Verfassungs- und Sozialgeschichte*, 45–63, at 54–5; O. Brunner,

'Vom Gottesgnadentum zum monarchischen Prinzip', ibid., 160–86, at 178–9; J. Van Horn Melton, 'The Nobility in the Bohemian and Austrian Lands, 1620–1780', in *The European Nobilities in the Seventeenth and Eighteenth Centuries*, II, 110–43, at 143; Finer, *The History of Government*, 1454.

23 Thompson, 'The Nobility in Spain, 1600–1800', 193, 220–36 (quotations pp. 224, 225); Shennan, *Liberty and Order in Early Modern Europe*, 57–9; H. Nader, *Liberty in Absolutist Spain: The Habsburg Sale of Towns, 1516–1700* (Baltimore, 1990), 15–16.

24 E. Gellner, *Conditions of Liberty: Civil Society and its Rivals* (London, 1994), 74–5; Parker, *Class and State in Ancien Régime France*, 221, 259. Quotation from Shennan, *Liberty and Order in Early Modern Europe*, 19. See also Shennan, *The Origins of the Modern European State*, 99.

25 Cf. Chapter 3; Parker, *Class and State in Ancien Régime France*, 278 (quotation 276); J. V. Beckett, *The Aristocracy in England, 1660–1914* (Oxford, 1986), 403–6; G. E. Aylmer, 'The Peculiarities of the English State', *Journal of Historical Sociology* 3 (1990), 91–108, at 105; C. S. R. Russell, 'Monarchies, Wars, and Estates in England, France, and Spain, c.1580-c.1640', *Legislative Studies Quarterly* 7 (1982), 205–21; O. Di Simplicio, 'La nobiltà europea', in *La storia: I grandi problemi dal Medioevo all'Età contemporanea*, vol. 3, *L'Età moderna*, i, *I quadri generali*, 487–526, at 508, 517–18; J. Cannon, 'The British Nobility, 1660–1800', in *The European Nobilities in the Seventeenth and Eighteenth Centuries*, I, 53–81, at 75–6.

26 Cf. G. Chittolini, 'The "Private," the "Public," the State', in *The Origins of the State in Italy 1300–1600*, ed. J. Kirshner (Chicago, 1996), 34–6, at 50–1; R. R. Harding, *Anatomy of a Power Elite: The Provincial Governors of Early Modern France* (New Haven, 1978), 216; Parker, *Class and State in Ancien Régime France*, 221–2, 278–9.

27 Cf. W. Beik, *Absolutism and Society in Seventeenth-Century France: State Power and Provincial Aristocracy in Languedoc* (Cambridge, 1985), 332, 335–6, 338; Jouanna, *Le devoir de révolte*, 221–2; B. Yun Casalilla, 'The Castilian Aristocracy in the Seventeenth Century: Crisis, Refeudalisation, or Political Offensive?', in *The Castilian Crisis of the Seventeenth Century*, ed. I. A. A. Thompson and B. Yun Casalilla (Cambridge, 1994), 277–300, especially 287–8, 298.

28 Finer, *The History of Government*, 47–9; Shennan, *Liberty and Order in Early Modern Europe*, 33–5; D. Outram, *The Enlightenment* (Cambridge, 1995), 109–13. Quotations from C. de Secondat, Baron de Montesquieu, *The Spirit of the Laws*, ed. and trans. A. M. Cohler, B. C. Miller and H. M. Stone (Cambridge, 1989), 17, 18.

29 Shennan, *Liberty and Order in Early Modern Europe*, 34–5, 36–9; Brunner, 'Vom Gottesgnadentum zum monarchischen Prinzip', 178–9; A. Jouanna, 'Die Legitimierung des Adels und die Erhebung in den Adelsstand in Frankreich (16.-18. Jahrhundert)', in *Ständische Gesellschaft und soziale Mobilität*, ed. W. Schulze (Munich, 1988), 165–77, at 172–3; Sieyès, *What is the Third Estate?*, 59–60. Quotation from J. Cannon, *Aristocratic Century: The Peerage of Eighteenth-Century England* (Cambridge, 1984), 168.

30 Jouanna, *Le devoir de révolte*, 222. See also Chapter 5; Beik, *Absolutism and Society in Seventeenth-Century France*, 338.

31 Beckett, *The Aristocracy in England*, 406–11, 434–5; H. Berghoff, 'Adel und Bürgertum in England 1770–1850: Ergebnisse der neueren Elitenforschung', in *Adel und Bürgertum in Deutschland*, 95–127; M. Thompson, 'The Landed Aristocracy and Business Elites in Victorian Britain', in *Les noblesses européennes au xixe siècle*, 267–79. See also Cannon, 'The British Nobility', 80–1. Quotation from Berghoff, 'Adel und Bürgertum in England', 102 (citing W. D. Rubinstein, *Men of Property: The Very Wealthy in Britain since the Industrial Revolution* [London, 1981], 61).

32 Beckett, *The Aristocracy in England*, 461; Berghoff, 'Adel und Bürgertum in England', 102, 108–9. W. Bagehot, *The English Constitution*, edn of 1928 (London), 83.

Select bibliography

Anderson, P. *Lineages of the Absolutist State*. London, 1974.

Arriaza, A. J. 'Nobility in Renaissance Castile: The Formation of the Juristic Structure of Nobiliary Ideology'. University of Iowa PhD thesis, 1980.

Asch, R. G. 'Introduction: Court and Household from the Fifteenth to the Seventeenth Centuries.' In *Princes, Patronage, and the Nobility: The Court at the Beginning of the Modern Age c. 1450–1650*, ed. R. G. Asch and A. M. Birke, 1–38. Oxford, 1991.

Asch, R. G. *Der Hof Karls I. von England: Politik, Provinz und Patronage, 1625–1640*. Cologne, 1993.

Asch, R. G. 'Kriegsfinanzierung, Staatsbildung und ständische Ordnung in Westeuropa im 17. und 18. Jahrhundert'. *Historische Zeitschrift* 268 (1999), 635–71.

Aylmer, G. E. 'The Peculiarities of the English State'. *Journal of Historical Sociology* 3 (1990), 91–108.

Basin, T. *Histoire de Charles VII*. Edited by C. Samaran. Vol. 2. Paris, 1965.

Beceiro Pita, I. 'Doléances et ligues de la noblesse dans la Castile de la fin du moyen âge (1420–1464)'. In *Genèse médiévale de l'Espagne moderne: Du refus à la révolte: Les résistances*, ed. A. Rucquoi, 107–26. Nice, 1991.

Beckett, J. V. *The Aristocracy in England, 1660–1914*. Oxford, 1986.

Beik, W. *Absolutism and Society in Seventeenth-Century France: State Power and Provincial Aristocracy in Languedoc*. Cambridge, 1985.

Beik, W. 'A Social Interpretation of the Reign of Louis XIV'. In *L'état ou le roi: Les fondations de la modernité monarchique en France (xive–xviie siècles)*, ed. N. Bulst, R. Descimon and A. Guerreau, 145–60. Paris, 1996.

Berghoff, H. 'Adel und Bürgertum in England 1770–1850: Ergebnisse der neueren Elitenforschung'. In *Adel und Bürgertum in Deutschland, 1770–1850*, ed. E. Fehrenbach, 95–127. Munich, 1994.

Bernard, G. W. 'La noblesse anglaise sous Henri VIII'. In *Pouvoir et institutions en Europe au XVIème siècle*, ed. A. Stegmann, 153–62. Paris, 1987.

Bernard, G. W. 'Introduction: The Tudor Nobility in Perspective'. In *The Tudor Nobility*, ed. G. W. Bernard, 1–48. Manchester, 1992.

Billacois, F. 'La crise de la noblesse européene (1550–1650): Une mise au point'. *Revue d'histoire moderne et contemporaine* 23 (1976), 258–77.

Bittmann, K. *Ludwig XI und Karl der Kühne: Die Memoiren des Philippe de Commynes als historische Quelle*. 2 vols. Göttingen, 1964–70.

Bois, G. 'Noblesse et crise des revenues seigneuriaux en France aux XIVᵉ et XVᵉ siècles: Essai d'interprétation'. In *La noblesse au moyen âge, XIᵉ–XVᵉ siècles: Essais à la mémoire de Robert Boutruche*, ed. P. Contamine, 219–33. Paris, 1976.

Bouchard, C. B. *'Strong of Body, Brave and Noble': Chivalry and Society in Medieval France*. Ithaca, 1998.

Brady, T. A. Jr. *Turning Swiss: Cities and Empire, 1450–1550*. Cambridge, 1985.

Brewer, J. *The Sinews of Power: War, Money and the English State, 1688–1783*. Cambridge, MA, 1988.

Brunner, O. *Adeliges Landleben und europäischer Geist: Leben und Werk Wolf Helmhards von Hohberg 1612–1688*. Salzburg, 1949.

Brunner, O. *Neue Wege der Verfassungs- und Sozialgeschichte*. 3rd edn. Göttingen, 1980.

Calabria, A. *The Cost of Empire: The Finances of the Kingdom of Naples in the Time of Spanish Rule*. Cambridge, 1991.

Cannon, J. 'The British Nobility, 1660–1800'. In *The European Nobilities in the Seventeenth and Eighteenth Centuries*, ed. H. M. Scott, vol. 1, 53–81. London, 1995.

Caron, M.-T. *Noblesse et pouvoir royal en France: XIIIᵉ–XVIᵉ siècle*. Paris, 1994.

Carpenter, C. *The Wars of the Roses: Politics and the Constitution in England, c.1437–1509*. Cambridge, 1997.

Casey, J. *Early Modern Spain: A Social History*. London, 1999.

Chaunu, P. 'L'état.' In *Histoire économique et sociale de la France*, ed. F. Braudel and E. Labrousse, vol. 1, *L'état et la ville*, 9–228. Paris, 1977.

Chittolini, G. 'The "Private," the "Public," the State'. In *The Origins of the State in Italy 1300–1600*, ed. J. Kirshner, 34–61. Chicago, 1996.

Clark, S. *State and Status: The Rise of the State and Aristocratic Power in Western Europe*. Cardiff, 1995.

Commynes, P. de. *Memoirs: The Reign of Louis XI, 1461–83*. Translated by M. Jones. Harmondsworth, 1972.

Constant, J.-M. *La noblesse française aux XVIᵉ et XVIIᵉ siècles*. Paris, 1985.

Contamine, P. *Guerre, état et société à la fin du moyen âge: Études sur les armées des rois de France 1337–1494*. Paris, 1972.

Contamine, P. 'France at the End of the Middle Ages: Who Was then the Gentleman'. In *Gentry and Lesser Nobility in Late Medieval Europe*, ed. M. Jones, 201–16. Gloucester, 1986.

Contamine, P. *La noblesse au royaume de France de Philippe le Bel à Louis XII: Essai de synthèse*. Paris, 1997.

Cooper, J. P. 'General Introduction'. In *The New Cambridge Modern History*, vol. 4, *The Decline of Spain and the Thirty Years War, 1609–48/59*, ed. J. P. Cooper, 1–66. Cambridge, 1970.

Dessert, D. 'Le rôle de la noblesse dans le finances royales sous le règne de Louis XIV'. In *La fiscalité et ses implications sociales en Italie et en France au XVIIᵉ et XVIIIᵉ siècles, 175–90*. Rome, 1980.

Dessert, D. *Argent, pouvoir et société au Grand Siècle*. Paris, 1984.

Devyver, A. *Le sang épuré: Les préjugés de race chez les gentilshommes français de l'Ancien Régime, 1560–1720*. Brussels, 1973.

Dewald, J. *Aristocratic Experience and the Origins of Modern Culture: France, 1570–1715*. Berkeley, 1993.

Dewald, J. *The European Nobility, 1400–1800*. Cambridge, 1996.

Dios, S. de. *El Consejo Real de Castilla (1385–1522)*. Madrid, 1982.

Dipper, C. 'La noblesse allemande à l'époque de la bourgeoisie: Adaptation et continuité'. In *Les noblesses européennes au xixᵉ siècle*, ed. G. Delille, 165–97. Rome, 1988.

Discours d'un genti-homme François à la Noblesse de France, sur l'ouverture de l'assemblee des Estats generaux dans la ville de Paris en ceste annee 1614. Avec deux advertissemens particuliers à Mʳˢ les Deputez du Clergé & de la Nobleße. N.p., 1614.

Di Simplicio, O. 'La nobiltà europea'. In *La storia: I grandi problemi dal Medioevo all'Età contemporanea*, vol. 3, *L'Età moderna, i, I quadri generali*, ed. N. Tranfaglia and M. Firpo, 487–526. Turin, 1987.

Di Simplicio, O. 'Istituzioni e classi sociali: L'egemonia nobiliare.' in *La storia: I grandi problemi dal Medioevo all'Età contemporanea*, vol. 3, *L'Età Moderna, i, I quadri generali*, ed. N. Tranfaglia and M. Firpo, 527–51. Turin, 1987.

Dobson, R. B. (ed.). *The Peasants' Revolt of 1381*. London, 1970.

Donati, C. *L'idea di nobiltà in Italia: Secoli XIV–XVIII*. Bari, 1988.

Dravasa, E. '"Vivre noblement": Recherches sur la dérogeance de noblesse du XIVᵉ au XVIᵉ siècle'. Parts 1 and 2. *Revue juridique et économique du Sud-Ouest, série juridique* 16 (1965), 135–93; 17 (1966), 23–129.

Elliott, J. H. 'Revolution and Continuity in Early Modern Europe'. In his *Spain and its World 1500–1700: Selected Essays*, 92–113. New Haven, 1989.

Elliott, J. H. 'The Court of the Spanish Habsburgs: A Peculiar Institution'. In his *Spain and its World 1500–1700: Selected Essays*, 142–61. New Haven, 1989.

Engels, O. 'Die Krise in Kastilien während des 14. Jahrhunderts'. In *Europa 1400: Die Krise des Spätmittelalters*, ed. F. Seibt and W. Eberhard, 257–66. Stuttgart, 1984.

Ernst, F. *Eberhard im Bart: Die Politik eines deutschen Landesherrn am Ende des Mittelalters*. 1933. Reprint, Darmstadt, 1970.

Ertman, T. *Birth of the Leviathan: Building States and Regimes in Medieval and Early Modern Europe*. Cambridge, 1997.

Evans, R. J. W. *The Making of the Habsburg Monarchy 1550–1700: An Interpretation*. Oxford, 1979.

Fayard, J., and Gerbet, M.-C. 'Fermeture de la noblesse et pureté de sang en Castille: À travers les procès de *hidalguía* au XVIème siècle'. *Histoire, économie et société* (1982), 51–75.

Finer, S. E. *The History of Government from the Earliest Times*. 3 vols. Oxford, 1997.

Froissart, J. *Chronicles*. Edited by G. Brereton. Harmondsworth, 1978.

Gaussin, P.-R. 'Les conseillers de Charles VII (1418–61): Essai de politologie historique'. *Francia* 10 (1982), 67–130.

Gaussin, P.-R. 'Les conseillers de Louis XI (1461–83).' In *La France de la fin du XVe siècle: Renouveau et apogée*, ed. B. Chevalier and P. Contamine, 105–34. Paris, 1985.

Genet, J.-P. 'L'état moderne: Un modèle opératoire?' In *Genèse de l'état moderne: Bilans et perspectives*, ed. J.-P. Genet, 261–81. Paris, 1990.

Genet, J.-P. 'Which State Rises?' *Historical Research* 65 (1992), 119–33.

Genet, J.-P. 'Féodalisme et naissance de l'état moderne: À propos des thèses de Charles Tilly'. In *Villes, bonnes villes, cités et capitales: Études d'histoire urbaine (XIIe–XVIIIe siècles) offertes à Bernard Chevalier*, ed. M. Bourin, 2nd edn, 239–46. Caen, 1993.

Genicot, L. 'La noblesse au moyen âge dans l'ancienne "Francie": Continuité, rupture ou évolution'. *Comparative Studies in Society and History* 5 (1962–3), 52–9.

Genicot, L. 'La noblesse médiévale: Encore!' *Revue d'histoire ecclésiastique* 88 (1993), 173–201.

Gerbet, M.-C. *Les noblesses espagnoles au moyen âge: XIe–XVe siècle*. Paris, 1995.

Given-Wilson, C. *The English Nobility in the Late Middle Ages: The Fourteenth Century Political Community*. London, 1987.

Greengrass, M. 'Noble Affinities in Early Modern France: The Case of Henri I de Montmorency, Constable of France'. *European History Quarterly* 16 (1986), 275–311.

Greengrass, M. 'Property and Politics in Sixteenth-Century France: The Landed Fortune of Constable Anne de Montmorency'. *French History* (1988), 371–98.

Greengrass, M. 'Functions and Limits of Political Clientilism in France before Cardinal Richelieu'. In *L'état ou le roi: Les fondations de la modernité monarchique en France (xive–xviie siècles)*, ed. N. Bulst, R. Descimon and A. Guerreau, 69–82. Paris, 1996.

Greindl, G. 'Der alte Adel in der bayerischen Landschaft des 16. Jahrhunderts'. In *Aus Bayerns Geschichte: Forschungen als Festgabe zum 70. Geburtstag von Andreas Kraus*, ed. E. J. Greipl *et al.*, 217–43. St Ottilien, 1992.

Guéry, A. 'Le roi dépensier: Le don, la contrainte, et l'origine du système financier de la monarchie française d'Ancien Régime'. *Annales: E.S.C.* 39 (1984), 1241–69.

Gunn, S. J. *Early Tudor Government, 1485–1558*. Basingstoke, 1995.

Guy, J. A. 'The French King's Council, 1483–1526'. In *Kings and Nobles in the Later Middle Ages: A Tribute to Charles Ross*, ed. R. A. Griffiths and J. Sherborne, 274–94. Gloucester, 1986.

Haigh, C. *Elizabeth I*. London, 1988.

Haliczer, S. 'The Castilian Aristocracy and the Mercedes Reform of 1478–1482'. *The Hispanic American Historical Review* 55 (1975), 449–67.

Hamon, P. *L'argent du roi: Les finances sous François Ier*. Paris, 1994.

Harding, R. R. *Anatomy of a Power Elite: The Provincial Governors of Early Modern France*. New Haven, 1978.

Harriss, G. L. *King, Parliament, and Public Finance in Medieval England to 1369*. Oxford, 1975.

Harriss, G. L. 'Political Society and the Growth of Government in Late Medieval England'. *Past and Present* 138 (1993), 28–57.

Harsgor, M. 'Maîtres d'un royaume: Le groupe dirigeant français à la fin du XVe siècle'. In *La France de la fin du XVe siècle: Renouveau et apogée*, ed. B. Chevalier and P. Contamine, 135–46. Paris, 1985.

Henneman, J. B. *Royal Taxation in Fourteenth Century France: The Development of War Financing, 1322–1356*. Princeton, 1971.

Henneman, J. B. *Royal Taxation in Fourteenth-Century France: The Captivity and Ransom of John II, 1356–1370*. Philadelphia, 1976.

Henneman, J. B. 'The Military Class and the French Monarchy in the Late Middle Ages'. *The American Historical Review* 83, 4 (1978), 946–65.

Henneman, J. B. 'Nobility, Privilege and Fiscal Politics in Late Medieval France'. *French Historical Studies* 13, 1 (1983), 1–17.

Henneman, J. B. *Olivier de Clisson and Political Society in France under Charles V and Charles VI*. Philadelphia, 1996.

Henshall, N. 'Early Modern Absolutism 1550–1700: Political Reality or Propaganda?' In *Der Absolutismus – ein Mythos?: Strukturwandel monarchischer Herrschaft in West- und Mitteleuropa (ca. 1550–1700)*, ed. R. G. Asch and H. Durchhardt, 25–53. Cologne, 1996.

Hinrichs, E. 'Abschied vom Absolutismus?: Eine Antwort auf Nicholas Henshall'. In *Der Absolutismus – ein Mythos?: Strukturwandel monarchischer Herrschaft in West- und Mitteleuropa (ca. 1550–1700)*, ed. R. G. Asch and H. Durchhardt, 353–71. Cologne, 1996.

Hörsch, W. 'Adel im Bannkreis Österreichs: Strukturen der Herrschaftsnähe im Raum Aargau-Luzern'. In G. P. Marchal, *Sempach 1386: Von den Anfängen des Territorialstaates Luzern: Beitrag zur Frühgeschichte des Kantons Luzern*, 353–402. Basel, 1986.

Jago, C. J. 'Aristocracy, War, and Finance in Castile, 1621–1665: The Titled Nobility and the House of Béjar during the Reign of Philip IV'. Cambridge University PhD thesis, 1969.

Jago, C. J. 'The Influence of Debt on the Relations between Crown and Aristocracy in Seventeenth-Century Castile'. *The Economic History Review* 26 (1973), 218–36.

Jago, C. J. 'The "Crisis of the Aristocracy" in Seventeenth-Century Castile'. *Past and Present* 84 (1979), 60–90.

Jahss LeGates, M. 'The Knights and the Problem of Political Organizing in Sixteenth-Century Germany'. *Central European History* 7 (1974), 99–136.

Johnson T. and Dandeker, C. 'Patronage: Relation and System'. In *Patronage in Ancient Society*, ed. A. Wallace-Hadrill, 219–42. London, 1989.

146 *Select bibliography*

Jones, M. 'The Late Medieval State and Social Change: A View from the Duchy of Brittany'. In *L'état ou le roi: Les fondations de la modernité monarchique en France (XIVe-XVIIe siècles)*, ed. N. Bulst, R. Descimon and A. Guerreau, 117–44. Paris, 1996.

Jordan, W. K. *Edward VI: The Young King: The Protectorship of the Duke of Somerset*. London, 1968.

Jouanna, A. 'Die Legitimierung des Adels und die Erhebung in den Adelsstand in Frankreich (16.-18. Jahrhundert)'. In *Ständische Gesellschaft und soziale Mobilität*, ed. W. Schulze, 165–77. Munich, 1988.

Jouanna, A. *Le devoir de révolte: La noblesse française et la gestation de l'État moderne, 1559–1661*. Paris, 1989.

Jouanna, A. 'La noblesse gardienne des lois du royaume: Un modèle politique proposé pendant les Guerres de Religion en France'. In *Nobilitas: Funktion und Repräsentation des Adels in Alteuropa*, ed. O. G. Oexle and W. Paravicini, 177–92. Göttingen, 1996.

Kaminsky, H. 'Estate, Nobility, and the Exhibition of Estate in the Later Middle Ages'. *Speculum* 68 (1993), 684–709.

Keen, M. *Chivalry*. New Haven, 1984.

Kennedy, P. *The Rise and Fall of the Great Powers: Economic Change and Military Conflicts from 1500 to 2000*. London, 1988.

Kettering, S. *Patrons, Brokers, and Clients in Seventeenth-Century France*. Oxford, 1986.

Kettering, S. 'The Decline of Great Noble Clientage during the Reign of Louis XIV'. *Canadian Journal of History* 24 (1989), 157–77.

Ladero Quesada, M. A. 'Ingresso, gasto y política fiscal de la Corona de Castilla: Desde Alfonso X a Enrique III (1252–1406)'. In his *El siglo XV en Castilla: Fuenetes de renta y política fiscal*, 13–57. Barcelona, 1982.

Ladero Quesada, M. A. 'La genèse de l'état dans les royaumes hispaniques médiévaux (1250–1450)'. In *Le premier âge de l'état en Espagne (1450–1700)*, ed. C. Hermann, 9–65. Paris, 1989.

Lagomarsino, P. D. 'Court Faction and the Formulation of Spanish Policy towards the Netherlands (1559–67)'. Cambridge University, PhD thesis, 1973.

Lander, J. R. *Crown and Nobility, 1450–1509*. London, 1976.

McFarlane, K. B. *The Nobility of Later Medieval England: The Ford Lectures for 1953 and Related Studies*. Oxford, 1973.

MacHardy, K. J. 'The Rise of Absolutism and Noble Rebellion in Early Modern Habsburg Austria, 1570–1620'. *Comparative Studies in Society and History* 34 (1992), 407–38.

Machiavelli, N. *The Discourses*. Edited by B. Crick. Harmondsworth, 1970.

Machiavelli, N. *The Prince*. Edited by Q. Skinner and R. Price. Cambridge, 1988.

MacKay, A. *Spain in the Middle Ages: From Frontier to Empire, 1000–1500*. London, 1977.

Major, J. R. *From Renaissance Monarchy to Absolute Monarchy: French Kings, Nobles and Estates*. Baltimore, 1994.

Maltby, W. S. *Alba: A Biography of Fernando Alvarez de Toledo, Third Duke of Alba, 1507–1582*. Berkeley, 1983.

Menjot, D. 'L'établissement du système fiscal étatique en Castilla (1268–1342)'. In *Génesis medieval del estado moderno: Castilla y Navarra (1250–1370)*, 149–72. Valladolid, 1987.

Molho, A. *Marriage Alliance in Late Medieval Florence*. Cambridge, MA, 1994.

Molho, A. 'The State and Public Finance: A Hypothesis Based on the History of Late Medieval Florence'. In *The Origins of the State in Italy 1300–1600*, ed. J. Kirshner, 97–135. Chicago, 1996.

Moraw, P. *Von offener Verfassung zu gestalteter Verdichtung: Das Reich im späten Mittelalter 1250 bis 1490*. Frankfurt am Main, 1985.

Moraw, P. 'Fürstentum, Königtum und "Reichsreform" im deutschen Spätmittelalter'. *Blätter für deutsche Landesgeschichte* 122 (1986), 117–36.

Morsel, J. 'Die Erfindung des Adels: Zur Soziogenese des Adels am Ende des Mittelalters – das Beispiel Frankens'. In *Nobilitas: Funktion und Repräsentation des Adels in Alteuropa*, ed. O. G. Oexle and W. Paravicini, 312–75. Göttingen, 1997.

Mourier, J. 'Nobilitas, quid est?: Un procès à Tain-l'Hermitage en 1408'. *Bibliothèque de l'École des Chartes* 142 (1984), 255–69.

Moxó, S. de. 'De la nobleza vieja a la nobleza nueva: La transformación nobiliaria castellana en la Baja Edad Media'. *Cuadernos de Historia* 3 (1969), 1–210.

Müller, R. A. *Der Fürstenhof in der Frühen Neuzeit*. Munich, 1995.

Müller, U. *Die ständische Vertretung in den fränkischen Markgraftümern in der ersten Hälfte des 16. Jahrhundert*. Neustadt an der Aisch, 1984.

Nader, H. 'Noble Income in Sixteenth-Century Castile: The Case of the Marquises of Mondéjar, 1480–1580'. *The Economic History Review*, 2nd ser., 30 (1977), 411–28.

Nader, H. *The Mendoza Family in the Spanish Renaissance, 1350 to 1550*. New Brunswick, NJ, 1979.

Nader, H. *Liberty in Absolutist Spain: The Habsburg Sale of Towns, 1516–1700*. Baltimore, 1990.

Neuber, W. 'Adeliges Landleben in Österreich und die Literatur im 16. und im 17. Jahrhundert'. In *Adel im Wandel: Politik, Kultur, Konfession 1500–1700*, ed. H. Knittler, G. Stangler and R. Zedlinger, 543–53. Vienna, 1990.

Nierop, H. F. K. van. 'Willem van Oranje als hoog edelman: Patronage in de Habsburgse Nederlanden?' *Bijdragen en mededelingen betreffende de geschiedenis der Nederlanden* 99 (1984), 651–76.

Nierop, H. K. F. van. *The Nobility of Holland: From Knights to Regents, 1500–1650*. Translated by M. Ultee. Cambridge, 1993.

Oberhammer, E. (ed.) *Der ganzen Welt ein Lob und Spiegel: Das Fürstenhaus Liechtenstein in der frühen Neuzeit*. Munich, 1990.

Orlea, M. *La noblesse aux États généraux de 1576 et de 1588: Étude politique et sociale*. Paris, 1980.

Oudendijk, J. K. 'Den coninck van Hispaengien heb ick altijt gheeert'. In *Dancwerc: Opstellen aangeboden aan Prof. Dr D. Th. Enklaar*, 264–78. Groningen, 1959.

Paravicini, W. *Guy de Brimeu: Der burgundische Staat und seine adlige Führungsschicht unter Karl dem Kühnen*. Bonn, 1975.

Parker, D. *Class and State in Ancien Régime France: The Road to Modernity?* London, 1996.

Parker, G. 'The Emergence of Modern Finance in Europe, 1500–1700'. In *The Fontana Economic History of Europe*, vol. 2, *The Sixteenth and Seventeenth Centuries*, ed. C. M. Cipolla, 527–94. Glasgow, 1974.

Parker, G. *The Dutch Revolt*. Rev. edn. Harmondsworth, 1985.

Parrott, D. 'Richelieu, the *Grands*, and the French Army'. In *Richelieu and his Age*, ed. J. Bergin and L. Brockliss, 135–73. Oxford, 1992.

Phillips, W. D. Jr. *Enrique IV and the Crisis of Fifteenth-Century Castile, 1425–1480*. Cambridge, MA, 1978.

Press, V. *Kaiser Karl V., König Ferdinand und die Entstehung der Reichsritterschaft*. 2nd edn. Wiesbaden, 1980.

Press, V. 'Adel im Reich um 1600: Zur Einführung'. In *Spezialforschung und 'Gesamtgeschichte': Beispiele und Methodenfragen zur Geschichte der frühen Neuzeit*, ed. G. Klingenstein and H. Lutz, 15–47. Vienna, 1981.

Price, J. L. 'The Dutch Nobility in the Seventeenth and Eighteenth Centuries'. In *The European Nobilities in the Seventeenth and Eighteenth Centuries*, ed. H. M. Scott, vol. 1, 82–113. London, 1995.

Reinhard, W. 'Kriegsstaat – Steuerstaat – Machtstaat'. In *Der Absolutismus – ein Mythos?: Strukturwandel monarchischer Herrschaft in West- und Mitteleuropa (ca. 1550–1700)*, ed. R. G. Asch and H. Durchhardt, 277–310. Cologne, 1996.

Rodríguez-Salgado, M. J. *The Changing Face of Empire: Charles V, Philip II and Habsburg Authority, 1551–1559*. Cambridge, 1988.

Root, H. L. *The Fountain of Privilege: Political Foundations of Markets in Old Regime France and England*. Berkeley, 1994.

Rosenfeld, P. 'The Provincial Governors of the Netherlands from the Minority of Charles V to the Revolt'. *Anciens pays et assemlbées d'états – Standen en landen* 17 (1959), 1–63.

Rothwell, H. (ed.) *English Historical Documents, 1189–1327*. London, 1975.

Round, N. *The Greatest Man Uncrowned: A Study of the Fall of Don Alvaro de Luna*. London, 1986.

Runciman, W. G. 'The Origins of the Modern State in Europe and as a Topic in the Theory of Social Selection'. In *Visions sur le développement des états européens: Théories et historiographies de l'état moderne*, ed. W. Blockmans and J.-P. Genet, 45–60. Rome, 1993.

Rupprecht, K. *Ritterschaftliche Herrschaftswahrung in Franken: Die Geschichte der Guttenberg im Spätmittelalter und zu Beginn der Frühen Neuzeit*. Neustadt a.d. Aisch, 1994.

Sacks, D. H. 'The Paradox of Taxation: Fiscal Crises, Parliament, and Liberty in England, 1450–1640'. In *Fiscal Crises, Liberty, and Representative*

Government, 1450–1789, ed. P. T. Hoffman and K. Norberg, 7–66. Stanford, CA, 1994.

Saul, N. *Richard II*. New Haven and London, 1997.

Schalk, E. *From Valor to Pedigree: Ideas of Nobility in France in the Sixteenth and Seventeenth Centuries*. Princeton, 1986.

Schalk, E. 'The Court as "Civilizer" of the Nobility: Noble Attitudes and the Court in France in the Late Sixteenth and Early Seventeenth Centuries'. In *Princes, Patronage, and the Nobility: The Court at the Beginning of the Modern Age c. 1450–1650*, ed. R. G. Asch and A. M. Birke, 245–63. Oxford, 1991.

Schmid, P. *Der Gemeine Pfennig von 1495: Vorgeschichte und Entstehung, verfassungsgeschichtliche, politische und finanzielle Bedeutung*. Göttingen, 1989.

Schubert, E. *Fürstliche Herrschaft und Territorium im späten Mittelalter*. Munich, 1996.

Scott, H. M. 'Conclusion: The Continuity of Aristocratic Power'. In *The European Nobilities in the Seventeenth and Eighteenth Centuries*, ed. H. M. Scott, vol. 2, 274–91. London, 1995.

Secousse, D. F. *et al.* (eds). *Ordonnances des roys de France de la troisième race recueillis par ordre chronologique*. 21 vols. Paris, 1723–1849.

Shennan, J. H. *The Origins of the Modern European State, 1450–1725*. London, 1974.

Shennan, J. H. *Liberty and Order in Early Modern Europe: The Subject and the State 1650–1800*. London, 1986.

Sieyès, E. J. *What is the Third Estate?* Edited by S. E. Finer. Translated by M. Blondel. London, 1963.

Stone, L. *The Crisis of the Aristocracy, 1558–1641*. Oxford, 1965.

Sturmberger, H. *Georg Erasmus Tschernembl: Religion, Libertät und Widerstand. Ein Beitrag zur Geschichte der Gegenreformation und des Landes ob der Enns*. Linz, 1953.

Swann, J. 'The French Nobility, 1715–1789'. In *The European Nobilities in the Seventeenth and Eighteenth Centuries*, ed. H. M. Scott, vol. 1, 142–73. London, 1995.

Thompson, I. A. A. *War and Government in Habsburg Spain 1560–1620*. London, 1976.

Thompson, I. A. A. 'The Nobility in Spain, 1600–1800'. In *The European Nobilities in the Seventeenth and Eighteenth Centuries*, ed. H. M. Scott, vol. 1, 174–236. London, 1995.

Tilly, C. 'War Making and State Making as Organized Crime'. In *Bringing the State Back In*, ed. P. B. Evans, D. Rueschemeyer and T. Skocpol, 169–91. Cambridge, 1985.

Tilly, C. *Coercion, Capital, and European States, AD 990–1992*. Oxford, 1992.

Toboso Sánchez, P. *La deuda pública castellana durante el Antiguo Régimen (juros) y su liquidación en el siglo XIX*. Madrid, 1987.

Ulrichs, C. *Vom Lehnhof zur Reichsritterschaft: Strukturen des fränkischen Niederadels am Übergang vom späten Mittelalter zur frühen Neuzeit.* Stuttgart, 1997.

Valdeón Baruque, J. 'Las crisis del siglo XIV en la Corona de Castilla'. In *La historia en el contexto de las ciencias humanas y sociales: Homenaje a Marcelo Vigil Pascual*, ed. M. J. Hidalgo de la Vega, 217–35. Salamanca, 1989.

Vale, M. G. A. *Charles VII.* London, 1974.

Van Horn Melton, J. 'The Nobility in the Bohemian and Austrian Lands, 1620–1780'. In *The European Nobilities in the Seventeenth and Eighteenth Centuries*, ed. H. M. Scott, vol. 2, 110–43. London, 1995.

Walker, S. 'Autorité des magnats et pouvoir de la *gentry* en Angleterre à la fin du moyen âge'. In *L'état et les aristocraties (France, Angleterre, Ecosse): XIIe–XVIIe siècle*, ed. P. Contamine, 189–211. Paris, 1989.

Walser, F. *Die spanischen Zentralbehörden und der Staatsrat Karls V.: Grundlagen und Aufbau bis zum Tode Gattinaras.* Edited by R. Wolhlfeil. Göttingen, 1959.

Wansink, H. (ed.) *The Apologie of Prince William of Orange against the Proclamation of the King of Spaine.* Leiden, 1969.

Waquet, J.-C. 'Who Profited from the Alienation of Public Revenues in Ancien Régime Societies?: Some Reflections on the Examples of France, Piedmont and Naples in the XVIIth and XVIIIth Centuries'. *Journal of European Economic History* 11, 3 (1982), 665–73.

Waquet, J.-C. *Le Grand-Duché de Toscane sous les derniers Médicis: Essai sur le système des finances et la stabilité des institutions dans les anciens états italiens.* Paris, 1990.

Weary, W. A. 'La maison de La Trémoille pendant la Renaissance: Une seigneurie agrandie'. In *La France de la fin du XVe siècle: Renouveau et apogée*, ed. B. Chevalier and P. Contamine, 197–212. Paris, 1985.

Weinfurter, S. 'Herzog, Adel und Reformation: Bayern im Übergang vom Mittelalter zur Neuzeit'. *Zeitschrift für Historische Forschung* 10 (1983), 1–39.

Willard, C. C. 'The Concept of True Nobility at the Burgundian Court'. *Studies in the Renaissance* 14 (1967), 33–48.

Win, P. de. 'The Lesser Nobility of the Burgundian Netherlands'. In *Gentry and Lesser Nobility in Late Medieval Europe*, ed. M. Jones, 95–118. Gloucester, 1986.

Winkelbauer, T. 'Krise der Aristokratie?: Zum Strukturwandel des Adels in den böhmischen und niederösterreichischen Ländern im 16. und 17. Jahrhundert'. *Mitteilungen des Instituts für österreichische Geschichte* 100 (1992), 328–53.

Wood, J. B. *The Nobility of the 'Election' of Bayeux, 1463–1666: Continuity through Change.* Princeton, 1980.

Young, C. R. *The Making of the Neville Family in England, 1166–1400.* Woodbridge, 1996.

Yun Casalilla, B. 'The Castilian Aristocracy in the Seventeenth Century: Crisis, Refeudalisation, or Political Offensive?' In *The Castilian Crisis of the Seventeenth Century*, ed. I. A. A. Thompson and B. Yun Casalilla, 277–300. Cambridge, 1994.

Index